Beyond Rights

Beyond Rights

The Nisga'a Final Agreement and the Challenges of Modern Treaty Relationships

CAROLE BLACKBURN

© UBC Press 2021

All rights reserved. No part of this publication may be reproduced, stored in a retrieval system, or transmitted, in any form or by any means, without prior written permission of the publisher, or, in Canada, in the case of photocopying or other reprographic copying, a licence from Access Copyright, www.accesscopyright.ca.

30 29 28 27 26 25 24 23 22 21   5 4 3 2 1

Printed in Canada on FSC-certified ancient-forest-free paper (100% post-consumer recycled) that is processed chlorine- and acid-free.

Library and Archives Canada Cataloguing in Publication

Title: Beyond rights : the Nisga'a Final Agreement and the challenges of modern treaty relationships / Carole Blackburn.
Names: Blackburn, Carole, author.
Description: Includes bibliographical references and index.
Identifiers: Canadiana (print) 20210307757 | Canadiana (ebook) 20210318023 | ISBN 9780774866453 (hardcover) | 9780774866460 (softcover) | ISBN 9780774866477 (PDF) | ISBN 9780774866484 (EPUB)
Subjects: LCSH: Nisga'a Nation. Treaties, etc. 1999 April 27. | LCSH: Niska Indians – Legal status, laws, etc. | LCSH: Niska Indians – Government relations. | LCSH: Niska Indians – Claims.
Classification: LCC KE7749.N5 B53 2021 | LCC KF5662.N58 B53 2021 kfmod | DDC 346.71104/3208997412 – dc23

Canadä

UBC Press gratefully acknowledges the financial support for our publishing program of the Government of Canada (through the Canada Book Fund), the Canada Council for the Arts, and the British Columbia Arts Council.

This book has been published with the help of a grant from the Canadian Federation for the Humanities and Social Sciences, through the Awards to Scholarly Publications Program, using funds provided by the Social Sciences and Humanities Research Council of Canada.

Printed and bound in Canada by Friesens
Set in Myriad and Sabon by Apex CoVantage, LLC
Copy editor: Deborah Kerr
Proofreader: Judith Earnshaw
Indexer: Margaret de Boer
Cover designer: JVDW Designs

UBC Press
The University of British Columbia
2029 West Mall
Vancouver, BC V6T 1Z2
www.ubcpress.ca

Contents

Acknowledgments / vii

Introduction / 3

1 We Have Always Made Laws: Defending the Right to Self-Government / 27

2 Aboriginal Title, Fee Simple, and Dead Capital: Property in Translation / 55

3 Treaty Citizenship: Negotiating beyond Inclusion / 93

4 The Treaty Relationship: Reconciliation and Its Discontents / 118

Conclusion / 143

Notes / 149

References / 167

Index / 181

Acknowledgments

This book has taken several years to complete and would not have been possible without the support and encouragement of many people. I am most indebted to the Nisg̱a'a Nation and to the many Nisg̱a'a citizens, elders, and treaty negotiators who were willing to discuss the origins and implications of the Nisg̱a'a Final Agreement in varying ways. Without their generosity, this book would not exist. I cannot name everyone here but would like to thank Ed Allen, Collier Azak, Les Clayton, Eric Grandison, the late Nelson Leeson, Corrine McKay, Kevin McKay, Nita Morven, Deanna Nyce, Emma Nyce, Harry Nyce Jr., Harry Nyce Sr., and Gary Tait. I am honoured to have spent time with the late James Gosnell and the late Rod Robinson, both of whom were leaders of great strength who sacrificed much for the final realization of the treaty. I also thank Nisg̱a'a Lisims Government and the Wilp Wilx̱o'oskwhl Nisg̱a'a Institute for initial permission to conduct research in the Nass Valley. For patient legal explanations I owe a huge debt to Jim Aldridge. I would also like to thank Peter Baird and the late Bob Spence, both of whom kindly facilitated many important introductions after I arrived in Ottawa to watch the treaty bill being debated in the House of Commons. I am grateful for the opportunity to interview former BC Supreme Court justice Thomas Berger, during which he shared his recollections of his first meeting with Frank Calder and the Nisg̱a'a Tribal Council.

viii *Acknowledgments*

This research has taken me through a variety of offices, and I am grateful to the many people at the Federal Treaty Negotiating Office in Vancouver, the BC Ministry of Indigenous Relations and Reconciliation in Victoria, the former Department of Indian Affairs and Northern Development, and the federal Department of Justice who generously shared their expertise and knowledge of land claims agreements and federal and provincial policies related to their negotiation. I am also grateful to people from the First Nations Summit, the BC Union of Indian Chiefs, the Assembly of First Nations in Ottawa, and the former Aboriginal Healing Foundation in Ottawa who took the time to talk to me and share their knowledge and their concerns. Any errors in interpretation, whether of the treaty's legal contents or cultural and social implications, are mine alone.

I am deeply grateful to the late Lorene Plante, whose Lava Lodge was a welcoming home for me in Gitlaxt'aamiks. Lorene was a woman of great presence and strength. I would also like to thank Ron and Jackie Nyce for their warm hospitality, wonderful food, and good humour while I stayed with them in Gitwinksihlkw. Robert and Donna Miles also gave me much-needed accommodation and conversation on more than one occasion. They have left the valley, but I am indebted to them for their hospitality and to Robert for driving me around and sharing his knowledge of early church history in the area.

I presented various parts of what would become chapters in this book at meetings of the American Anthropological Association, the Law and Society Association, the American Society for Ethnohistory, at the Max Planck Institute for Social Research in Halle, Germany, the Peter Wall Institute for Advanced Study at the University of British Columbia, and most recently at a workshop on Indigenous sovereignties and self-determination sponsored by the Faculty of Law, Laval University, and hosted by the Huron-Wendat First Nation in Wendake, Quebec. I am grateful to Kiera Ladner, Geneviève Motard, and Martin Papillon for encouragement at this last event, coming as it did when I was close to finishing the manuscript. Simon Picard's presentation at this workshop on the ramifications of the Huron-British Treaty of 1760 was a compelling reminder of the importance of honouring treaty relationships.

This research was supported by the Social Sciences and Humanities Research Council of Canada, for which I am very grateful. Additional research support was provided by the Mellon Foundation, the American Philosophical Society, the Cultural and Social Anthropology Department at Stanford University, the Behavioural Research Ethics boards of both Stanford and the University of British Columbia, and with the permission of Wilp Wilxo'oskwhl Nisga'a Institute.

I would like to thank friends and colleagues in the Department of Anthropology at the University of British Columbia for their support and insight over the years, including but not limited to Alexia Bloch, Millie Creighton, Nicola Levell, Sabina Magliocco, Bruce Miller, Shaylih Muehlmann, and Leslie Robertson. I have also benefitted from conversations with the wonderful graduate students who have worked with me, including Emma Feltes, Lauren Harding, Fumiya Nagai, and Maia Wikler. I thank Renisa Mawani for her support and intellectual encouragement over many years, Coll Thrush, and Doug Harris for clarifying comments on the nature of fee simple and English property law.

At UBC Press, I would like to thank editors Darcy Cullen, Karen Green, and the entire production team for their professional guidance and patient support of the manuscript. I am particularly indebted to the two anonymous reviewers whose careful readings and comments helped improve this work immensely. Last but not least, I thank my family for their love and support over the last several years.

Beyond Rights

Introduction

> We want the words and hands of the chiefs on both sides, Indian and Government, to make a promise on paper – a strong promise – that will be not only for us, but for our children and forever ... But we want a solemn promise – a treaty.
>
> – Charles Russ, resident of Laxgalts'ap, speaking to Commissioners Cornwall and Planta, 1887[1]

Since 1975, the Canadian government has concluded over two dozen land claims agreements with First Nations and Inuit peoples covering approximately 40 percent of the country's land mass.[2] These are known as "modern treaties" to distinguish them from the historic treaties made between European newcomers and Indigenous peoples from the onset of contact, trade, and exploration through to the beginning of the twentieth century.[3] Though both forms are legally and politically binding, many Canadians are not aware of their ongoing importance and role in the development of this country (Asch 2018). Historic treaties in particular are sometimes dismissed as dusty artifacts of the past, as an exchange of promises made in another era and not relevant today. Yet the relationship between Indigenous peoples and the rest of Canada lurches from crisis point to crisis point, often because historic treaty rights and the treaty principles of sharing land and respecting Indigenous governance are not taken seriously. Treaties are foundational to Canada's formation as a country and are at the heart of what many Indigenous people consider their special relationship with the Crown. Indigenous peoples have used treaties to create relationships with newcomers from the very beginnings of contact and exploration on this continent (Asch 2014; Coyle 2017; Craft 2013; Miller 2009; Mills 2017; Leanne Simpson 2008; Williams 1999). When the Truth and Reconciliation Commission on Indian residential schools released its final report in 2015, it spoke to the importance of rebuilding the political relationship between Indigenous peoples and Canadian governments by recovering some of the principles of these early treaty relationships. The report authors wrote, "It is important for all Canadians to understand that without Treaties, Canada would have no legitimacy as a nation. Treaties between Indigenous nations and the Crown established the legal and constitutional foundation of this country" (Truth and Reconciliation Commission of Canada 2015, 33).

In this book, I look at the promises and pitfalls of contemporary treaty making as a means of reforming relationships between Indigenous peoples and the state. I do this through an examination of the Nisga'a Final Agreement, also known as the Nisga'a treaty, which came into effect on May 11, 2000. It is the first modern treaty made in British Columbia. It covers the traditional territories of the Nisga'a Nation, which lie in the Nass River Valley on the northwestern coast of British Columbia. The Nass empties into the Pacific Ocean through Portland Inlet near the southern tip of the Alaska Panhandle. The treaty is the result of over one hundred years of Nisga'a men and women protesting, petitioning, litigating, and then negotiating with federal and provincial governments for recognition of their rights and land title in the form of a treaty. It defines all the Aboriginal rights of the Nisga'a people, including the right to self-government, and recognizes Nisga'a ownership of 2,000 square kilometres in northwestern British Columbia and other treaty rights over 27,000 square kilometres that are known as the Nass Wildlife Area.

This book focuses on the meaning and implications of three main aspects of the treaty: the nature and source of self-government, the nature and source of Aboriginal title, and citizenship. These were among the most difficult and legally complex elements to negotiate because they touch on fundamental matters such as state sovereignty, the underlying title of the Crown, and the distribution of differing rights across diverse political communities within one state. They are also critical points in the past and present relationship between Indigenous peoples and the rest of Canada. For Nisga'a, negotiating the treaty required revisiting and trying to repudiate key assumptions of a century and a half of Indigenous policy in Canada. The self-government provision in the Nisga'a Final Agreement was possibly its most controversial feature when it was debated in the House of Commons and the Senate and by the public in print media, on radio call-in shows, and in public hearings. Critics and political opponents argued that the provision created a third order of government and was an unconstitutional division of power, as I shall discuss in Chapter 1. But it is also significant that during the years that the treaty was negotiated, the inherent right of Aboriginal self-government and its place in the Canadian Constitution was a particularly important question of policy and law for federal and provincial governments. In some respect, the analysis I offer here serves as a bit of a time capsule because the commitment of federal and provincial governments to making treaties that would deal comprehensively with large, complex legal issues and a multiplicity of rights is waning. They are now looking toward less jurisdictionally complicated sectoral agreements with Indigenous peoples – things such as revenue-sharing agreements and agreements on isolated issues of governance capacity – that are quicker to achieve but are not treaties and are therefore not constitutionally protected. This shift is happening despite recommendations from the Truth and Reconciliation Commission and the work of scholars who point to treaties as a key mechanism of substantive reconciliation in Canada.

Scholarly work on treaty making in North America has addressed the origins, benefits, and drawbacks of historic and modern treaties from a range of disciplinary perspectives. Historians and scholars working to recover Indigenous views on treaties show us that multiple forms of treaty making and treaty relationships have existed since the first days of contact, trade, and exploration (Miller 2009; Promislow 2014; Ray, Miller, and Tough 2000).[4] Treaties were made to signify political or military alliances, to permit trading relationships, and to allow land settlement after Confederation in 1867. The Indigenous peoples who entered into them did so from a variety of political and economic contexts, sometimes from positions of strength and sometimes while facing the onset of disorienting change, but they nevertheless expected treaties to result in a binding relationship of mutual support and obligation between the partners (Asch 2014; Cardinal and Hildebrandt 2000; Craft 2013; Lyons 2010; Leanne Simpson 2008). They would not have made them otherwise. There is a common misconception that Indigenous people were tricked or duped to give up much for very little in return (Asch 2018; Craft 2013, 20; Promislow 2014). This is a historical misrepresentation and a misunderstanding of the expectations that Indigenous parties brought to treaty making.

Modern treaty making in Canada is a complex affair. Whereas historic treaties were completed over the course of a week and are a few pages long, their modern counterparts can take up to twenty years to negotiate and are usually over two hundred pages long. Research on modern treaties has examined the process of negotiations and the consequences of treaties for the communities who made them. This work reveals that negotiating a treaty is fraught with conflicting expectations, is divisive for communities, and takes up far too much time and resources (Alcantara 2013; de Costa 2008; Egan 2012; Penikett 2006; Woolford 2005). Indigenous communities that negotiate treaties are required to make significant compromises on lands and resources, and the mandates of federal and provincial negotiators have been too fixed on certainty and finality (Penikett 2006; Woolford 2005). Other scholars have addressed social and cultural consequences of land claims and self-government agreements. In analyzing the impact of the land claims agreements among the Kluane First Nation in Yukon, Paul Nadasdy (2017, 87) argues that these agreements make First Nations governments state-like in their adoption of statist concepts of nation, sovereignty, and citizenship, and in their transformation into small-scale bureaucracies. As Nadasdy (2012) and Thom (2014) also illustrate, the land claims process requires Indigenous peoples to define fixed boundaries around their territories that are not representative of historically more fluid territorial relationships. Some scholars criticize contemporary land claims and self-government agreements as mechanisms of territorial dispossession and assimilation that confine Indigenous peoples to small bits of their traditional lands in exchange for a limited range of self-government (Alfred 2009; Corntassel 2012; Coulthard 2014). Taiaiake Alfred (2005, 39) states, for example, that self-government and Aboriginal rights are "the benefits accrued by indigenous peoples who have agreed to abandon autonomy to enter the state's legal and political framework."

This is the persistent dilemma for Indigenous peoples who use state mechanisms and state institutions such as the courts, or the political process, to defend their rights or negotiate governance and matters of economic development and environmental protection in their homelands (Hale 2020). The question becomes whether or not these kinds of engagements lead to deeper incorporation within state structures and paradigms and a corresponding loss of Indigenous values. For Indigenous communities and governments who spend years in courts and treaty negotiations, this challenge is very real. However, I do not propose that it has been the inevitable result of the Nisg̱a'a treaty. Nisg̱a'a and other First Nations in British Columbia and Canada have strategically interacted with governments, missionaries, and traders since at least the time of first exploration and contact (Cooper 1993; Lutz 2008; Patterson 1992; Robertson with the Kwagu'ł Giẋsam Clan 2012). The Nisg̱a'a have always been confident in their ability to do this. Seeing these engagements as either always constitutive of Indigenous resistance or as always complicit in the perpetuation of non-Indigenous hegemony may not be the most fruitful approach (Richland 2008, 159). I am writing about a treaty that has already been made and about people who mostly want it to work. As Sherry Ortner (2006, 142) explains, people on the margins of power pursue goals that are informed by their "own social and political relations, and by their own culturally constituted intentions, desires, and projects" all the time, with results that are complicated assemblages of resistance, accommodation, and strategic exercises of agency (Feit 2010; Robertson with the Kwagu'ł Giẋsam Clan 2012). In her analysis of the self-government negotiations between the Dene of the Northwest Territories and the federal and territorial governments, Irlbacher-Fox (2009, 164) describes how during the nineteenth century, the Dene took their furs to various traders to incite competition between the traders and to postpone when they had to repay their debts. She suggests that contemporary Dene negotiators approach land claims and self-government agreements equally strategically, as things that can provide some useful tools to help their communities. Writing about the James Bay Cree, who negotiated the first modern treaty in Canada in 1975, Harvey Feit (2010, 54) also maintains that the Cree continue to engage government and industry in their territory through "a pattern of partial opposition, partial negotiation, and continuing relationships."

Any treatment of Indigenous action around land and governance in a contemporary settler state is incomplete without a consideration of the theoretical framework of settler colonialism (Veracini 2010; Wolfe 2006, 2011). Settler colonial theory is now prominent in Native American and Indigenous Studies, although it does not refer solely to the situation of Indigenous peoples. The term "settler colonialism" was coined in 1965 by a US-based Palestinian scholar in a book about Palestine (Kauanui 2016). Settler colonialism is a "land-centred project" that involves permanent settlement and is distinct from other colonialisms that focus on extracting resources (Wolfe 2006, 393). Canada, Australia, New Zealand, and the United States are all examples of settler states, and scholars continue to use the theoretical framework of settler colonialism to describe the occupation of Palestinian territories by Israel (Barakat 2018; Veracini 2010, 2015; Wolfe 2006). Australian scholar Patrick Wolfe's (2006, 2011) formulation of the features of settler colonialism has been particularly influential. Wolfe (2006, 388) argues that settler colonialism is a "structure rather than an event" to emphasize its continuity in ongoing state projects of land acquisition, usually for resource extraction, and Indigenous dispossession. Wolfe (2006) also states that a logic of elimination is inherently tied to settler colonialism's imperative of obtaining and maintaining territory. Elimination encompasses physical genocide but is also manifest in the government emphasis on assimilation through such things as residential schools, compulsory enfranchisement, and other coercive projects to remove the collective and legally distinct identities of Indigenous people.

Although the settler colonialism framework gives us critical insight into the features of this particularly land-centred colonial project, some scholars have argued that it is too rigid and forecloses possibilities of Indigenous resistance, survival, and resurgence (Carey 2020, 25; Kauanui 2016). The theoretical framework of settler colonialism informs this book because the denial of Aboriginal title in a place like British Columbia has been explicitly about the removal of Indigenous peoples from their territories. However, my analysis also aligns with the work of scholars who highlight the plurality, heterogeneity, and incompleteness of settler governance and sovereignty. This is because much of the debate, political controversy, struggle, and accomplishments of the Nisga'a treaty reveal settler sovereignty to be an unfinished and imperfect project (McHugh and Ford 2012). Indigenous peoples are in fact counting on its incompleteness. Socio-legal scholar Renisa Mawani (2016, 114) points out that though Wolfe's logic of elimination "rightfully emphasizes the intensity of political and legal violence that indigenous dispossession demanded," it affords "too much power to colonial states." Of special relevance for my analysis here, Mawani (2016, 114) contends that attempts to eliminate "indigenous people relied on legal processes that were themselves a fulcrum of struggle that did not always achieve their desired or state objectives." Law has always been a central component of colonial rule, but it is also used in resistance by colonized peoples everywhere in ways that contest its authority and application (Hale 2020; Merry 1991). Treaties themselves are the "product of the encounter between two separate legal orders" (Coyle 2017, 47). When the Nisga'a Tribal Council went to court in 1967 to argue that Nisga'a title had never been extinguished, the resulting Supreme Court judgment in *Calder* altered Canadian law.[5] It also initiated a body of jurisprudence that categorizes Aboriginal title as a unique right that is produced by the interaction between the Crown and Indigenous peoples (Slattery 2006). One consequence of this jurisprudence is that the content of Aboriginal title itself is not fixed but continues to evolve.

Debates about reconciliation have become part of a global trend in settler states, and Canada is no exception. Reconciliation has taken on particular prominence in the wake of the recent Truth and Reconciliation Commission on Indian residential schools. The word "reconciliation" is everywhere in public discourse and political parlance, lending its value to how varying levels of governments and organizations talk about changing relationships with Indigenous people. Federal and provincial government representatives now commonly refer to modern treaties as mechanisms of reconciliation. When I began research on the Nisga'a treaty, I heard it repeatedly and fulsomely referred to as a form of reconciliation – as, for example, an "important step toward reconciliation and the dream of true equality."[6] The federal government has recently stated that it "is committed to achieving reconciliation with Indigenous peoples through a renewed, nation-to-nation, government-to-government, and Inuit-Crown relationship based on recognition of rights, respect, co-operation, and partnership as the foundation for transformative change."[7] In this book, I hold that to fully understand reconciliation in Canada, and the way it is linked to modern treaty negotiations, we must understand its genesis in the Supreme Court judgments of the 1990s that directed governments to use treaties to reconcile the constitutional rights of Indigenous peoples with the sovereignty of the Crown. As many have pointed out, the Supreme Court idea of reconciliation has foregrounded the supremacy of Crown title and sovereignty, meaning that Aboriginal rights must be defined in ways that do not challenge this supremacy (Asch 1999; McNeil 2003; Dale Turner 2013). This has put the burden of reconciliation on Indigenous peoples, as they are required to accommodate their rights and interests to those of the much more powerful Crown. Historically, Indigenous peoples who made treaties did so with the reasonable expectation that the relationship into which they had entered was not one of subordination. Treaties and treaty making are important elements in the work of reconciliation, but they need to be implemented and understood as relationships of mutual obligation and reciprocity rather than a strictly contractual set of rights.

Context and Location

The valley of the Nass River is the centre of the traditional territory of the Nisg̱a'a people. The Nisg̱a'a, who call the river K̲'alii-aksim Lisims, have lived at many village sites on its banks and up its forested slopes since time immemorial. Historically, they followed a pattern of seasonal movement as they harvested resources throughout the year, returning to semi-permanent villages for the winter. There are currently four main villages along the river – Gingolx, Lax̱galts'ap, Gitwinksihlkw, and Gitlax̱t'aamiks. All were Indian reserves before the treaty came into effect on May 11, 2000. Gingolx, which sits at the mouth of the Nass, was formerly called Kincolith and was founded in 1867 by a group of

Nisga'a Christian converts who settled there with the Anglican missionary Robert Doolan (Patterson 1989). Before a logging road connected the upriver villages to the town of Terrace, Gingolx was the gateway to the Nass and an important focal point for political activity around the land question. Laxgalts'ap, the next upriver village, whose name means "village on village," is the site of several thousand years of settlement (Boston and Morven 1996, 63). It was formerly known as Greenville after the Methodist missionary Alfred Green. Gitwinksihlkw, which lies on the north side of the river, has also been called Canyon City because the river narrows into a canyon near its location. Access to Gitwinksihlkw was by a narrow suspension bridge until a car bridge was completed in 1998. The uppermost and largest village is Gitlaxt'aamiks, formerly New Aiyansh. Nisga'a also live in towns and cities throughout British Columbia and beyond, including the northern towns of Terrace and Prince Rupert, as well as Vancouver.

Gitlaxt'aamiks is the administrative seat of the government of the Nisga'a Nation. It sits on high ground on the south side of the river. This is a recent location and not the traditional site of the village. The original village of Gitlaxt'aamiks was on lower ground on the north side of the Nass River. It was home to Sgat'iin, a prominent *sim'oogit*, or chief, who is famous for having provincial government surveyors escorted off his lands at musket point in 1881. They were accompanying Indian reserve commissioner Peter O'Reilly on his first attempt to lay out reserves on the upper portion of the Nass. During the late 1800s, the Anglican missionary James B. McCullagh established the village of Aiyansh in a grassy meadow just a few kilometres downriver from Gitlaxt'aamiks. Aiyansh grew as a settlement but suffered from flooding. After one particularly bad flood in 1961, the Department of Indian Affairs relocated the village across the river to the higher ground and it became New Aiyansh. The new village site was bare and rocky. People spoke fondly about their life in the former Aiyansh and told me that the flooding was caused by upriver log jams resulting from clearcutting operations that had been ongoing in Nisga'a territory since the 1950s.

McCullagh aimed to construct an economically independent Christian village along the lines of the Tsimshian village of Metlakatla, founded by the Anglican missionary William Duncan. Among other things, Aiyansh had a sawmill that produced boards for the new Victorian houses that people were building, a tannery, a cannery, and a printing press (John Barker 1998, 441). McCullagh's approach was often combative, and people remember him for convincing their forefathers and foremothers to burn their ceremonial regalia and cut down their poles. Anglican and Methodist missionaries had reached the Northwest Coast during the mid- to late nineteenth century and invariably became embroiled in matters related to the land question in British Columbia. Some, such as the Methodist Alfred Green at Laxgalts'ap, supported the Nisga'a in their fight for recognition of their Aboriginal title and acted as a kind of cultural translator between them and government officials. Even McCullagh wrote to the superintendent general of Indian Affairs in 1876, saying that the peoples of the Nass and Skeena had come to the conclusion that "the government of the country was an organized system of land robbery" and that "every government official was to be suspected as a corrupt character and could be bought" (Cooper 1993, 387). Nisga'a converts brought traditional teachings into their interpretation of Christianity and were using the authority of the church to support their land claim by the mid-twentieth century (John Barker 1998).

Outside the Nass Valley, Terrace is the nearest town accessible by road from any of the villages. Terrace is on the Skeena River along Highway 16, which is also known as the Highway of Tears. More than two dozen mostly Indigenous women and girls have gone missing or been murdered along its isolated stretches. The 105-kilometre road from Terrace into the Nass Valley was built in 1958 by Columbia Cellulose, an American company headquartered in New York (Rajala 2006). The company pushed the road as far as the future site of New Aiyansh to facilitate access to Tree Farm Licence No. 1. This massive timber licence was granted to Columbia Cellulose by the provincial government in 1948. It covered 825,000 acres and approximately a third of Nisga'a traditional territory (Rajala 2006, 9). This road was unpaved until 2005. In May 2000, as I prepared to visit the Nass Valley for the first time, people repeatedly asked me if I knew how to change a flat tire because the road was so rough that punctures and flat tires were common. I was familiar with twisty gravel roads and the requirement of slow and careful driving; I was also lucky to have only one flat and to have help fixing it. In my case, this was a temporary inconvenience. For residents of the Nass Valley, the unpaved road with its choking dust in summer and slippery dangerous conditions in winter stood for just how excluded they were from the wealth of British Columbia and Canada more broadly. The roads in the four villages themselves were also unpaved before the treaty came into effect, producing a layer of nose-clogging dust that coated everything in people's homes all summer long. The road from Terrace is now labelled Nisga'a Highway 113, for the 113 years it took to resolve the Nisga'a land claim.

The lava beds near Gitlaxt'aamiks and Gitwinksihlkw are one of the most striking features of the valley. They are the result of a volcanic eruption that took place approximately three hundred years ago. The eruption began at a cinder cone along the Tseax River, a tributary of the Nass. Lava flowed eleven kilometres northward down the Tseax Valley into the Nass Valley, covering a village and fish camps and killing at least two thousand people on the way. The flow pushed the Nass River across the valley and stopped just below the present location of Gitwinksihlkw. According to Nisga'a oral history, the eruption was a supernatural punishment that came after children had been playing with the salmon that were swimming upriver to spawn (Boston and Morven 1996, 148). The "chiefs warned the children they were being disrespectful," but the children unfortunately did not heed the warning (Canada, British Columbia, Nisga'a Tribal Council 1993, 82). Not long afterward, the volcano erupted, spewing lava, smoke, and poisonous gas into the valley. Elder Rod Robinson told me of explorers' log books that chronicle attempting to ascend the Nass River but being stopped by a wind so hot it took the paint off their ship's masts.[8]

A memorial park now covers much of the lava beds, including the crater. Co-managed by the Nisga'a Nation and the Province, it has a visitor centre and a small campground. The road between Gitlaxt'aamiks and Gitwinksihlkw crosses the lava beds, and the park includes an auto-route tour with self-guided stops for tourists. Some of the lava formations have anthropomorphic shapes, and standing alone on these beds can be an eerie experience. Guided hikes to the volcanic crater are also available.

Under the terms of the treaty, the Nisga'a Nation owns approximately 2,000 square kilometres in the Nass Valley, including subsurface and

The lava beds.
Photograph by author.

mineral rights. These are the core treaty lands and consist of 1,930 square kilometres of transferred Crown land and 62 square kilometres of former Indian Act reserve land (Rose 2000, 28). The Nisga'a also have constitutionally protected rights and interests, including rights to hunt or fish for food, social, and ceremonial purposes in 27,000 square kilometres known as the Nass Wildlife Area. The treaty requires that they be consulted on any project in this area that could be expected to have an impact on Nisga'a citizens, treaty rights, and lands. The treaty also provided a cash settlement of approximately $250 million to be paid out over fourteen years. Nisga'a Lisims Government, which is the representative body for the Nisga'a Nation, put these monies in trust, where they remain today.[9] The 1,992 square kilometres in the core area constitute 7 percent of the land claimed by the Nisga'a Tribal Council in its negotiations. This number and the boundaries established by the treaty are disputed by neighbouring First Nations, and the matter of overlapping claims is a critical weakness of the treaty negotiating process in British Columbia and Canada today.[10] The text of the treaty is just over 250 pages long, with an additional 450 pages in appendices. It sets out all the rights and jurisdictional authorities of the Nisga'a people in areas such as governance, lands and title, wildlife, forest resources, fisheries, justice, taxation, and citizenship. Nisga'a governance under the treaty includes four village governments and three urban locals in Prince Rupert, Terrace, and Vancouver. The elected representatives of the village governments and an elected representative from the urban locals all serve in the larger nation government known as the Nisga'a Lisims Government.

The Nisga'a treaty is the result of approximately twenty years of negotiations that began after *Calder*, a landmark Supreme Court of Canada judgment of 1973. However, the Nisga'a struggle for recognition of their Aboriginal title goes much further back, beginning in the second half of the nineteenth century. Nisga'a first encountered Europeans much earlier than that. In 1793, Captain George Vancouver sailed up the coast of British Columbia looking for a northwest passage. He ventured into the mouth of the Nass and explored parts of Portland Inlet but did not ascend the river (McNeary 1976). He met several people in canoes, probably Nisga'a, who expressed an interest in trade. In 1831, the Hudson's Bay Company established a trading post on the Nass near the present village of Gingolx. It was called Port Simpson but was also known as Fort Nass (Patterson 1983, 41). Its site is now occupied by the Gingolx cemetery. The tides and weather made Fort Nass an unsuitable spot, however, and the company moved farther south to what is now the Tsimshian village of Lax Kw'alaams. The Nisga'a were disappointed with this development because having the fort at the mouth of the Nass gave them trade advantages. Cooper (1993, 107) writes that by the late 1820s, "the Nisga'a were well supplied with muskets by American traders and they had gained a reputation as an aggressive tribe who tolerated no intrusions upon their river." From the beginning of their interactions with Europeans, Nisga'a vigorously maintained their independence and territorial rights, while also engaging the newcomers in trade in ways that were to their best advantage. This practice of strategic engagement carried on into treaty negotiations during the twentieth century.

The Crown colony of British Columbia was formed in 1859. In 1871, the colony joined Canada as its westernmost province. The Nass Valley had already begun to attract settlers and the attention of the fishing, logging, and mining industries. First Nations throughout the new province were becoming increasingly worried about incursions into their territories and the theft of their resources. At the same time, provincial officials refused to acknowledge anything like Aboriginal title and declined to enter into treaties despite the precedent set in much of the rest of Canada. The history of the formation of British Columbia and the denial of Aboriginal title has been well told by others (see Fisher 1977; Foster 1995, 2007; Tennant 1990). Here I offer the main points of reference leading up to the negotiation of the Nisga'a treaty after 1973. I will return to aspects of this history at various times in the following chapters.

In 1881, Peter O'Reilly, the Indian reserve commissioner for British Columbia, travelled to the north coast to lay out reserves in Nisga'a and Tsimshian territory. At this time, many Nisga'a were particularly concerned about two new canneries that had opened at the mouth of the river. O'Reilly spent little more than one week on the Nass. Such a brief visit did not give him enough time to really consult with chiefs up and down the river. The reserves that he surveyed were "hastily allotted and ill considered" (Harris 2008, 73), and the whole process deeply alarmed the Nisga'a. They did not want reserves, they wanted recognition of their ownership and territorial rights. A few years later, in 1887, a group of Nisga'a and Tsimshian men travelled to Victoria to convey their concerns to Premier William Smithe. During their meetings with Smithe they expressed their desire to be "free" upon their land, asserting both their demand for recognition of their Aboriginal title and their authority to govern themselves outside of the Indian Act (Tennant 1990, 57). They asked for a public inquiry to be held into the land question and for a treaty. Smithe rejected their demands and said they were wrong to think they could get a treaty.

In 1907, Arthur Calder and Charles Barton spearheaded the formation of the Nisga'a Land Committee (Tennant 1990, 86). Calder structured the committee to include representatives from each of the four *pdeek* (tribes) and the four villages. The committee combined the essentials of Nisga'a tribal organization and hereditary leadership but was also a "planned political restructuring for the purposes of achieving greater effectiveness in dealing with the white political system" (Tennant 1990, 86). Along with several other Aboriginal rights organizations that were then forming in British Columbia, the committee's goal was to push the federal and provincial governments to recognize Aboriginal title and the obligations of treaty making (Tennant 1990). At a 1913 meeting in Gingolx, members of the Nisga'a Land Committee hired the lawyer and clergyman Arthur O'Meara to draft a petition to be sent to the British Privy Council. This petition asserted that the Nisga'a Nation held unsurrendered Aboriginal title, as a collective, and requested that the Privy Council rule on it (Haig-Brown 2005). A few years earlier, O'Meara had helped draft a similar petition for the Cowichan First Nation of Vancouver Island. Indeed, as the twentieth century began, multiple BC First Nations created petitions that "sought to revive the protective functions of the British Crown" (Feltes 2015; McHugh and Ford 2012, 32). The preamble to the Nisga'a petition included a statement that Nisga'a spokespersons have repeated time and again during their defence of the treaty:

> We are not opposed to the coming of the white people into our territory, provided this be carried out justly and in accordance with the British principles embodied in the Royal Proclamation. If therefore, as we expect, the aboriginal rights which we claim should be established by the decision of His Majesty's Privy Council, we would be prepared to take a moderate and reasonable position. In that event, while claiming the right to decide for ourselves the terms upon which we would deal with our territory, we would be willing that all matters outstanding between the Province and ourselves should be finally adjusted by some equitable method to be agreed upon which should include representation of the Indian Tribes upon any Commission which might then be appointed.[11]

The proclamation referred to here was issued by King George III in 1763, and I will discuss it in more detail in Chapter 2. It set out the basic requirements of treaty making between the Crown and Indigenous nations under British rule in North America. While they wanted to invoke the authority of the Crown at its highest level, the Nisga'a had to send their petition to the federal government in Ottawa first. In March 1914, the federal Cabinet passed an Order-in-Council stating that the government would refer the petition to the Judicial Committee of the Privy Council in England only if the Nisga'a and by extension all other BC First Nations accepted three conditions. First, if the courts did rule in favour of Aboriginal title, the Nisga'a "would surrender the title completely in return for the same sort of treaty benefits awarded elsewhere in Canada." Second, they would accept the recommendations of the upcoming McKenna-McBride Commission on reserve allocations. And third, if a court case arose, they would be represented by lawyers hired for them by Canada (Tennant 1990, 93; Wickwire 2005, 307). Not surprisingly, the Nisga'a did not agree to these conditions.

This Order-in-Council galvanized Indigenous resistance across the province. First Nations in British Columbia continued to organize to defend their land and demand treaties throughout the first decades of the twentieth century. In 1927, the federal government amended the Indian Act to make it illegal (by virtue of section 141) for any person to receive or solicit any payment from an Indigenous person for the purpose of prosecuting a claim against the government (Tennant 1990, 112). Written with men such as Arthur O'Meara in mind, the amendment made it impossible for any First Nation individual or organization to hire a lawyer to assist with a land claim (Haig-Brown 2005). Section 141 was not removed from the Indian Act until 1951. After its removal, Frank Calder spearheaded the formation of the Nisga'a Tribal Council in 1955 (Tennant 1990, 123). By this time, Calder was a BC MLA and the first Indigenous elected representative in any legislative assembly in the Commonwealth.[12] He became the first president of the Nisga'a Tribal Council and served in that position until 1974, when James Gosnell was elected. The tribal council was incorporated as a society in 1963. Its mandate covered a broad range of social and economic issues but concentrated on negotiating and settling the comprehensive land claim based on Nisga'a Aboriginal title. Rod Robinson (Sim'oogit Minee'eskw) was another early founder and member of the tribal council. When I spoke with him, he reflected on how the council had held its first annual convention in a house in Greenville in 1955. Initially, its mandate was to "settle with the white man" a just and reasonable solution to the land question and to improve living conditions in the valley.[13] Robinson recalled that ten years later, during the tenth annual convention in Canyon City, people said, "We've talked and talked, now let's test the white man's law, let's test British justice to see how just British justice is, let's go to court."[14]

In 1967 the Nisga'a Tribal Council took its case to the BC Supreme Court with the help of the young lawyer Tom Berger. In *Calder*, it sued for a declaration that Nisga'a Aboriginal title had never been lawfully extinguished in the province. It lost this case and then lost again in the BC Court of Appeal. In 1972, the tribal council took the case to the Supreme Court of Canada. The stakes in this case were particularly high. Losing would mean that the highest Canadian court had ruled against the presence of Aboriginal title in British Columbia, thereby quashing all other Aboriginal title claims in the province. When the Nisga'a decided to press ahead with their litigation, they lost many allies among BC First Nations. Of seven justices in the Supreme Court, six agreed that Nisga'a Aboriginal title had existed in the past. This was more than any BC government had ever agreed to. Three of the justices ruled that title had been extinguished by various ordinances, acts, and proclamations issued or passed by the colonial government of British Columbia before 1871, when the province joined Confederation (Godlewska and Webber 2007, 5).[15] Three others ruled that it had not been so extinguished. The seventh, Justice Pigeon, abstained on a technicality.[16] Even though the court split on the extinguishment decision, the *Calder* ruling opened the possibility that Aboriginal title still existed in British Columbia and elsewhere in Canada. The federal government responded to this development by establishing a process for receiving and negotiating comprehensive land claims where treaties had not previously been made, primarily British Columbia, Yukon, the Northwest Territories, and northern Quebec (Sanders 1999, 108). Completed comprehensive land claims are also known as modern treaties. Ottawa also began negotiating with the Nisga'a Tribal Council.

These negotiations started in 1976. The provincial government did not participate in them until 1990. Without the involvement of the province of BC, Nisga'a and federal government negotiators were confined to talking about things within federal jurisdiction, such as fishing and self-government on existing reserves. In Canada, the underlying title to Crown land – about which I will say more in Chapter 1 – is held in right of the provinces. The provincial government declined to join the negotiations because its elected officials refused to acknowledge the presence of unextinguished Aboriginal title. Their position was that there was nothing to discuss. Provincial leaders changed their approach to questions of Aboriginal land claims and the necessity of treaty making when the costs of uncertainty around land title in the provincial resource sector became too great to ignore (Blackburn 2005). In British Columbia, the late 1980s and early 1990s saw almost constant protests by First Nations against logging, mining, and oil and gas exploration in their traditional territories (Blomley 1996). This agitation was referred to as the "war in the woods." Blockades against logging on Lyell Island in Haida Gwaii and in Clayoquot Sound on the west coast of Vancouver Island permanently halted operations at these locations (Blomley 1996). The costs to these industries were significant and drove political change in the province more than social or moral considerations (Blackburn 2005). A 1990 study by Price Waterhouse estimated that "almost $1 billion of currently proposed mining and forest industry investments could be affected by the non-settlement of comprehensive land claims."[17]

In 1993, Victoria established the BC Treaty Commission to oversee the negotiation of treaties in the province. The Nisga'a negotiations were already under way, and the Nisga'a treaty is *not* a product of the BC treaty process. The first treaty to come out of the BC treaty process is the Tsawwassen Final Agreement. Signed by the federal and provincial governments and the Tsawwassen First Nation in 2007, it came into effect in 2009. The Maa-nulth Final Agreement was concluded in 2006 and came into effect in 2011. Five First Nations on the west coast of Vancouver Island are parties to this agreement. The Tla'amin Final Agreement was signed in 2014 and came into effect in 2016. These treaties share some key features with the Nisga'a Final Agreement, and the First Nations who concluded them struggle with many of the same issues involving implementation. The BC treaty process was supposed to hasten treaty making in the province, but this has not occurred, and the few First Nations that have concluded their agreements are the exceptions in what is a very difficult process. Currently, over fifty First Nations are involved in the process: fourteen have reached the final agreement stage, and thirty-six are negotiating an agreement in principle.[18] Others have walked away from the table due to costs, time delays, and insurmountable differences with federal and provincial negotiating mandates on matters of lands, governance, and the scope of rights (de Costa 2008).

Ottawa, Victoria, and the Nisga'a finalized an agreement in principle in 1996 and a final agreement in 1998. The treaty was approved by a special assembly of the Nisga'a Nation held between October 5 and 7 in 1998. A referendum on the final agreement was held for Nisga'a citizens on November 6 and 7 of that year. Voting took place in the four villages and in the urban locals of Vancouver, Terrace, and Prince Rupert. It was restricted only to those individuals who were eligible to be enrolled in the treaty, which was one reason eligibility criteria became so important early on, as I discuss in Chapter 3. In the referendum, acceptance or refusal of the treaty was determined by a simple majority of voters. Sixty-one percent of Nisga'a who were eligible to vote cast ballots in the referendum, 73 percent of whom voted in favour of the treaty. The final agreement was then brought to the BC legislature for debate and ratification. The legislature passed the bill in the spring of 1999 after a lengthy and acrimonious debate.

The treaty bill – Bill C-9 – was introduced in the House of Commons in October 1999 and moved into the Senate in February 2000. It was ratified, becoming law, on April 13, 2000, and then legally came into effect at midnight on May 10, 2000. At this time, the federal Liberal Party was in power and Jean Chrétien was the prime minister. The Reform Party under the leadership of Preston Manning was the Official Opposition. Reform was a right-of-centre party that began in Alberta and quickly rose to dominate the right in Canada. It built itself on a platform favouring free enterprise, lower taxation, private property, and minimal government spending. It opposed all forms of separate rights or collective rights for Indigenous people, Quebecers, or any minority. Reform MPs took every opportunity to oppose the treaty, dismissing it as a collection of race-based rights that entitled one set of Canadians at the expense of others.

In British Columbia, the treaty came into effect during the tenure of the New Democratic Party. Espousing left-of-centre politics, the New Democrats supported the agreement, and Premier Glen Clark played an important role in getting it through the legislature even though he made the mistake of calling it a template for future treaties in the province. This comment would haunt Clark but was also not how the Nisga'a negotiators wanted their treaty to be viewed by other First Nations. In the provincial election of 2001, the Liberal Party won a huge majority and would remain in power for the next sixteen years. At this time, the BC Liberal Party had much more in common with the federal Reform Party than with the federal Liberals. They had not supported the treaty when they were in Opposition, and they had promised to hold a public referendum on treaty making in the province if they were elected. They delivered on their promise in 2002, and I will return to these events and the reasoning behind them in Chapter 1. Before they were elected, Liberal leader Gordon Campbell launched a court case challenging the constitutionality of the Nisga'a Final Agreement. The Liberals' election in May 2001 was consistent with public perception around Aboriginal rights, title, and treaty making in British Columbia. More specifically, it was consistent with a vast amount of suspicion, resentment, and lack of awareness about the legal realities of Aboriginal rights and title. The Liberal Party now speaks a language of new relationships and reconciliation in respect of Indigenous issues but maintains a strong pro-industry, pro-resource-development orientation in all its governing and policy positions. It was in power from 2001 to 2017, at which point it was toppled by a coalition of the NDP and the Green Party.

Chapter Summary

The Nisga'a Final Agreement states that the Nisga'a Nation "has the right of self-government, and the authority to make laws" (Canada, British Columbia, Nisga'a Nation 1998, ch. 11, s. 1). Chapter 1 examines the legal arguments over the source of this authority and the place of Indigenous government alongside federal and provincial governments. In Canada, this issue has drawn the attention of legal and constitutional scholars, as well as the highest courts. It has also prompted decades of Indigenous activism (Papillon 2014). The struggle to implement Indigenous juris-dictions is a struggle to make Indigenous legal orders possible within Canada. The Nisga'a treaty does not create any exclusive jurisdiction for the Nisga'a Nation, but it does establish concurrent jurisdiction through which Nisga'a lawmaking is paramount in fourteen areas.

Traditionally, Nisga'a territory was divided into approximately forty segments or House territories. These are the *ango'oskw*. When the treaty came into effect, the Nisga'a Nation became the owner of 2,000 square kilometres of territory, representing 7 percent of their total claim. In the process, its Aboriginal title was modified into the Western property law concept of fee simple. Chapter 2 explores how the state's criteria of legibility imposed this prerequisite but also how Nisga'a negotiators pushed for a broader, fuller fee simple to signal their ancestral inheritance and temporal priority on their territory. Throughout this chapter, I trace the complicated legal, political, and economic factors underwriting the transformation of property regimes on Nisga'a land.

Since 1975, all modern land claims agreements in Canada have included sections on enrolment and eligibility, which set out who is entitled to receive treaty benefits. To be enrolled as a citizen of the Nisga'a Nation and have access to the treaty rights, a person must have a Nisga'a maternal ancestor within four generations. The Nisga'a argue that this entails a return to traditional matrilineal practices and a rejection of patrilineal identity requirements of the Indian Act. Critics saw it as a proxy for blood, itself a signifier for race, and accused the Nisga'a of enacting race-based membership criteria. Some disparaged the treaty itself as a set of race-based "special rights" that violates democratic principles. In Chapter 3, I show that matrilineal ancestry is not the same as blood, but that ideas about it are tainted by the past and present racialization of Indigenous people in Canada (Kauanui 2008; Sturm 2002). The misreading of genealogical forms of reckoning used by Indigenous peoples reduces them to the status of a racial minority (Kauanui 2008). The treaty creates a form of treaty citizenship for Nisga'a that should reflect the importance of treaties as mechanisms that mediate the respective rights, duties, and relational obligations between treaty partners.

Chapter 4 discusses the treaty relationship between the Nisga'a and the federal government, which has proved disappointing to the Nisga'a. Broadly speaking, governments see a treaty as a legal mechanism whose purpose is to produce certainty around the scope and nature of

24   *Beyond Rights*

Aboriginal rights (Blackburn 2005). The Nisga'a criticism of the government's approach is that while it may fulfill the legal and technical requirements of the treaty, it does not fulfill the broader spirit and intent. They are now active in the Land Claims Agreements Coalition (LCAC), attempting to improve treaty implementation, and appear to be making some progress. Together, the members of LCAC have developed a model framework for a Modern Treaties Implementation Review Commission, and though they continue to lobby the federal government to develop this commission, their momentum is slipping as Ottawa turns its focus to the creation of a Rights Recognition Framework.

Notes on the Research

The research for this book began in 1999, when the Nisga'a Final Agreement was introduced in the House of Commons. My approach was multi-sited from necessity, as the legal document and the people who had worked on it were moving between the Nass Valley, Vancouver, and Ottawa (Marcus 1995). I began in Ottawa, where members of the Nisga'a Tribal Council had gathered as Bill C-9 was debated in the House and the Senate. During the fall of 1999, I watched the debate in the House of Commons and attended the meetings on Parliament Hill of the Standing Committee on Aboriginal Affairs as it reviewed the bill. I met members of the Nisga'a, provincial, and federal negotiating teams as this process unfolded. In early 2000, I travelled to Vancouver and Victoria, and then to Terrace, Prince Rupert, and the Nass Valley, following the routes that the treaty negotiators had taken as they logged miles between local, regional, provincial, and federal negotiating sites. I was in Gitlaxt'aamiks in May 2000 when the treaty came into effect, and I attended the celebrations in Gitwinksihlkw on May 11. The night before, I sat with a group of Nisga'a and non-Nisga'a treaty negotiators in Nass Camp as midnight approached, because the treaty would legally come into effect at the stroke of midnight. Nass Camp was a former logging camp that then featured a store, gas station, restaurant and pub, and trailers for rent. There was a lot of enthusiasm in the cabin that night among the lawyers and negotiators who had gathered for celebrations the following day. On May 11, I walked across the Gitwinksihlkw suspension bridge while the helicopter carrying BC premier Ujjal Dosanjh flew overhead and landed in one of the few flat places by the river, delivering him for the festivities.

I returned to the Nass Valley in 2006, 2007, and 2011. I began following the work of the Land Claims Agreements Coalition in 2010 and first discussed its goals with elected Nisg̲a'a officials Kevin McKay, who was the chief executive officer of Nisg̲a'a Lisims Government, and Nelson Leeson, then president of the Nisg̲a'a Nation, in Gitlax̲t'aamiks in 2011. I attended two coalition conferences on treaty implementation in Ottawa. Both were critical to my appreciation of the goals of other First Nations and Inuit in Canada who have made modern treaties and the challenges they face regarding implementation.

Many, many Nisg̲a'a women and men worked on the treaty negotiations over many years. Along with a core team of negotiators, specialized committees and working groups drew on expertise across the Nisg̲a'a communities. Some examples are the Nisg̲a'a Government Committee, the Lands and Resources Committee, the Fiscal and Implementation Working Group, the Nisg̲a'a Constitution and Laws Working Group, the Lands, Access and Environmental Working Group, the Fisheries Committee, the Wildlife Working Group, and more. These and at least twenty other bodies were organized under the umbrella of the Nisg̲a'a Tribal Council.[19] The village governments also sent observers to the treaty talks, and representatives of other important community services, such as the Health Board, the Nisg̲a'a School Board, and Wilp Wilx̲o'oskwhl Nisg̲a'a Institute (the Nisg̲a'a House of Learning), participated in the working groups leading up to the final agreement. Wilp Wilx̲o'oskwhl Nisg̲a'a Institute is a pioneering post-secondary educational facility in the Nass Valley, now located in Gitwinksihlkw.

Among Nisg̲a'a citizens there are many differing opinions and experiences of the treaty. I would not expect consensus in any community or set of communities, especially not on something this legally complicated and so fraught with the weight of historical injustice and hope and expectations for the future. While some of these differences become apparent in this book, I do not claim to capture the full gamut of community views on and experiences of the treaty. These views and experiences are diverse and changing, as one would expect. During my research, I spoke with treaty negotiators, politicians, bureaucrats, political activists, Nisga'a citizens and government workers, lawyers for the Province, lawyers for the federal government, and lawyers for the Nisga'a. People shared a range of perspectives on the treaty: some were for it, others against it, and some wanted to see how it all evolved over time. Most interviews and conversations were on a not-for-attribution basis to ensure that people could comment freely. I am indebted to the negotiators on all sides who spent long hours explaining legal complexities to me. In places throughout this book, I discuss some aspects of Nisga'a culture in relation to provisions of the treaty. I base these passages on the generous explanations given me by elders, as well as on written sources including the invaluable four-volume *Ayuukhl Nisga'a Study* produced by the Nisga'a Tribal Council in 1984 and then republished in 1995. Another important source was *From Time before Memory*, a book produced by Nisga'a School District No. 92 (Boston and Morven 1996). These sources represent the knowledge and expertise of generations of Nisga'a men and women. Any errors of characterization are mine alone.

We Have Always Made Laws: Defending the Right to Self-Government

1

On May 11, 2000, the newly created Nisga'a Lisims Government sat for the first time in the old recreation hall in the village of Gitwinksihlkw. It consisted of the former band councillors from the four villages (eight each), a representative from the urban locals of Terrace, Prince Rupert, and Vancouver, and the elected officials of the Nisga'a Tribal Council. The first order of business was to pass eighteen pieces of legislation to make the Nisga'a government operational.[1] With a court challenge on the treaty's constitutionality starting in Vancouver in a matter of days, negotiators on all sides agreed that there should be no phase-in period in making it operational.[2] Sim'oogit Minee'eskw, Rod Robinson, spoke to the assembled crowd before the official business began. He said that the self-government they were about to embark on was "nothing new" for the Nisga'a. He reminded his listeners that the Nisga'a had been governing themselves and making laws since time immemorial, and he referred to the years of Indian Act administration as a "brief interruption" of their powers. After Nisga'a Lisims Government passed the bills, the crowd milled around outside the hall. A CBC Television news crew was in attendance, recording the event. I watched as reporter Terry Milewski spoke into the camera, saying "these people have a reason to be smiling ... They've just passed their first laws without having to ask Ottawa."[3]

The reporter and Rod Robinson were both referring to the Nisga'a experience with the Indian Act, the band council system of reserve governance, and the Department of Indian Affairs, which was headquartered in Ottawa. The Indian Act was and is a mechanism of state encompassment that extended the reach of the federal government into virtually every nook and cranny of First Nations peoples' lives. Rod Robinson's remark that self-government was not new to the Nisga'a was echoed time and again in my conversations with Nisgsa'a citizens about the treaty. "We've always had self-government," one elder explained to me at a settlement feast in Laxgalts'ap, shortly after the treaty had come into effect.[4] A settlement feast takes place shortly after someone passes away and is a complex ceremony during which the family of the deceased publicly settles all debts incurred in the funeral preparations (Roth 2002). The elder noted that Nisga'a used to have self-government without welfare payments, without family allowances, when everything they had was hand-made by themselves – their houses, their food, their education, everything. She said they were made wards of the government and did not want to be. She referred to the feast itself – where I watched detailed financial accounting read into the public record – as a mechanism of governance and an expression of Nisga'a law. Other individuals shared their thoughts about the Nisga'a as a "proud self-governing people" in the past and mentioned the challenge of showing the world that they could be that kind of people again.

In Canada, modern-day treaty making involves Indigenous communities in complex negotiations around the scope and place of Indigenous self-government in relationship with federal, provincial, and territorial governments. It encompasses questions about the source of Indigenous governing authority and the place it can occupy within, or alongside, Canadian sovereignty. Legal and constitutional scholars and practitioners have also addressed these issues, as have the highest courts, and they have inspired decades of activism by Indigenous peoples. In this chapter, I examine the nature of the governing arrangement put in place by the Nisga'a Final Agreement. The first modern treaty to include self-government, the treaty establishes the ability of Nisga'a government to make laws with paramount authority in fourteen areas of jurisdiction. The inclusion of self-government in the treaty means that it is protected by

Celebrating the treaty coming into effect, Sim'oogit Minee'eskw (Rod Robinson) in the foreground. Gitwinksihlkw, May 12, 2000.

Photograph by author.

the Constitution and that it is not delegated to the Nisga'a by the Crown. Instead, it is recognized as an inherent, pre-existing collective right of the Nisga'a Nation. The agreement creates space for Nisga'a lawmaking and a form of legal pluralism, expressed in concurrent jurisdiction, which recognizes that the authority of Nisga'a to govern themselves comes from them and not the state. While Nisga'a government under the treaty is not the subordinate exercise of a municipal-style government, as some critics suggest, it is contained within the framework of Canadian federalism. Even this gain in the recognition of the inherent right to self-government was hard-won against the tide of incredible resistance on the part of federal and provincial governments, politicians, and whole swaths of public opinion that refused to accept anything other than delegated authority and the supremacy of the Crown.

The Indian Act Arrives on the Northwest Coast

Getting rid of the Indian Act and its system of band council governments was one of the main things I saw people celebrating when the Nisga'a treaty came into effect on May 11, 2000. The Indian Act has managed the lives of Nisga'a and other Northwest Coast First Nations for more than a century, and it is inescapably part of what people talk about when they consider the pros and cons of treaty governance. The first version of the Indian Act dates from 1876 and was a consolidation of previously existing legislation and Imperial policies. It set out the basic parameters of an elective system of band council government for status Indians who lived on reserves. This included a three-year term of office for chiefs and councillors, the exclusion of women from voting, and the ability of government officials to remove elected chiefs and councillors for "dishonesty, intemperance or immorality" (Daugherty and Madill 1984, 2). Women could not vote in band council elections until 1951. When the Indian Act was created, federal policy makers assumed that elected municipal-style governments would contribute to the civilization and advancement of the First Nations who adopted them. Ottawa also expected that band councils would weaken and replace Indigenous governance. The band council system has partly achieved this goal though not uniformly so. Indigenous forms of governance and legal orders have endured, in some cases by going underground or by running parallel to band councils, or because people have elected hereditary leaders to blend traditional and band council governance (Borrows 2010, 43; Ladner 2006).[5]

In 1888, Indian Agent Charles Todd took up his post in the Tsimshian village of Metlakatla (Cooper 1993). Todd was the first agent for the Northwest Coast Agency, and his advent marked the formal arrival though not the full implementation of the Indian Act in this part of Canada. One year before his arrival, Clement Cornwall and Joseph Planta had visited Nisga'a and Tsimshian communities as representatives of the Indian Reserve Commission, formally known as the Commission to Enquire into the Conditions of the Indians of the North-West Coast. The federal and provincial governments created this commission to address the grievances of the Nisga'a and other First Nations on the north coast about the hasty, flawed, and inadequate allocation of reserves by Commissioner Peter O'Reilly.[6] Before Cornwall and Planta began their work, the provincial attorney general told them that they should not entertain any discussion of Aboriginal title. The commissioners were hard pressed to follow this proscription in the communities they visited, where the land was the main topic, and they concluded that the federal government needed to get an Indian agent up there as quickly as possible. They recommended that existing reserves be enlarged but also wrote that "the Indians of the North-West Coast have been left too much alone, almost isolated from proper Governmental regulations and control" (British Columbia 1888, 11). They worried that the missionaries had too much influence and blamed them for stirring people up about the land question.[7] In their opinion, leaving the Indians "to pursue their course unaided, uninstructed, as to the objects and purport of the law, and uncontrolled by the civil power, would be fatal to any probability of future peace" (British Columbia 1888, 11).

Nisga'a responses to Todd's appointment and the attempt to extend the Indian Act into their communities were mixed. Gingolx was the first village to adopt the band council system. With the assistance of Agent Todd, the residents of Gingolx elected a first council of five members, choosing Gints'aadax, a prominent sim'oogit of the Wolf tribe, as their chief councillor (Patterson 1989).[8] The Anglican missionary George Collison was a factor in all of this. Unlike the Methodists such as Alfred Green at Laxgalts'ap, the Anglicans generally supported cooperation with the federal government and its policies, including the establishment of reserves and the implementation of the Indian Act (Patterson 1983). Gingolx had previously had a village council that had been organized with the help of Collison. When the provincial government made these sorts of mission councils illegal in 1884 – because of suspicions that missionaries exerted too much political influence – the village had been obliged to abandon it. The chiefs at Gingolx were frustrated by this development and wanted something to replace the discontinued council. They also wanted to control access to the fisheries on the lower part of the Nass (Cooper 1993).[9] In meetings with Commissioners Cornwall and Planta, Gingolx chiefs said they were more powerful than the upriver people and that ownership of the Nass fishery should be theirs alone. They told the commissioners that "the Kincolith chiefs when it is theirs will take care of it and will let all other Indians fish there." Once their band council was established, they set about policing the lower river to assert their authority (Cooper 1993, 362).

The upriver villages of Laxgalts'ap and Aiyansh took on the band council system later, during the mid- to late 1890s (Patterson 1982). They adopted the system grudgingly and often refused to cooperate with the Indian agent, especially after hereditary leaders from all the villages formed the Nisga'a Land Committee in 1907 (Cooper 1993, 395). Like Gingolx, these villages elected hereditary leaders as a way of circumventing the erosion of traditional governance that the band council system was supposed to achieve. Although they adopted this strategy, they accepted the band council system for many of the same reasons that other First Nations did. By the end of the nineteenth century, most Indigenous people found that their tribal governments were almost powerless in dealing with federal and provincial governments (Little Bear, Boldt, and Long 1984). The federal government presented the system of elected band councils as a way in which people could regain some of their former self-governing authority in a changing world (Little Bear, Boldt, and Long 1984).

The truth was that band councils themselves had very limited power. They could do little except implement policies determined in Ottawa, a situation that did not greatly improve during the twentieth and twenty-first centuries. Then and now, the main decision-making power resides with the minister of the federal department responsible for Indigenous affairs. The name of this department has changed over the decades; when the Nisga'a treaty was negotiated, it was the Department of Indian Affairs and Northern Development (DIAND). Band bylaws can be rendered invalid by federal laws, federal regulations, or the DIAND minister (Ladner 2006).[10] With such limited powers, band councils cannot govern as effectively as they need to; they can only administer elements of the Indian Act. They are also placed in the almost impossible position of being accountable to DIAND, the source of all their funding, and to their communities. This is the very limited and constraining kind of governance that people such as Rod Robinson referred to and that the Nisga'a wanted to escape.

You Cannot Give It to Us: Self-Government as an Inherent Right

Three days after Nisga'a self-governance was re-inaugurated in Git-winksihlkw, representatives of the Nisga'a government had to appear in a Vancouver courtroom to defend it. The case of *Campbell v British*

Columbia (Attorney General) began in the BC Supreme Court on May 14, 2000.[11] As signatories to the treaty, Canada and British Columbia were also defendants in this case, putting the two senior governments on the same side as the Nisga'a. The main plaintiff, Gordon Campbell, was the leader of the BC Liberal Party, which was then the Official Opposition in the legislature. Campbell was joined as plaintiff by two of his Liberal colleagues, Michael de Jong and Geoffrey Plant. Michael de Jong was the Aboriginal affairs critic in Opposition, and Geoffrey Plant was the critic for the attorney general. In February 2000, de Jong had attended the Ottawa hearings of the Standing Senate Committee on Aboriginal Affairs, where he criticized the treaty's self-government provisions. Campbell also appeared before the Parliamentary Standing Committee on Aboriginal Affairs in November 1999 when it travelled to British Columbia as part of its review of Bill C-9 for the House of Commons. Whereas the federal Liberals supported the treaty, their provincial counterparts, a product of BC politics, aligned themselves more to the right of centre. Their arguments against the treaty were essentially the same as those of the Reform Party.

The first paragraph in the Governance chapter of the treaty states that "the Nisga'a nation has the right to self-government, and the authority to make laws, as set out in this agreement" (Canada, British Columbia, Nisga'a Nation 1998, 159). Indigenous peoples in Canada maintain that the right to self-government is inherent and that their practice of governing themselves predates the arrival of Europeans. This is what Rod Robinson meant when he stated that Nisga'a self-government was nothing new. To say that the right to self-government is inherent means that the Nisga'a automatically possess it, just as individuals automatically possess human rights. Such rights are not created by the state. The Nisga'a Final Agreement is the first modern treaty to include the right to self-government, of which I will say more below. Enshrining this right in a treaty means that it becomes constitutionally protected by virtue of section 35 of the Constitution. Section 35 asserts that the Aboriginal and treaty rights of Aboriginal peoples in Canada, including rights that are acquired in modern treaties, are protected and affirmed. The story of how section 35 came to be in the Canadian Constitution begins with Prime Minister Pierre Elliott Trudeau's initiative to repatriate the Constitution from the United Kingdom at the beginning of the 1980s. Indigenous people across the country responded to Trudeau's repatriation plan by demanding that a renewed Constitution both acknowledge and strengthen the nation-to-nation relationship between themselves and the Crown that predated Confederation.[12] Although section 35 was a compromise, it means every right set out in a modern treaty becomes a constitutionally protected right and cannot be removed or extinguished.

The plaintiffs in the *Campbell* case insisted that the Nisga'a treaty and any other treaties to be negotiated in the future should not include the right to self-government. In their statement of claim and arguments in court, they repeated many of the criticisms made against self-governance by Reform MPs and others in the House of Commons debate, the Senate debate, the House and Senate committee meetings, in the media, and during the treaty negotiation itself. Nisga'a politicians and citizens found the whole experience demoralizing. Here they were, after Parliament had ratified the treaty and it had legally come into effect, still having to answer the same questions and defend themselves against the same arguments – Did they really have a right to self-government? Was it inherent? Why couldn't they accept a delegated form of self-government? What kind of jurisdiction and lawmaking powers could an Indigenous government have, and how would that affect the sovereignty of the provincial and federal Crowns? Did the treaty create a third order of government that would disturb the constitutional division of powers between the federal and provincial governments? What were the risks, why was there so much fear? Over and over again, Nisga'a negotiators had to fight for recognition of the prior presence of Indigenous peoples in North America, organized as political entities whose self-governing authority did not vanish in a puff of smoke at the assertion of British sovereignty in 1846.

In *Campbell*, the lawyers for the plaintiffs contended that if an Aboriginal right to self-government had ever existed, it was "extinguished when the United Kingdom acquired sovereignty over the Northwest coast, or when English law was received in B.C. or when B.C. entered Confederation."[13] They stated that any right of self-government did not survive to 1982 and thus could not be one of the *existing* Aboriginal rights that were recognized and affirmed by section 35 of the Constitution. In British

Columbia, the courts have chosen 1846 as the date when the Crown asserted sovereignty. This was the year in which the United States and Britain signed the Oregon Boundary Treaty to settle their competing claims to the Pacific Northwest (McNeil 2018a, 301). Indigenous peoples in Canada were never conquered. Thus, to accept that British sovereignty became paramount merely because representatives of the Crown showed up and asserted it is to assume that Indigenous peoples had no sovereignty at the time, or had a very inferior form of it (Borrows 2010). The Nisga'a's legal team submitted a written statement of defence to the court in which they argued that before contact and colonization, Indigenous nations were independent political entities with the capacity to make laws and exercise jurisdiction over their territories. It referred to the 1996 report of the Royal Commission on Aboriginal Peoples, which described Indigenous nations as "autonomous political units living under the Crown's protection and retaining their internal political authority and their territories."[14] The lawyers argued that the right to self-government persisted after Confederation in 1867, surviving up to and through the 1982 entrenchment of Aboriginal rights in section 35 of the Constitution. To defend this reasoning, they cited precedents in which Canadian courts recognized the presence of Indigenous lawmaking authority after 1867, starting with the case of *Connolly v Woolrich*. In this case, a Quebec court ruled that a marriage between a white trader and a Cree woman, performed according to Cree customary law, was legally binding and not obviated by any Canadian law.[15] The Nisga'a also argued that lawmaking ability was the essence of self-government and that in recognizing the practice of Indigenous lawmaking the courts had recognized the ongoing practice of Indigenous self-government. In addition, they stressed that the right of self-government was "completely integral" to their ability to exercise all the other rights in the treaty (Edward Allen 2004, 243).

The main concern of the *Campbell* case was that the treaty should not include the right to self-government, because this would violate the distribution of powers allowable in the Constitution. The plaintiffs advocated that the federal and provincial governments should have created a local government for the Nisga'a through legislative enactment outside of the treaty, and that the Governance chapter should be struck from the final agreement. For them, and for many other critics, a form of delegated authority for First Nations outside of the protection of the Constitution would be acceptable. In fact, federal negotiators had proposed exactly this during the treaty talks. They wanted the Nisga'a to accept a form of self-government in what is known as a side agreement. Side agreements are not modern treaties or comprehensive land claims, and their provisions do not fall under section 35 of the Constitution. Thus, the right to self-government would not be protected. Other modern treaties, such as the Yukon Umbrella Final Agreement and the James Bay and Northern Quebec Final Agreement, do not include self-government. Nelson Leeson and Kevin McKay told me that during negotiations, "the federal government dangled a carrot in front of us."[16] In other words, it offered money to the Nisga'a Tribal Council to support its ability to negotiate self-government as a separate matter. The money would have paid for research, consultancy, travel, and all the things it takes for people to spend days on end, over years, working on negotiations. The council declined the offer because it knew that the side agreement would entail a delegated form of governing authority, which could be taken away. Delegated authority is loaned out and can be withdrawn. It is also fundamentally at odds with the Nisga'a position that their right to govern themselves is inherent and cannot be given to them in bits and pieces by the Crown.

At stake here is whether or not the Constitution has room for Indigenous governance and lawmaking authority, a question that is still a fundamental issue in Canada. By insisting that the treaty include their right to self-government and defending this in court, the Nisga'a were maintaining that it does and it must. The legal argument of the plaintiffs was that the Constitution has no room for Indigenous governance, and that all legitimate lawmaking authority in Canada flows only from the Crown. Sections 91 and 92 of the British North America Act 1867 (BNA Act), which is now the Constitution Act, divided lawmaking power in Canada between the federal and provincial governments, creating the division of powers that characterizes Canadian federalism. The *Campbell* plaintiffs held that when this division was made in 1867, it was exhaustive and exclusive, with no lawmaking authority left over (Edward Allen 2004, 242). The idea here is that, together, sections 91 and 92 result in 100 percent of governmental authority. If this were accurate, the only way in which an Indigenous government could possess any governing authority, apart from having it delegated, would be to get an amendment to the Constitution to enable a third order of government. Constitutional amendments require approval by the House of Commons, the Senate, and two-thirds or more of the provincial legislatures representing no less than 50 percent of the population. In November 1999, when Gordon Campbell spoke about the treaty at the hearings of the Standing Committee on Aboriginal Affairs, he said,

> This model of self-government is unconstitutional, for the Nisga'a treaty will create a brand-new third order of government with special status and paramount powers under our Constitution. In at least 14 areas of jurisdiction, Nisga'a laws will take precedence over federal and provincial laws; they will be legally superior. No other aboriginal government in Canada has such constitutionally entrenched status. Our Constitution says that all powers are exhaustively held by only two levels of government, the federal government and the provincial governments, yet this treaty attempts to effectively amend our Constitution through the back door.[17]

The inference here is that if Indigenous governments are to exercise any lawmaking power, it must be delegated to them by the Crown. This approach assumes that sovereignty in a settler state is exclusive to settler governments and cannot come from Indigenous peoples themselves. When this court case was taking place, I was in Gitlaxt'aamiks. One evening I went for a drive with a matriarch of the Wolf tribe, who said that people who opposed the treaty just did not want Indigenous people to have anything. They want to keep us like this, she said, and she squashed her thumb down on the dashboard. In court, the Nisga'a argued that the division of powers was not exhaustive and that another political authority had been present in Canada in 1867 – an authority that was not acknowledged when the Constitution was drafted but which existed, nevertheless. Their written statement of defence declared that "the Parliament at Westminster, in enacting the Constitution Act, 1867, set up a new dominion, but it did not thereby extinguish the aboriginal right of self-government that had survived to 1867."[18] The exercise of the right may have been impaired, but the right itself was not eradicated. They also argued that distributing legislative jurisdiction and extinguishing Indigenous political autonomy *are not the same thing*, and that the treaty did not create a third order of government because section 35 in itself has made room for an Aboriginal right of self-government as expressed and established through the Nisga'a treaty.[19]

Justice Williamson concurred. In his ruling, he said that the powers distributed by sections 91 and 92 belonged to the British colonies in Canada. It did not follow that this distribution cancelled out any other sovereign powers. He agreed with the Nisga'a that when the Constitution was drawn up in 1867, another power existed that was not considered. He reasoned that anything "not encompassed by sections 91 and 92 remained outside the power of Parliament and the legislative assemblies" to disburse (Edward Allen 2004, 244). Another way of saying this is that the division of powers in sections 91 and 92 was internal to the Crown. Indigenous people were not at the table when the BNA Act was drafted and did not consent to any extinguishment of their authority. For these reasons, Justice Williamson stated, their authority survived the coming into force of the BNA Act. He wrote that "although the right of aboriginal people to govern themselves was diminished, it was not extinguished." He also noted that after 1982, any Aboriginal rights to self-government "cannot be extinguished, but they may be defined (given content) in a treaty. The Nisga'a Final Agreement does the latter expressly."[20] Williamson also found that land rights and self-government are closely linked, and that because of this an Indigenous nation's decision-making authority over its lands was necessarily governmental in nature (Edward Allen, 2004).

Campbell was a victory for everyone who had struggled to achieve the treaty, and to have it include self-government, for more than twenty years. The court recognized that the Nisga'a had self-governing authority that survived the arrival of Europeans and the creation of Canada in 1867. Moreover, it could still have a place in modern-day Canada. It had been circumscribed and contained but not extinguished. If the *Campbell* ruling had been different, the consequences would have resonated negatively through all other treaty-making attempts in British Columbia and would have eroded the incremental recognition in the courts of an inherent and unextinguished right of self-government. Instead, the

Supreme Court of Canada has ruled more explicitly on Indigenous self-government: in its 2004 rulings in *Haida Nation* and *Taku River Tlingit*, the court acknowledged pre-existing and unextinguished Aboriginal sovereignty (McNeil 2018a, 302).[21]

The *Campbell* plaintiffs did not appeal. When the Liberals won the provincial election in 2001, Gordon Campbell became the premier and Geoffrey Plant became the attorney general. This gave them a different platform from which to challenge the terms of treaty making in British Columbia. In 2002, the Liberal government held a mail-in referendum in which it solicited public response to questions about the mandate of treaty negotiations. There were eight questions on the referendum ballot; seven of these affirmed principles that were *already part* of treaty negotiations, including, for example, that no private property would be expropriated for the purposes of treaty settlements. The sixth question asked voters if they agreed "that aboriginal self-government should have the characteristics of local government, with powers delegated from Canada and British Columbia" (Penikett 2006, 131). Many voters boycotted this referendum. Thirty-five percent of the electorate sent in a ballot; of these, 87 percent answered "yes" to question six (Penikett 2006, 136). This was a victory of sorts for the Liberals, who had campaigned on the promise of holding the referendum. However, the law on the legitimacy of the self-government provisions in the Nisga'a treaty remains determined by Justice Williamson's ruling in the *Campbell* case.[22] Subsequent treaties made in British Columbia, including the Tsawwassen Final Agreement (2009), the Maa-nulth Final Agreement (2011), and the Tla'amin Final Agreement (2014), all include self-government.

Another challenge to the constitutional validity of the Nisga'a Final Agreement and its self-government provisions came from within Nisga'a communities. This highlights some of the difficult community dynamics that can result from land claims and treaty negotiations. In 2005, James Robinson and Mercy Thomas, both from the village of Gingolx, brought a case to the BC Supreme Court challenging the constitutional legitimacy of the treaty. Robinson holds the name of Chief Mountain, Sim'oogit Sga'nisim. Both he and Mercy Thomas had spoken out against the treaty prior to its ratification in 2000. Robinson stated that his *wilp* (House) lost vital territories to the north of Gingolx in Portland Canal and that the Nisga'a Tribal Council did not have the authority to negotiate a treaty with this result. When the tribal council was formed under the Societies Act of British Columbia in 1963, it took as part of its mandate the negotiation of a resolution to the land question. Before this, in 1907, Nisga'a chiefs put all their traditional territories into a "common bowl" to prosecute the land claim from a collective and thereby stronger position; the nature of this agreement was not raised in the BC Supreme Court case but is important historical context to which I return in Chapter 2. Mercy Thomas testified to the Standing Senate Committee on Aboriginal Affairs when it deliberated on Bill C-9 in the spring of 2000; her testimony drew on a mixture of traditional ownership and governance, Indian Act reserve boundaries, band council governance, and principles of Canadian law to create a unique amalgamation upon which to assert the exclusive rights of the residents of Gingolx.

Initially, the lawyers for the plaintiffs were Paul Jaffe and John Weston. In 2000, Weston was active in the group Canfree, which stands for Canadians for Reconciliation, Equality and Equity (Rose 2000). Weston and Canfree played an important role in getting former Supreme Court justice Willard Estey to testify to the Senate committee studying Bill C-9. As a former justice, Estey would not normally be expected to take a strong position on a political matter. He testified before the committee on March 23, 2000, the same day as Mercy Thomas, telling his listeners that the treaty was unconstitutional. Weston also helped establish the Canadian Constitution Foundation (CCF) in 2002. The CCF is a registered charitable organization that describes itself as dedicated to defending the constitutional freedoms of Canadians in both the courts and public opinion. It identified Chief Mountain as one of its clients and supported his case financially.[23] By 2007, Weston had been replaced on the case by John Carpay, who was then the CCF executive director, along with CCF member Jeffrey Rustand. In 2009, Paul Jaffe became the lawyer of record on the case.

The case moved in fits and starts and did not get its first hearing in the BC Supreme Court until 2005. Back in 2001, Justice Wong of the court had struck down portions of the plaintiffs' statement of claim due to its inconsistencies. These inconsistencies showed that there were discrepancies between the goals of James Robinson and Mercy

Thomas and those of their legal team. Wong wrote that "in the first part of the claim the plaintiffs allege the existence of certain inherent aboriginal rights of self-government. In the second part of the claim, as reflected in their prayer for relief, the plaintiffs allege that there is no room in the Canadian Constitution for an inherent aboriginal right of self-government."[24] Robinson's initial argument was that the rights of hereditary chiefs to exercise exclusive authority over their ango'oskw still existed, but this logic implied the existence of inherent, unextinguished Aboriginal rights of self-government and jurisdiction, as well as unextinguished Aboriginal title. When the case came to trial in 2005, the pleadings focused on the claim that the treaty provisions for self-government were unconstitutional for the same reasons presented in *Campbell* – that an inherent right to self-government did not exist, that if it ever had existed it was extinguished by the assertion of Crown sovereignty, and that Indigenous governments in Canada should operate only through delegated authority.

The case dragged on until 2013, when the BC Court of Appeal dismissed it in a unanimous ruling. The court stated that it is "a misinterpretation of the treaty to view it as involving the abdication of exclusive lawmaking authority by Canada and British Columbia." It also argued that the appellants "mischaracterize the effect of the Treaty in material ways" and that "to put the matter baldly, the treaty does not do what they say it does."[25] The Supreme Court of Canada declined to hear an appeal.

In Gingolx and the other Nass villages, opinions are mixed about this case.[26] Some Gingolx residents did not approve of the treaty, because they felt strongly that Gingolx was overlooked and underserved in political decision making among the four villages. In this, they shared some of the sentiments expressed by Robinson and Thomas. Some were skeptical about the motivations of the plaintiffs. The decades-long process of negotiating the treaty and the layering of band council governance over traditional forms of governance has generated tensions within and across communities that both produced this dispute and made it so difficult to actually resolve. The Nisga'a have a history of turning to Western legal procedures to deal with threats to their territory; in fact, they are pioneers in this regard. In this case, Chief Mountain applied the same tactic to address an internal matter that was partially produced by the land claims struggle as well as contestations regarding rightful ownership of hereditary privileges and conduct between chiefs. Ultimately, the lawyers who took the case had no concern for the preservation of the traditional territories of any Nisg̱a'a sim'oogit. They wanted to quash the treaty for the same reasons that Gordon Campbell and others did; they thought that Indigenous people had no inherent rights that had survived the assertion of Crown sovereignty and that Indigenous governments in Canada should exercise only delegated authority.

Space, Law, and Territory: The Struggle over Jurisdiction

Long before explorers, traders, missionaries, and settlers arrived on the Northwest Coast, Nisg̱a'a followed a legal code known as the Ayuuḵhl Nisg̱a'a. This is reflected in the name of their legislative body – Wilp Si'ayuuḵhl Nisg̱a'a (WSN), or the Nisg̱a'a House of Laws. When Rod Robinson talked about the history of Nisg̱a'a government in the community hall when the treaty came into effect, he linked self-government to the ability to make laws. Later, when all the media attention had died down and Wilp Si'ayuuḵhl Nisg̱a'a convened officially for the second time, Frank Calder spoke to the elected representatives about their renewed responsibility to pass laws. He too emphasized the centrality of lawmaking to self-government and urged WSN members not to take this responsibility lightly. Over the years, Nisg̱a'a leaders have also consistently linked self-government with their possession of Aboriginal title. This title is both the source of lawmaking authority and dependent upon it. Commenting on the issues at the heart of the *Campbell* case, former negotiator Edward Allen (2004, 235) notes that "from the beginning, our relationship to the land and our governance in respect of the land has always been one, singular and indivisible concept."

The Ayuuḵhl Nisg̱a'a was one of many Indigenous legal orders in place when Europeans arrived in North America (Macklem 2016, 19). During the initial stages of exploration and trade, when European settlements were small and Indigenous nations were powerful, legal pluralism remained the norm. In his classic article on legal pluralism, John Griffiths (1986, 6) calls it a "fixture" of colonial experience. In North America, the historical record provides many examples of settlers, traders, and explorers turning to Indigenous law to resolve disputes, work out trading agreements, and, as affirmed by the case of *Connolly v Woolrich*, get married (Borrows 2010, 134; Lisa Ford 2010; Loo 1995; Promislow 2013).[27] The treaty making that took place during these early stages of contact, trade, and military alliances is informed by Indigenous legality and did not subordinate either party to the laws of the other; certainly, Indigenous people did not foresee creating such a relationship with any treaty partner (Asch 2014, 90; Macklem 2016). Exclusive lawmaking authority became more important to settler sovereignty in Canada and the United States during the mid-nineteenth century, as settlement increased and the need for land intensified the processes of Indigenous dispossession. This kind of territorial jurisdiction is a critical component of settler colonialism because it links sovereignty and territory (Pasternak 2014b, 146). Over time, settler governments worked to subordinate Indigenous laws and lawmaking power and to displace Indigenous governance (Joanne Barker 2005). This process was incremental, however, and not uniform in Canada or other settler states (McHugh and Ford 2012). Indigenous legalities, sovereignties, and governance values persisted, nested in an uneasy and increasingly confrontational relationship with the state (Audra Simpson 2014). The challenge of contemporary treaty making is to work out forms of political community that acknowledge the source and legitimacy of Indigenous governance and share sovereignty across Indigenous, provincial, federal, and territorial orders, rather than fusing it into uniform territorial jurisdiction (Nettelbeck et al. 2016, 219).

Through the treaty, the Nisga'a have recovered their lawmaking ability, but they do not possess exclusive jurisdiction. Instead, Nisga'a Lisims Government now has concurrent jurisdiction with the federal and provincial governments. The Tsawwassen (2009), Maa-nulth (2011), and Tla'amin Final Agreements (2014) also establish this form of jurisdiction. Concurrent jurisdiction means that for every area where the Nisga'a government can make a law, a federal or provincial law may already be in place on the same subject; they exist concurrently with laws the Nisga'a will make. In this situation, the rules of paramountcy setting out whose law will prevail on any given subject are critical, and Nisga'a laws are paramount in fourteen areas. Edmund Wright (2003, 10), formerly the secretary-treasurer of Nisga'a Lisims Government and a long-serving member of the Nisga'a negotiating team, explains that Nisga'a laws are paramount when they "deal with matters that are internal to the Nisga'a Nation, integral to Nisga'a culture or essential to the operation of Nisga'a government or the exercise of other Nisga'a treaty rights." This entails the administration and operation of Nisga'a government, the management of Nisga'a lands, including forests, fisheries, wildlife, and other resources, the management of Nisga'a assets, Nisga'a citizenship, and matters relating to Nisga'a culture and language (Borrows 2010).[28] These matters are internal to the Nisga'a Nation but are also essential for the operation of the treaty.

When the Nisga'a team was negotiating the governance aspects of the treaty, it insisted that concurrent jurisdiction would be acceptable only if it included these rules of priority, making Nisga'a laws paramount in the fourteen key areas, as noted above. If Nisga'a government had no exclusive jurisdiction, and if federal and provincial laws would always be paramount, any law passed by the Nisga'a could potentially be trumped by a federal or a provincial law. This situation would differ little from living under the Indian Act, when the minister could overrule band bylaws. Time and again, Nisga'a negotiators insisted that the Nisga'a wanted to form a government, not to be a band, and that the essence of self-government was the ability to make laws without interference.

Concurrent jurisdiction does not mean that federal and provincial laws do not apply on Nisga'a lands. Although Nisga'a lawmaking authority prevails in the fourteen areas mentioned above, federal and provincial laws apply in other areas. In fact, the Province actually gained lawmaking authority on Nisga'a lands. This was a critical and underemphasized point amid all the concern that opponents raised over loss of federal and provincial power. When Nisga'a were organized as Indian bands, their reserves were governed by the Indian Act, which is a piece of federal legislation. Most provincial laws do not apply on Indian reserves, not even concurrently; Indian reserves are held in trust by the federal government and lie outside of most provincial jurisdictions. Important provincial laws such as the Wildlife Act, the Highways Act, and the Schools Act now apply on Nisga'a land, whereas before the treaty they did not. During the Senate committee hearings, UBC law professor Doug Sanders argued "that the Nisga'a treaty will integrate Nisga'a government into the Constitutional order of Canada, and in particular will normalize or structure its relationship to provincial governments, something that the present system does not do adequately." Sanders aptly pointed out that many First Nations critics of the treaty felt that it created "too much integration."[29]

Other critics nevertheless used the fact of Nisga'a paramountcy in the fourteen areas to suggest that this treaty and others like it would create mini-sovereign states in which neither federal nor provincial laws would apply. This was an irresponsible exaggeration that misrepresented the kind of lawmaking authority and self-government created by the agreement and others like it, and it returns us to the issue of the source of governing authority. Treaty opponents complained about the "giving" away or improperly "ceding" and surrendering of federal and provincial authority, indicating that the only source of sovereignty and lawmaking power in Canada could be the Crown. In the House of Commons, Mike Scott, the Reform MP for the Skeena riding that included the Nass Valley and nearby Terrace and Prince Rupert, referred inaccurately to the "exclusive legislative jurisdiction" that "has been handed over" in the treaty.[30] Senators complained that the agreement "cedes powers from both the provincial and the federal governments to the Nisga'a" and that the treaty "give[s] the Nisga'a government paramount legislative jurisdiction in a number of areas. This legislative jurisdiction is not delegated; it is ceded or forfeited from the provincial and federal governments."[31] In a piece on the Chief Mountain case, the Canadian Constitution Foundation went further in describing the Nisga'a Nation and Nisga'a Lisims Government as a "quasi-sovereign state residing in Canada with the ability to pass laws that supersede Canadian law."[32]

These kinds of statements pandered to the worst fears of people who were unclear about the nature of Aboriginal rights and the ultimate results of Aboriginal self-government but who generally suspected that they stood to lose something by it. They also reveal assumptions about sovereignty that are historically and culturally specific and entwined in the mythology of the state. The first of these is that sovereignty is necessarily exclusive to the Crown and needs to be uniformly exerted over a territory, as discussed above. The contemporary state system rests on the idea that states have territorially based sovereignty extending over a mapped area, rather than over a set of subjects as was the case for much of the pre-modern world (Biolsi 2005, 240). This form of sovereignty is "fully, flatly and evenly operative over each square centimeter of a legally demarcated territory" (Anderson 1991, 19).[33] A Reform MP expressed precisely this vision of territorial sovereignty when he said,

> The problem ... is the question of who is ultimately supreme with regard to the functioning of society within geographic boundaries. I believe it is purported by the government that the boundaries of Canada are still from the Queen Charlotte Islands, past Victoria, right through to Newfoundland and past Prince Edward Island. This contiguous land mass is meant to be governed by this parliament.[34]

Second, such statements reveal an understanding of sovereignty as a zero-sum game wherein whatever one party gets the other party loses (Lightfoot and MacDonald 2017). They replicate the false choice of "destruction or denial," which Kevin Bruyneel (2007, 219) sees as so detrimental to forging a space for Indigenous governance in settler states. The false choice is that "either indigenous tribes and nations must become sovereign states, thereby destroying the settler states within which they reside, or their citizens must accept unambiguous inclusion in the settler polity" (Bruyneel 2007, 217).

Nisga'a negotiators rejected the zero-sum game. Indeed, the treaty would have been impossible to negotiate with such a view. They also distanced themselves from the sovereignty concept. This was partly a negotiating strategy and partly an assessment of whether "sovereignty" represented what they were striving to achieve through the treaty. When the treaty was being debated in the House of Commons, I asked Joseph Gosnell and Nelson Leeson how they positioned it in relation to sovereignty. Gosnell replied that "the objective of the exercise is to secure the rights that our people will enjoy within the context of Canadian law." He knew that other First Nations thought the Nisga'a did not get enough in the treaty, in land and jurisdiction, but they negotiated it for themselves. "Sovereignty," he said, "what are they referring to? It's a word that people throw around without understanding its meaning." Nelson Leeson explained that the Nisga'a "were not looking to be sovereign but *were looking for autonomy*." The goal is "to get toward self-sufficiency again."[35]

Osage scholar Jean Dennison (2017, 686) writes that sovereignty "is one of the most debated concepts in Native American and Indigenous studies." What people in communities actually want it to look like, in governance practices, varies enormously but is not well captured through the word "sovereignty." When a delegation of Nisga'a travelled to Victoria to meet with Premier Smithe in 1887, to which I will return in the next chapter, they spoke of wanting to be "free" upon their lands. They did not refer to rights, self-government, or self-determination. These terms came into use after the Second World War and are linked to colonial independence movements and international concern for minority rights (Joanne Barker 2005). The etymological origins of "sovereignty" go further back into the sixteenth century, in theories of divine authority that were transported into the political realm (Joanne Barker 2005; Deloria 1979; Dennison 2017; Lyons 2010). The term derived its meaning in a primarily European context, and this meaning is not reflective of Indigenous governance practices and values. Sovereignty is associated with independent states, closed borders, and exclusive territoriality, none of which adequately describe how Indigenous peoples governed themselves before contact or how they seek to create relationships with non-Indigenous governments today.

Some scholars argue for rejecting the term "sovereignty" entirely or deconstructing it in favour of a relational approach to governance. A relational approach acknowledges interdependence between polities and people, along with "freedom, respect and autonomy" (Alfred 2005, 33; Catellino 2008). Rauna Kuokkanen (2012, 229) calls this "relational self-determination," whereas political theorist Iris Marion Young (2001, 31) writes of "relational autonomy in the context of non-domination." In discussing the exercise of sovereignty by the Osage Nation of Oklahoma, Jean Dennison (2017, 687) states that sovereignty is a practice that entangles Indigenous nations with other polities and requires continual work to maintain. She contends that the Osage Nation has maintained sovereignty only by becoming more involved with other structures of power, "such as French and US trade networks, oil and gas extraction,

US congress lawmaking, environmental impact statements," and so on (Dennison 2017, 689). These kinds of interconnections are at the core of how sovereignty functions, in part because through them the state is also entangled with the Osage Nation.

Concurrent jurisdiction creates a layered relationship of laws on Nisg̱a'a territory (Pasternak 2014b). The relationship between these laws changes according to the subject matter. Concurrent jurisdiction disrupts the goal of flat and uniform territorial jurisdiction and creates space for the enactment of Nisg̱a'a laws that have primacy in fourteen areas. Here, the Nisg̱a'a exercise lawmaking outside of the oversight of federal and provincial governments. Although critics felt that their authority was too great, as mentioned above, the more important question for the Nisg̱a'a and other First Nations is whether it is enough, both in principle and day-to-day practice. This question is best answered by the Nisg̱a'a and other Indigenous communities who have concluded treaties with similar concurrent jurisdiction arrangements. Many people who work in government at the village or nation level have spoken positively about the scope and practice of treaty self-governance, especially if they had previously tried to get things done under the band council system of the Indian Act. People who worked in band councils and who experienced the paternalism and lack of any real decision-making power compare treaty self-government quite favourably to that. As one Nisg̱a'a elected official said to me, "it takes off the whole top layer," by which he meant the top layer of Indian Affairs bureaucracy. A village councillor explained that "before the treaty the Department of Indian Affairs could do anything it wanted around here." Waving his hands, he said "they could demolish this house if they wanted to." He recalled being on the band council before the treaty, making plans, and then presenting them to Indian Affairs, which always had the power to change or veto them. He said that the process often seemed like a waste of time and wondered why Indian Affairs staff didn't simply come up to the Nass and make all the plans and decisions themselves. Now, he said, "Indian Affairs can't do that anymore. We control it. Now when we plan something it doesn't get changed ... This is the difference the treaty makes." He added, "We are a government now ... We are no longer a band of Indians." Other elected officials said similar things about how the treaty gave them more power to determine what happened on their core lands, as well as on the much larger Nass Wildlife Area.

Other Nisga'a did not feel that their lives had changed for the better in the last several years. One resident of Gitlax̱t'aamiks said, "well, let's look at everything we got after the treaty. Roads are paved. Housing is better." It is not "a typical reservation situation" of high poverty rates and bad infrastructure. But we "still have all the social issues," and there is "nothing to do here, no jobs." He tells his kids to move elsewhere. "Where's the opportunity for jobs?" asked a long-time resident of Gingolx. "The opportunities are there for those politicians and their relatives," she said. "My way of life has not changed. I still have to work hard for what I want. I still have to do the cultural things that I need to do to survive. I never had any handouts from anybody."[36] People sometimes complained that their government did not do enough for them, but they also mentioned being over-governed. Expectations typically run high after the conclusion of land claims and self-government agreements, but nothing changes overnight, and in fact the socio-economic benefits do not appear in the short or even medium term (Papillon 2008; Warry 1998). At the Land Claims Agreements Coalition conference in 2020, a representative of the Huu-ay-aht First Nations spoke to these kinds of discrepancies, saying that "treaties are very good at creating advantages and success for the government but it's a lot harder to find the success for each individual citizen."[37] In 2010, the Frontier Centre for Public Policy conducted a survey that found that ten years into treaty self-government, Nisga'a citizens felt slightly more satisfaction than dissatisfaction (Quesnel and Winn 2011). This survey was not designed with any input from either Nisga'a Lisims Government or the village governments. More of this kind of research needs to be done, but communities must be involved in designing it and using the data to their benefit.[38] Nisga'a Lisims Government is now developing a quality of life survey based on indicators derived from community consultation (Bouchard et al. 2019). The goal is to identify culturally relevant indicators and to measure impacts of the treaty on things that community members decide are important.

The Ayuukhl Nisga'a and the Challenge of Plural Legal Orders

The treaty creates a new system of governance on Nisga'a lands that is no longer beholden to Indian Act regulations and bureaucracy, but it is not a return to pre–Indian Act forms of governance through chiefs and matriarchs and the Yukw, or feast system. Wilp Si'ayuukhl Nisga'a is the legislative arm for the whole nation (Hoffman and Robinson 2010). It is composed of all the councillors and chief councillors from the four Nisga'a village governments, as well as two representatives from each of the Nisga'a urban local associations in Terrace, Vancouver, and Prince Rupert. It includes the Nisga'a Lisims Government Executive, which is made up of the elected positions of president, the chairperson, the secretary-treasurer, and the chairperson of the Council of Elders. Nisga'a villages all have their own village charters with the authority to make laws on local matters.[39] They administer local programs and services and are responsible for economic development (Hoffman and Robinson 2010).

Nisga'a negotiators and government officials said that they intended their government to be modern and democratic but informed by the values represented in the legal code of the ayuukhl. The Ayuukhl Nisga'a includes laws of inheritance pertaining to land and other forms of property, as well as rules of conduct for war and peace, for trade with other nations, marriage and divorce, restitution for injury, and proper behaviour. Chiefs and matriarchs had a fundamental role in implementing the law, and for this reason it is also called *ayuukhl simgigat*. In the past, as I was told, the law was *in* the chiefs, whose training made them "finished with the law." Their role was to hold the law and look after the land, whereas the role of the matriarchs – the *sigidimhaanak'* – was to hold the stories and use them to remind the chiefs of where the law came from.[40] According to the treaty, "'law' includes federal, British Columbia, and Nisga'a legislation, acts, ordinances, regulations, orders in council, bylaws, and the common law, but, for greater certainty, does not include *Ayuukhl Nisga'a* or *Ayuuk* [traditional Nisga'a laws and customs]" (Canada, British Columbia, Nisga'a Nation 1998, 8). The treaty refers to the ayuukhl only in its preamble, where it states that the "Parties acknowledge the ongoing importance to the Nisga'a Nation of the *Simgigat* and *Sigidimhaanak* (hereditary chiefs and matriarchs) continuing

Nisga'a Lisims Government Building, Gitlaxt'aamiks.
Photograph by author.

to tell their *Adaawak* (oral histories) relating to their *Ango'oskw* (family hunting, fishing, and gathering territories) in accordance with the *Ayuuk* (Nisga'a traditional laws and practices)" (Canada, British Columbia, Nisga'a Nation, 1998, 1).

There was strong resistance to codifying the ayuukhl, and the decision was taken not to include it in the treaty. A primary and critical reason for this is that the ayuukhl is not easily codifiable. It is a set of laws and norms of conduct, but it is also ethics and worldview and values; it is about matters that are as much cultural and spiritual as legal. To write the ayuukhl into the treaty would mean having to codify it in a more final and rigid way. This was problematic because such codification could not possibly capture the context-specific nature of the application of the rules and principles of the ayuukhl. In addition, if the ayuukhl were written into the treaty, it would become subject to interpretation by Canadian courts. Three court challenges have already brought the treaty under legal scrutiny, and provision 7 of the Nisga'a constitution states that "the validity of a Nisga'a law may be challenged in the

Supreme Court of British Columbia."[41] Other Indigenous nations that have negotiated treaties during the recent past have been very cautious about bringing their law into the formal legality of these treaties. This reticence is grounded in fears that their legal systems will be constrained and misappropriated, an unsurprising attitude given that the systems survived by being kept underground.[42] In a report prepared by the Ayuukhl Nisga'a Department of Nisga'a Lisims Government the ayuukhl is described as an "all encompassing set of laws which governs our way of life as evidenced through our customs and traditions." There are "laws which relate to how we live on our traditional lands and to how we manage the resources on our lands."[43] The text explains the processes of teaching and storytelling through which the ayuukhl are orally transmitted. It outlines some of the key principles of the ayuukhl, such as that of respect, but it is intended for community use, not as a final written document of Nisga'a law.

The Council of Elders brings the precepts embedded in the ayuukhl, through their living knowledge of it, into conversation with the lawmaking authority and mechanisms created by the treaty. The council consists of eight elders, two from each village, with each person serving for a two-year term. It provides guidance to Nisga'a Lisims Government as the latter makes and implements new laws. One member of the council said to me, "We are the watchdogs of what they do, to make sure they don't infringe on our ayuukhl and to give advice."[44] This advising role for the Council of Elders is also written into the Nisga'a Constitution. Some council members told me that the elected leaders at WSN passed laws too quickly, without consulting them enough, but it is apparent from talking to negotiators and a reading of the constitution and the treaty documents that the Nisga'a expect a dialogue to exist between traditional legal norms and present-day lawmaking activity. They are "confident that their customary law can adapt to the new legal environment and that, in turn, Nisga'a statute law can be fashioned so as to minimize conflicts with custom" (Otis 2014, 330). This is the work that needs to be done now, outside of the glare of the treaty negotiations.

One criticism of modern treaties is that they create Euro-Canadian styles of government and enable the erosion of Indigenous cultures and methods of governance (Alfred 2005; Coulthard 2014). Nisga'a and other

Indigenous peoples involved in negotiation and implementing modern treaties are faced with creating governing arrangements that provincial, territorial, and federal governments will ratify, through which they can engage with other entities of state and civil society. The Nisga'a chose not to revitalize governance through the feast system and the wilp, in which there are no elections, and did not bring that model of governance for ratification to the House of Commons and Senate in 1999 and 2000. There is a range of scholarly observations on best practices for revitalizing Indigenous governance, just as communities and nations will adopt differing approaches to self-determination as a collective action. Taiaiake Alfred (2005) argues that if Indigenous governments are to be accountable and effective, they need to revitalize their traditional philosophies and methods of leadership. Jeff Corntassel (2008, 108) suggests that for Indigenous self-determination to be sustainable, it should be economically, environmentally, and culturally viable, and should involve restoration of Indigenous livelihoods and relationships with the land. Cornell and Kalt (1998, 188) show that the governance institutions that work the best in Indigenous nations feature a cultural "match" with communities. Coffey and Tsosie (2001, 202) advocate for an approach to tribal sovereignty that depends on "an understanding of where we have been (e.g., how we constitute tradition) and where we are going (e.g., our contemporary interpretation and use of these things to ensure the survival of our Indian people)." They point to the possibility of cultural values informing and strengthening communities but in new ways.

The approach outlined by Coffey and Tsosie best characterizes that taken by the Nisga'a to date. The enrolment and eligibility provisions of the treaty are an example of this. Nisga'a negotiators won the authority to define their own citizenship only after an arduous and lengthy campaign, and their laws on the subject constitute an effort to revitalize cultural norms and practices. Before the treaty came into effect, the Nisga'a Tribal Council created eligibility and enrolment criteria to determine who could be a beneficiary of the treaty rights. These criteria prioritize matrilineal descent. As Bill C-9 moved through the House and Senate, the Nisga'a took a huge amount of criticism regarding this decision but defended their ability to determine their membership in culturally relevant ways (I return to this topic in Chapter 3). The citizenship criteria were drafted in the years leading up to the treaty by an Elders Advisory Committee and brought forward for community consultation every year through the conventions held by the Nisga'a Tribal Council. The Citizenship Act was one of the first pieces of legislation passed by Nisga'a Lisims Government on May 11, the first day of what Rod Robinson referred to as the renewal of Nisga'a self-government. The act is significant because it brings culturally specific criteria into Nisga'a lawmaking within one of the paramount areas of jurisdiction, and the Nisga'a defended it as an appropriate exercise of their self-governance.

Conclusion

This chapter has revealed how difficult it was for Nisga'a negotiators to get self-government included in the treaty, where it would become a constitutionally protected right. Their work here was groundbreaking because all treaties made in British Columbia following the Nisga'a Final Agreement include self-government and concurrent jurisdictional arrangements. The public and political opposition to the inclusion of self-government during the ratification of Bill C-9 and the two court challenges to the constitutionality of the treaty expressed, in often hostile terms, the idea "that the state is the exclusive site and form of legitimate political authority" (Bruyneel 2007, 225). Resisting this idea continues to be all-important to reconfiguring settler states. If contemporary treaties are to provide a mechanism for restoring Indigenous governance and re-creating relationships based on mutual respect, as recommended by the Truth and Reconciliation Commission's calls to action, a recognition of the plurality of the *source* of governing authority in Canada is critical. Referring to "ceding," "giving away," and "forfeiting" are all ways of saying that the sovereignty of the Crown is primary and that any governing authority possessed by Indigenous peoples must be given to them from the Crown. This argument betrays a lack of knowledge of the important role played by Indigenous peoples in the legal and political development of Canada. The relationship it envisions is one of inequality and subordination, rather than one informed by the partnership that was a living potential in earlier treaty relationships.

Aboriginal Title, Fee Simple, and Dead Capital: Property in Translation

2

Historically, treaty making between Indigenous peoples and the Crown in North America has been about a number of things, including trade, military and political alliances, and sharing land and other resources. This chapter outlines the struggle of the Nisga'a Tribal Council to get Aboriginal title recognized and the challenges it faced in trying to keep it. The courts have defined Aboriginal title as a *sui generis* right that is not known to English common law or any Indigenous system of law. *Sui generis* means that it is unique and does not fit into existing legal categories or classifications. As a legal concept, Aboriginal title flows "from the distinct set of rules that bridge the gap between English and Indigenous legal systems and provided for their interaction" (Slattery 2006, 258). Although the courts have recognized that Aboriginal title exists, in land claims negotiations its content must be politically negotiated, translated, or exchanged.

Traditionally, Nisga'a territory was divided into approximately forty ango'oskw, owned by several matrilineages, or *huwilp*. When the treaty came into effect, the Nisga'a Nation became the recognized owner of a 2,000-square-kilometre portion of this territory, which was achieved by legally modifying its collectively held Aboriginal title into fee simple. In 2012, Nisga'a Lisims Government implemented the Landholding Transition Act to make it possible for individual Nisga'a citizens to apply for and own property in fee simple. Nisga'a politicians explain that the act is an expression of their lawmaking and self-governing authority. Throughout this chapter, I trace the economic imperatives underwriting the transformation of property regimes on Nisga'a land, beginning with the state's refusal to acknowledge Nisga'a ownership and concluding with Nisga'a attempts to create a property regime that is conducive to sustainable economic development.

"Every Chief Has a Hunting Ground"

In February 1887, a delegation of Nisga'a and Tsimshian men travelled to Victoria to meet with Premier William Smithe to lay out their concerns about their land. Their goal was to press their claim for a treaty and to ask for a government inquiry into the question of Aboriginal title in British Columbia. The Nisga'a and Tsimshian Nations had already encountered provincial surveyors who were visiting their territories to mark out reserves, and they were deeply troubled by many aspects of that process. They were alarmed that reserve allocation did not acknowledge the extent of their territories, the fact of their original ownership, or the nature of this ownership (Cooper 1993). In addition, they had quickly realized that once a reserve was laid out, government officials, such as an Indian agent, could prevent them from harvesting wood and other necessities outside its borders (Cooper 1993).

Smithe met the delegation at his home in Victoria on February 3 and 8. The Nisga'a delegation included Charles Barton; John Wesley, who was the son of Chief Mountain; Matthew Naas; and Arthur Gurney (Patterson 1983, 44). They were accompanied by John Ryan and Richard Wilson, both from the Tsimshian village of Fort Simpson. Commissioner Peter O'Reilly, the provincial attorney general A.E.B. Davie, and federal superintendent general of Indian Affairs Israel Wood Powell also attended the meetings. A full transcript exists for both days because the Nisga'a and Tsimshian asked that one be made so they could take it back to their communities. The Methodist missionary Thomas Crosby, who was working with the Tsimshian community in Port Simpson, came along to serve as interpreter. At this time, Smithe and most other government officials blamed missionaries for stirring up the land question on the Northwest Coast (Foster 1995, 49). They did not want Crosby involved and refused to let him translate. Charles Barton was pressed into service as the translator instead.

Barton said they had come for nothing more than to see about the land that they knew was theirs. They were not interested in the reserve space laid out for them, which was not enough, and they felt they were "not free upon it."[1] Barton emphasized that they were willing to obey the laws of Queen Victoria but with a treaty that recognized their ownership of the land and their ability to be self-governing. He explained the Nisg̱a'a system of land tenure:

> By the laws among the Indians every chief has a hunting ground, and fishing ground, and goes there to dry salmon all the winter; and that they do not want to be interfered with on that account, but they never refuse anyone to go on that ground to hunt. These chiefs keep these hunting grounds free, not to themselves, and quarrels have never been known upon them yet; but there is a chief on every inlet, and he calls it his own where he hunts.[2]

The hunting grounds Barton referred to are the ango'oskw, the territories owned by the wilp and stewarded by the chiefs for the collective benefit of the wilp. They were often identified by an inlet, stream, or particular fishing site, as Barton said, but they also encompassed the valley in which these geographic features sat. Thus, ango'oskw typically stretch from mountain top to mountain top. Anthropologist Wilson Duff described this in 1969, when he testified as an expert witness in the *Calder* case at the BC Supreme Court:

> The ownership of the mouth of the stream and the seasonal villages, or habitations that were built there, signify the ownership and use of the entire valley. It would be used as a fishing site itself and a fishing site on the river, but in addition to that the people who made use of this area would have the right to go up the valley for berry picking up on the slopes, for hunting and trapping in the valley and up to forest slopes, usually for the hunting of mountain goats. In other words they made use, more or less intensive use of the entire valley rather than just the point at the mouth of the stream.[3]

This system of land tenure and ownership had no parallel in the English land law with which Premier Smithe and the others at this meeting were familiar. What Barton described, and the legal system underpinning it, was not acknowledged as property ownership by policy makers and politicians in British Columbia. The overriding prejudice of the day was that Indigenous people were not civilized enough to have rights in property or a legal system that reflected these rights. After Barton spoke, the premier asked Peter O'Reilly to clarify what he had just said. O'Reilly replied that it was "very easily explained." He stated that the delegation's claims were "impossible" and dismissed what Barton and others referred to as the "laws among the Indians" as mere "habit." He said,

> They each have a little spot which they are in the habit of calling their own. Every inlet is claimed by some one, and were I to include all these, it would virtually declare the whole country a reserve; this arrangement I could not justify. To lay out all the inlets pointed out and claimed by them, would be impossible. They were given the right to all streams which run through their reserves, and every fishing ground pointed out by them, of every sort or kind, was reserved for them. There was no difficulty in doing this, as the fish of special value to the Indians the white men do not care for, therefore their interests do not clash. But to declare every inlet, nook and stream an Indian reserve would virtually be to declare the whole country a reserve.[4]

Smithe did not give the delegation any reassurance that his government would change its approach to the land question. He declared that all the land belonged to the queen and that the Nisga'a and Tsimshian had the right to hunt on it while it remained unoccupied and not yet purchased by a white man, but that they could not own hunting territories exclusively. He also told them that they were better off than white men because the government actually gave them land. According to him, "The Indians, indeed, are specially favoured. When a white man comes into the country no land is given to him, no reserve is made for him, and he does not own a single inch until he has paid for it."[5] Then, resorting to an argument that would exasperate generations of Nisga'a and other BC First Nations people, the premier explained that "the Queen gives it to her Indian children because they do not know so well how to make their own living, the same as a white man, and special indulgence is extended to them and special care shown. Thus, instead of being treated as a white man, the Indian is treated better."[6]

Smithe told the men that they were wrong to think they had any possibility of getting a treaty. Ignoring the precedents of treaty making that had been ongoing in Canada since at least the Royal Proclamation of 1763, he said, "There is no such law either English or Dominion that I know of" and added that "the Indians or their friends have been misled on that point."[7] His refusal to talk about a treaty or to recognize Aboriginal title was the position upheld by the BC government for more than a century (Culhane 1998). Smithe referred instead to Ottawa's enfranchisement policy, saying that any First Nation man "who may become so far advanced as to read and write may be authorized by Order in Council to pre-empt and occupy land like a white man, and earn his living upon it, – not in common with the rest of the tribe, but individually."[8] Pre-emption was a process through which individuals were provisionally granted a piece of Crown land that they had to improve, transforming it through their labour, after which they had the option of purchasing it from the Crown at a reduced rate. In British Columbia, Indigenous people were not permitted to pre-empt property either on or off reserves until 1953. By this time, settlers had taken up most of the land available for pre-emption (Tennant 1990). The Province's refusal to recognize Aboriginal title and the limitations on pre-emption effectively secured the majority of arable land for settlers. Crown land, which in British Columbia comprises about 97 percent of the land base, was made available for resource industries such as logging and mining.

Smithe stressed the necessity of *individual* property ownership and the need for Nisga'a and Tsimshian individuals to separate themselves from tribal affiliations. This emphasis on individual ownership has been an enduring element in government strategies of assimilation in Canada and the United States. Smithe said that eventually Nisga'a and Tsimshian would be able to pre-empt land like white settlers, but that "if you take this position you at once separate yourself from the tribe, and no longer have any common interest in the reserve or with the tribe in any way. You come out from your tribe as a separate individual, as a white man, and entirely on your own responsibility."[9] Federal policy, as reflected in Smithe's comments, was built on the assumption that civilizing Indigenous people required transforming them into self-contained independent modern subjects, able to function as individuals in a market economy. This self was the condition for property ownership, as well as the result of it, then as now. One reason that settlers and politicians did not recognize Indigenous land-ownership in British Columbia is because they did not see this kind of self among Indigenous people. They saw what they perceived as lack of productive use of the land that they themselves desired. The need for land "is settler colonialism's specific, irreducible element" and the motivating factor behind its various modalities – removal, physical genocide, or assimilation (Wolfe 2006, 388). Assimilationist policies in Canada and the United States were similarly focused on dismantling tribes and eliminating their collectively held lands.

Nisga'a Land Tenure

When settlers and explorers arrived in what is now British Columbia, the Nisga'a had lived in the Nass Valley for thousands of years.[10] Carbon dating from sites near the village of Laxgalts'ap shows ten thousand years of occupation. The Nisga'a, like the neighbouring Tsimshian and Gitxsan, practised a system of land tenure that interwove territorial prerogatives with social relationships, cosmology, law, and governance. Land was held collectively by the matrilineal kinship group known as the wilp, or "House." Socially, legally, and politically, the wilp (plural huwilp) is the most important unit in Nisga'a society. Each wilp holds two sets of ranked names, one for men and one for women, as well as other property in songs, crests, and stories. Names stay in the wilp and are passed on through the generations according to matrilineal descent, meaning that a man's name would pass first to a younger brother, and then to his sister's son, or maternal nephew (Nisga'a Tribal Council, 1984c, 7). The highest-ranking man in a wilp is the sim'oogit (plural simgigat); the highest-ranking woman is the sigidimnak̲' (plural *sigidimhaanak̲'*).

In English terminology, these are the chiefs and matriarchs of Nisga'a society.

Ango'oskw are the collective property of the wilp, but the title to an ango'oskw is vested in the chief. It is "tied to the chief's name" (Nisga'a Tribal Council 1984a, 12). When he passes away, the responsibility for the ango'oskw is transferred along with the name to his successor, who is usually a younger brother or a nephew. The sim'oogit's role was one of stewardship of the territory on behalf of the wilp. He was a caretaker of the land, not an owner. The wealth in resources that comes from the land supports and feeds the wilp; it also feeds the name and prestige of the chief and the wilp in the feast hall, where the food offered to guests demonstrates the wealth of the territories (Drucker 1965, 50). A chief's responsibility "was always to be as successful and wealthy as his lands and the efforts of his wilp could make him, thereby gaining prominence for his wilp within Nisga'a society" (Nisga'a Tribal Council 1984a, 21). There are other rights that give access to an ango'oskw; one of the most important derives from the law of *amnigwootkw*, or the privilege that a father gives to his son(s), granting them temporary use of his land. This privilege automatically ends when the father dies. Another, *Hagwin-yuu-wo'oskw*, is a plot of land granted to a bride on her wedding day by a maternal uncle or grandfather so that her husband has access to their land for the benefit of the children.[11] An ango'oskw could also be lost in warfare, to pay compensation for an offence, or if the wilp was unable to produce enough wealth to perform its ceremonial responsibilities.

The role of the simgigat and sigidimhaanak' in governance is tied to the management of territory. The simgigat would meet to discuss the condition of their ango'oskw and, as they discussed the status of the land and the animals, plan what would occur on their territories with respect to hunting and gathering activities. They gave permission in advance for these uses, between each other on their respective ango'oskw. Trespassing onto an ango'oskw without proper permission was a very serious infraction and, as I heard many times, could be punished by death. A sim'oogit had to know the boundaries and condition of his territory, as well as its resources and how those changed from year to year (Sterritt et al. 1998, 11). He also had to know the *adaawak* that tell of the historic migrations of the ancestors across the land. Adaawak̲, or oral records, contain the history of encounters between ancestors and the spirits of the land and are taught to those who are in line for the highest-ranking names. These encounters invested the ancestors with power and responsibility; they are the origins of rights to crests and songs and establish an enduring connection with the places in which they occurred (Robinson 1999, 48). The sigidimhaanak̲' are critical in holding and passing on the knowledge held in these oral records.

As is the case in other First Nations on the Northwest Coast, before inheriting a name, a person was groomed for the position by learning the features and boundaries of the relevant ango'oskw. Anyone in line for a high-ranking name also had to be instructed in proper behaviour. This tutoring often took place on the land. At the 2014 special assembly in Gitwinksihlkw, Joe Gosnell reflected on this critically important practice when he spoke movingly about all the things his father, the late Eli Gosnell, taught him when they were on their territory. He explained that when his father took him hunting and trapping as a young man, he was "always talking and teaching ... always talking. We travelled the river on the trapline, on the hunting grounds, he was always talking. Talking about the land. The names of the mountains. Every little creek that ran into the river has a name."[12] Joe Gosnell added that during all this, his father took the opportunity to teach him the skills necessary for leadership. Once Eli Gosnell died, his children's ability to use his territories ceased, in keeping with the matrilineal principle and with the principle of amnigwootkw described above, but the instruction that he gave to them on the land and about the land endured.

The ango'oskw were vital to survival. They were both a source of sustenance and a sacred trust and something with which chiefs had a physical bond. Describing this relationship between chiefs and their ango'oskw, one elder said, "they hold it," "it is precious." Everything had to come from the ango'oskw, which is why it was so important for chiefs to safeguard them. The elder recalled that her father referred to their ango'oskw as "their million-dollar place" that "will never run out."[13] He told his children never to let go of it, to look after it, and always to share its bounty if they were asked.

K'ayukws, thin strips of salmon, drying in the smokehouse, Gitlaxt'aamiks. Photograph by author.

Aboriginal Title in Canadian Common Law

The scope and source of Aboriginal property rights have been the subject of legal debate and political consideration in what is now Canada since at least the Royal Proclamation of 1763. Premier Smithe's flat refusal even to consider discussing a treaty and Aboriginal title is contrary to the willingness of both the Imperial Crown and the federal government to make treaties before Smithe was alive. George III issued the proclamation in 1763 after Britain defeated France in the Seven Years' War and took over French possessions in North America. Sometimes referred to as the Indian Magna Carta, the proclamation was an executive order having the force and effect of an act of Parliament. As a result, it has enduring legal significance as an enactment of the Crown. The proclamation dealt with multiple issues of governance then facing Britain in its new territories, including matters concerning Indians and Indian land. At the time, settlers and speculators wanted that land. The proclamation recognized that Indigenous peoples living under the Crown's protection "had the exclusive right to any territories they possessed that had not been ceded to the Crown" (Slattery 2006, 260). Most importantly, it set out the guidelines that informed treaty making in Canada through to and following Confederation in 1867 (McNeil 2006). This included the requirement that Indigenous people could cede land to representatives of the Crown only in a public gathering held especially for that purpose, as noted in the proclamation:

> And whereas great Frauds and Abuses have been committed in purchasing Lands of the Indians, to the great Prejudice of our Interests, and to the great Dissatisfaction of the said Indians; in order, therefore, to prevent such Irregularities for the future, and to the end that the Indians may be convinced of our Justice, and determined Resolution to remove all reasonable Cause of Discontent, We do, with the Advice of our Privy Council, strictly enjoin and require, that no private Person do presume to make any Purchase from the said Indians of any Lands reserved to the said Indians, within those parts of our Colonies where We have thought proper to allow Settlement; but that if, at any Time any of the Said Indians should be inclined to dispose of the said Lands, the same shall be Purchased only for Us, in our Name, at some publick Meeting or Assembly of the said Indians to be held for that Purpose by the Governor or Commander in Chief of our Colonies respectively, within which they shall lie.[14]

Representatives of the Crown applied these guidelines when they made treaties with Indigenous people in British North America and then Canada. These historic treaties cover military and political alliances, peace and friendship, trade, and territory. Some peace and friendship treaties, such as those completed in Nova Scotia between the Mi'kmaq and the British Crown, predate the proclamation. The territorial treaties were the last to be made and were entered into by the federal Crown in the interest of opening lands for settlement and resource extraction. They include the eleven numbered treaties negotiated by Ottawa and First Nations between 1871 and 1922, covering parts of Ontario westward through to Alberta and parts of the Northwest Territories (Asch 2014; Miller 2009). The northeast portion of British Columbia is included in Treaty 8, which was signed in 1899. This is the only historic treaty to cover any part of British Columbia except for those made by James Douglas when he was governor of the colony of Vancouver Island and chief factor of the Hudson's Bay Company. Between 1850 and 1854, Douglas made fourteen small treaties, styled as land purchases, that together cover approximately 930 square kilometres of Vancouver Island (Harris 2008, 21).

The royal proclamation mentioned "Indian lands" and "hunting grounds" but not Aboriginal title per se. The concept of Aboriginal title that exists in Canadian common law today does not refer to actual Indigenous systems of land tenure but is rather used by the courts to characterize a general Aboriginal property interest in relation to that of the Crown. The first judicial recognition of Aboriginal title in Canada came in the case of *St. Catharines Milling and Lumber Co v R*.[15] This case involved a dispute between the Province of Ontario, the St. Catharines Milling and Lumber Company, and the federal government. Their disagreement focused on whether Ottawa had the authority to grant a timber licence to the lumber company on lands that it believed First Nations had surrendered when they signed Treaty 3. In Canada, the terms of the BNA Act gave provincial governments ownership of Crown lands, which means that underlying Crown title in these lands is held by the Provinces. The federal government argued that when more than two dozen First Nations in northern Ontario had signed Treaty 3, they surrendered their Aboriginal title, at that time ill defined, to the Crown in right of Canada. After all, Canada, not the Province of Ontario, was the Crown party to the treaty. The Province suggested instead that the interest had simply gone away, leaving Ontario with the unencumbered title over which Ottawa had no rights.

The Judicial Committee of the Privy Council ruled in favour of the Province. It said that the land in Ontario was subject to an Aboriginal interest before Treaty 3 but that the treaty extinguished it. The council ruled that the source of Aboriginal title was the Royal Proclamation of 1763, and it characterized this title as a personal and usufructuary right. A usufruct is a legal right to use, occupy, and benefit from property that belongs to someone else. Importantly, the court did not say that there was a common law source for Aboriginal title grounded in occupation.

Instead, it stated that Aboriginal title was dependent upon the good will of the sovereign (Slattery 2006, 276). It held that Crown title was superior to Aboriginal title because "there has been all along a substantial and paramount estate, vested in the Crown, underlying the Indian title" (Borrows 2002, 7).[16]

This litigation informed legal thinking about Aboriginal title in Canada for several decades, in fact until Frank Calder and the Nisga'a Tribal Council appeared before the Supreme Court of Canada in *Calder*. In that case, six of the seven justices found that Aboriginal title existed when Crown sovereignty was asserted in what is now British Columbia. As mentioned in Chapter 1, the courts take 1846 as the date for this. Three judges – Judson, Martland, and Ritchie – found that Aboriginal title had been extinguished through ordinances and proclamations made by the BC government both before and after the province entered Confederation (Godlewska and Webber 2007, 5). Three others, in the ruling led by Justice Hall, said that it had not been so extinguished. As Justice Hall wrote, it was "beyond question that the onus of proving that the Sovereign intended to extinguish the Indian title lies on the [government] and that intention must be 'clear and plain.'"[17] Hall found that no proof existed to show this clear and plain intention. The seventh judge refused to rule on any aspect of the case because the Nisga'a had not obtained permission from the BC attorney general before launching their lawsuit. This three-three ruling was not an unqualified victory for the Nisga'a Tribal Council, but it did change the judicial understanding of the source of Aboriginal title, as well as some of its characteristics. It also raised the possibility that Aboriginal title still existed where treaties had never been made.

The *Calder* ruling overturned the notion that Aboriginal title was a usufruct right that originated in the royal proclamation, one that was dependent on the good will of the sovereign. It opened the legal door to the recognition that Aboriginal title arises from the presence of Indigenous people on their lands prior to European contact and any assertion of sovereignty. Writing for Maitland and Ritchie, Justice Judson stated,

> The fact is that when the settlers came, the Indians were there, organized in societies and occupying the land as their forefathers had done

for centuries. This is what Indian title means and it does not help one in the solution of this problem to call it a personal or usufructuary right. What they are asserting in this action is that they had a right to continue to live on their lands as their forefathers had lived and that this right has never been lawfully extinguished. There can be no question that this right was dependent on the good will of the sovereign.[18]

Justice Hall wrote, "In enumerating the *indicia* of ownership, the trial judge overlooked that possession is of itself proof of ownership. *Prima facie*, therefore, the Nishgas are the owners of the lands that have been in their possession from time immemorial and, therefore, the burden of establishing that their right has been extinguished rests squarely on the respondent."[19]

Calder was a turning point in the development of the legal recognition of Aboriginal title. Without it, there would be no Nisga'a treaty and no treaty process in British Columbia today. The ruling meant that the Nisga'a had rights that were recognizable in common law, not just rights that the government *had created for them* by legislative enactment or executive order (Borrows 2007). It "entrenched in Canadian law the existence of an Indian title" derived from Indigenous possession (Sanderson 2018, 343). After *Calder*, the next most significant ruling on Aboriginal title was the 1997 Supreme Court of Canada judgment in *Delgamuukw v British Columbia*.[20] The appellants in this case were the hereditary chiefs of the Gitxsan and Wet'suwet'en First Nations from northwestern and northcentral British Columbia. Like the Nisga'a, they sued for recognition of their title over their traditional territories, a combined area of approximately 58,000 square kilometres. After losses in the BC Supreme Court and the BC Court of Appeal, they took their case to the Supreme Court of Canada.

The court ruled that Aboriginal title continued to exist in British Columbia and affirmed that it was a right to the land itself, not merely a right to use and occupy the land. The court stipulated that Aboriginal title is held communally and is inalienable except to the Crown, meaning that it cannot be transferred, sold, or surrendered to anyone other than the federal government. In the majority ruling, Chief Justice Lamer wrote that "Aboriginal title has been described as *sui generis* in order to distinguish it from 'normal' proprietary interests, such as fee simple." Continuing on, Lamer stated that "it is also *sui generis* in the sense that its characteristics cannot be completely explained by reference either to the common law rules of real property or to the rules of property found in aboriginal legal systems. As with other aboriginal rights, it must be understood by reference to both common law and aboriginal perspectives." Building on the *Calder* ruling, Lamer specified that the source of Aboriginal title is not the Royal Proclamation of 1763 but rather "the prior occupation of Canada by aboriginal peoples."[21] In the common law, occupation is proof of possession in law, but what makes Aboriginal title *sui generis* is that it arises from possession *before* the assertion of British sovereignty. All other property interests in the common law arise afterward.

Delgamuukw moved Canadian jurisprudence on Aboriginal title forward, but it set significant limitations on the uses to which Aboriginal title lands could be put, and this affected how the Nisga'a went about negotiating the legal characteristics of their landownership in the treaty. A lawyer whom I interviewed described *Delgamuukw* as giving with one hand while taking away with the other. For example, the ruling said that Aboriginal title lands could not be used "in a manner that is irreconcilable with the nature of the claimants' attachment to those lands."[22] So, for example, if lands are claimed on the basis of being a hunting territory, they cannot be transformed into a strip mine. These limits are supposed to preserve the claimants' special interest in their land and to prevent uses that would destroy its ability to sustain future generations. The court emphasized that Aboriginal title lands are not an alienable commodity.[23] This is consistent with what many Indigenous people say about their relationship to their lands, but the *sui generis* nature of Aboriginal title as defined by the courts sets the lands apart in ways that Nisga'a negotiators found constraining. It is partly due to the *Delgamuukw* ruling that the Nisga'a ended up modifying their Aboriginal title into fee simple. John Borrows (2002, 100) argues that the *Delgamuukw* restriction "undermines Aboriginal title because it compels Aboriginal peoples to surrender their lands to the Crown if they want to use them for certain 'non-Aboriginal' purposes." Nisga'a negotiators, though forced into a corner, refused to surrender Nisga'a Aboriginal title. The result of this refusal was the development of the modification technique, to which I return below.

The court in *Delgamuukw* did not rule on the specific title claim of the Gitxsan and Wet'suwet'en. The only Supreme Court of Canada ruling to result in an actual finding of Aboriginal title in a specific area – rather than a theoretical finding of its unextinguished presence – is *Tsilhqot'in Nation v British Columbia*.[24] In this key 2014 case, the court ruled unanimously that the Tsilhqot'in Nation had Aboriginal title to 1,900 square kilometres of traditional territory in the BC interior. The Tsilhqot'in launched this case in the BC Supreme Court after the Province issued a timber licence to Carrier Lumber in 1983 that enabled the lumber company to log on their territory. The court also ruled that the British Columbia Forest Act did not apply on Tsilhqot'in title lands, because the Tsilhqot'in, not the Province, owned the forest on those lands. The court expanded the definition of Aboriginal title, saying that it "confers ownership rights similar to those associated with fee simple, including: the right to decide how the land will be used; the right of enjoyment and occupancy of the land; the right to possess the land; the right to the economic benefits of the land; and the right to proactively use and manage the land."[25]

Aboriginal Title, Fee Simple, and the Problem of Translation

The treaty transforms the Aboriginal title of the Nisga'a Nation into an estate in fee simple. It does this by "modifying" it. Section 25 of the General Provisions of the treaty states that "the aboriginal title of the Nisga'a Nation anywhere that it existed in Canada before the effective date [when the treaty comes into effect] is modified and continues as the estates in fee simple to those areas identified in this Agreement as Nisga'a Lands or Nisga'a Fee Simple Lands."[26] This modification clause appears in subsequent BC treaties, including the Tsawwassen Final Agreement (2009), the Maa-nulth Final Agreement (2011), and the Tla'amin Final Agreement (2014). Treaty negotiators also referred to the modification clause as the "certainty" language. Modification is called "certainty" because transforming the Aboriginal title and other undefined section 35 Aboriginal rights of a First Nation into defined treaty rights is said to create certainty about the nature and scope of these rights (Blackburn 2005). Formerly, the Canadian government used treaties to achieve what it saw as certainty by extinguishing Aboriginal rights and title, in exchange for other rights granted to the First Nation. The territorial treaties made by the government, whose purpose was to free up lands for settlement and resource extraction, all included a clause of cede, release, and surrender. Such a clause stated that the First Nation gave up all of its rights to the Crown, including its title to the land, in exchange for a different set of rights, promises, and guarantees. This was also called extinguishment, or extinguishment and exchange.

Treaty 8, for example, which was signed in 1899 by representatives of the Dunne Za in northern Alberta, northern Saskatchewan, and northeastern British Columbia, includes the following: "the said Indians DO HEREBY CEDE, RELEASE, SURRENDER AND YIELD UP to the Government of the Dominion of Canada, for her Majesty the Queen and her successors forever, all their rights, titles and privileges whatsoever" to the lands as specified in the treaty and "to all other lands wherever situated in the North-West Territories, British Columbia, or in any other portion of the Dominion of Canada."[27] In exchange for these surrenders, the First Nations who made treaties with the Crown were promised certain rights and benefits as set out in the treaty. These benefits encompassed provisions for education, health care, assistance with farming that included tools and livestock, and yearly treaty annuities (Asch 2014). Elders who were young children when the numbered treaties were completed say that there was no talk of extinguishment when their forefathers met with government representatives to negotiate treaty terms (Asch 2014, 107; Morin 2018). We know from oral history and living memory that the oral deliberations did not convey this sense of total and final surrender, even though it does appear in the written text of treaties (Cardinal and Hildebrandt 2000; Miller 2009, 172).

The Canadian government carried the requirement of extinguishment over into the post-1973 treaty-making period that began after the Supreme Court ruling in *Calder*. Although the *Calder* decision acknowledged the existence of Aboriginal title, Ottawa's immediate response was to go about getting that title extinguished rather than allowing such recognition to stand. For a time, its preferred policy procedure was extinguishment and exchange, whereby the Indigenous nation entering into a treaty would be granted rights in return for everything it gave up. Ottawa's 1981 Native Claims Policy was clear on this, saying that its point "is to exchange undefined aboriginal land rights for concrete rights and benefits" (Hamilton 1995, 19). In the government's revised 1986 Comprehensive Land Claims Policy, "extinguishment" was deleted, but the phrase "cede, release, and surrender" was retained, as was the principle of exchange of rights. The James Bay and Northern Quebec Agreement is the first post-1973 treaty in Canada, ratified in 1975. It contains a surrender and exchange clause, stating that "in consideration of the rights and benefits herein set forth in favour of the James Bay Crees and the Inuit of Quebec," they each "cede, release, surrender and convey all their native claims, rights, titles and interests, whatever they may be, in and to land in the Territory and Quebec."[28] The Yukon Umbrella Final Agreement, which was concluded in 1990, also contains the language of surrender. Chapter 2, section 2.5.0, of the agreement stipulates that its beneficiaries "cede, release and surrender their aboriginal claims, rights, titles and interests" to all lands outside the settlement lands provided in the agreement and also to the "mines and minerals within all settlement lands."[29] For the Nisga'a and other Indigenous peoples who were looking for treaty agreements with federal and provincial governments, removing the references to extinguishment while keeping "cede, release, and surrender" was not much of an improvement and ultimately boiled down to the same thing.

First Nations whose ancestors signed historic treaties containing the cede, release, and surrender language state that the signatories did not understand and never imagined they were extinguishing their rights for all time (Borrows 2002, 113). They saw treaties as creating relationships of mutual support and obligation between themselves and the European newcomers, akin to a social contract that was also legally binding (Craft 2013; Miller 2009). This is the true spirit and intent of treaties made between Indigenous peoples and the Crown. When rights are extinguished, they are cancelled or destroyed. The Nisga'a and other Indigenous peoples in Canada argue that their title and rights are fundamental to their identity and see any demand to extinguish these as extinguishing who they are as a people (Asch and Zlotkin 1997, 215).

In 1995, Ottawa commissioned Associate Chief Justice A.C. Hamilton of the Manitoba Queen's Bench to prepare a report on alternatives to extinguishment. Titled *Canada and Aboriginal Peoples: A New Partnership*, it is known as the Hamilton Report. The Nisga'a Tribal Council sent in a written submission in which it asserted that "extinguishment severs a First Nation's links with [its] past" (Hamilton 1995, 49–50). Extinguishment also privileges the Crown as the source of whatever rights the Indigenous party possesses after the treaty is concluded. This is the consequence of the exchange of rights. After surrendering everything, the Indigenous nation acquires a set of treaty rights, including designated lands, but these entitlements come from the Crown. They do not flow from the inheritance of ancestral territories or the internationally recognized inherent nature of Indigenous rights. This is a legally and symbolically profound difference.

Indigenous peoples in Canada have always insisted that their title and other rights do not come from any Crown grant and that the government cannot give them rights but can only recognize rights that they already have. This was at the crux of the argument over the inherent right to self-government, discussed in Chapter 1. Nisga'a leaders made this point to Commissioners Cornwall and Planta in 1887, they said it during the *Calder* case, and they said it throughout the negotiations of their treaty. The historical record is full of statements by outraged Nisga'a who were responding to the paternalistic assurances of government representatives that they would be "given" land on which to live. In 1887, Commissioners Cornwall and Planta told a group of Nisga'a assembled at Gingolx that the Province would always set apart land for their use. Charles Russ answered, "Set it apart, how did the Queen get the land from our forefathers to set it apart for us? It is ours to give to the Queen, and we don't understand how she could have it to give it to us."[30] At the same meeting, another chief by the name of Neis Puck, described in the transcript as elderly and blind, jumped to his feet to say, "I am the oldest man here and can't sit still any longer and hear that it is not our father's land. Who is the chief that gave this land to the Queen? Give us his name, we have never heard it."[31]

Nisga'a negotiators declared that if the government insisted on extinguishment, there would be no treaty. They did, however, accept that their Aboriginal rights and title could be "modified." The General Provisions chapter of the treaty thus contains paragraph 23, which states that the agreement exhaustively sets out the constitutionally protected section 35 rights of the Nisga'a, including their attributes, limitations, and geographic extent. This is followed by paragraphs 24 and 25, which explain that the Aboriginal rights and title of the Nisga'a are modified and continue as the rights set out in the treaty. Thus, the rights are not ceded in exchange for a different set of rights from the government. Instead, the undefined Aboriginal rights and title of the Nisga'a people are modified into the defined rights set out in the treaty and continue as such. Theoretically, they are transformed but their original source as the inherent rights of the Nisga'a people is not changed, and there is no initial surrender of the rights before the treaty takes effect. This modification occurred at the stroke of midnight between May 10 and May 11, 2000, when the treaty came into legal effect. Midnight in Ottawa occurred three hours earlier than in British Columbia, so the treaty took effect in the province only at midnight Pacific Standard Time.

An intense amount of legal energy and political concern went into developing the modification technique (Blackburn 2005). For the federal and provincial governments, it was essential that the model provide certainty; for Nisga'a negotiators, it was essential that the model not involve extinguishment. As a provincial negotiator remarked, there were more lawyers "dancing on the head of a pin" with respect to this issue than any other. "Certainty," he said, "was huge. It was a huge issue to do something that was not perceived as surrender by the First Nation but that provided governments with the certainty that we're not still dealing with undefined rights out there."[32] The issue was huge because it was legally complicated but also because concern about the economic, social, and governing uncertainty posed by the threat of unextinguished Aboriginal rights and title had intensified (Blackburn 2005; Woolford 2005). The recognition of Aboriginal title by the Supreme Court of Canada threw open issues of ownership and jurisdiction that heretofore had been considered settled, erroneously, thereby jeopardizing the Province's ability to secure lands for investment and resource development. In British Columbia and other resource-based provinces, economic certainty is pretty elusive at the best of times, however, and is affected by many more things than undefined Aboriginal rights. This includes shifting global markets and climate change and its associated economic disruptions, as well as jurisdictional disputes between provinces.

The Nisga'a negotiating team agreed to modify Aboriginal title because of the catch-22 created by the *Delgamuukw* ruling when it stipulated that Aboriginal title lands could not be alienated or used in a way that was inconsistent with what made them Aboriginal title lands. If the Nisga'a wanted to use their land differently, the only option coming out of *Delgamuukw* was to surrender it to the Crown and then have it returned to them under a different form of land tenure (Borrows 2002; McNeil 2006). In essence, this merely entailed a return to the extinguishment and exchange formula. The Nisga'a negotiating team accepted modification of Nisga'a title into fee simple because in that split second of midnight, there was no moment of surrender. Through the magic of legal technique, Nisga'a rights were modified and continued as modified. Although critics have suggested that modification is just extinguishment under another name, the Nisga'a negotiators felt that it preserved the integrity of the nation's original ownership; the Nisga'a did not have to give it up and then get it back. Philosophically, this was the most important thing. The negotiators also realized that Aboriginal title had to be modified for other reasons. As Joe Gosnell told me, he had always assumed that the Nisga'a could do as they pleased with Aboriginal title lands, but *Delgamuukw* changed that. *Delgamuukw*, he said, "would hold us in the same economic and political position we have been in since Canada became a country."[33] Indigenous people have a range of objectives for their land, but the ability to use both it and their resources in ways that support their economies and well-being is critical. Another negotiator spoke about the likelihood that non-Nisga'a institutions would want to see recognizable and legible forms of property rights that could fit within existing economic and legal structures. He said the Nisga'a would probably want to enter into transactions involving their land in the future and that those transactions

> have to have rules that are familiar to people who deal with this stuff every day ... They don't have to be identical; they just have to be

known. In order to do that the best way is to modify the interest into something that's familiar to the rules and the paradigms of the larger legal, economic, political system that we have.[34]

The questions that flow from the modification of Aboriginal title into fee simple concern the cultural dissonance of this process and what an estate in fee simple implies about the source of the ownership. To talk of fee simple is to enter into the doctrine of estates and the accompanying doctrine of tenures, both of which originated in feudal England. In the most basic terms, fee simple is an estate granted by the Crown on its underlying title. The doctrine of tenures that grants the Crown this underlying title dates back to the Norman Conquest of 1066 when William I defeated Harold II and became king of England. As king, William assumed ownership of all England in the form of radical or underlying title (Gray and Gray 2009, 56). The rights of existing lords and landowners were transferred into estates. As legal scholar Douglas Sanderson (2018, 325–26) clarifies, "Under a monarchial structure, landowners were made into lords who did not own their land – these belonged to the king – and the lords became a community of tenants who had jurisdiction over their lands and could demand various services from their tenants."[35] The lords in turn provided goods and services to the king, including military aid, in exchange for what were essentially sets of interests in land. The doctrine of tenures explains the king's underlying ownership as paramount lord of all England. The doctrine of estates refers to the sets of interests, including the time frame in which they are held, that are granted on top of Crown tenure.

The abstraction at the heart of the doctrine of estates is that the owner has "ownership of an intangible right (ie an estate) rather than ownership of a tangible thing (ie the land)" (Gray and Gray 2009, 57). An attorney for the Nisg̱a'a Tribal Council explained that, whereas private property owners may believe they own their land, "what [they] have is a bundle of rights, the right to occupy, to come on, to leave, to lease, to rent, to sell, to waste, which means destroy it. It's a bundle of rights ... But, the metaphysical notion is that the ownership of the soil is in the Crown, and what everybody else has is an estate."[36] Abstraction notwithstanding, an estate in fee simple is nevertheless the most extensive form of landownership possible in the common law (Gray and Gray 2009). It is "the closest approximation to absolute ownership found in the Anglo-Canadian system of landholding" (Ziff 2014, 172). One reason it is considered the largest estate in law is because it can be held indefinitely through successive inheritors. An estate is a quantity of interest in land that is defined in terms of time. The "doctrine of estates gave expression to the idea that each landholder owned not land but a slice of time in the land" and an estate in fee simple is the largest quantity of time in land (Gray and Gray 2009, 58). It has the potential to exist forever, unlike the fee tail or the life estate that are now much less common and limited in how they can be passed on to successors.

To return to the relationship between the fee simple of the Nisga'a Nation and the underlying title of the Crown, in Canadian common law the latter is a property right derived from the doctrine of tenures (McNeil 2018b, 276). In all recent court decisions on Aboriginal title, the courts proceed on the assumption that the Crown holds underlying title to all of Canada (Borrows 2016, 141). Aboriginal title is defined as a set of interests, unlike anything else in the common law, that sits on top of that title, and in this respect the courts have described it as an encumbrance or "burden" on Crown title (Borrows 1999b; Culhane 1998). In the landmark *Sparrow* decision of 1990, the Supreme Court of Canada held that

> it is worth recalling that while British policy towards the native population was based on respect for their right to occupy their traditional lands, a proposition to which the Royal Proclamation of 1763 bears witness, there was from the outset never any doubt that sovereignty and legislative power, and indeed the underlying title, to such lands vested in the Crown.[37]

More recent rulings in *Delgamuukw* and *Tsilhqot'in* affirm the presence of underlying Crown title and describe the crystallization of Aboriginal title upon the assertion of Crown sovereignty. In *Delgamuukw*, Chief Justice Lamer stated that "Aboriginal title is a burden on the Crown's underlying title. However, the Crown did not gain this title until it asserted sovereignty over the land in question. Because it does not make sense to speak of a burden on the underlying title before that title existed, aboriginal title crystallized at the time sovereignty was asserted."[38] Several years later in *Tsilhqot'in*, the Supreme Court stated that "at the time of assertion of European sovereignty, the Crown acquired radical or underlying title to all the land in the province. This Crown title, however, was burdened by the pre-existing legal rights of Aboriginal people who occupied and used the land prior to European arrival."[39]

The languages used to talk about title are rich in spatializing metaphors, locating the Crown's encompassing presence at what seems like an inescapably subterranean level but also horizontally, across the territorial expanse of the state (Ferguson and Gupta 2002). The prior ownership of lands by Nisga'a and other Indigenous peoples would seem to suggest that if anybody's title were to sit on top of anyone else's, it would be the Crown title sitting on top of Aboriginal title. On this point, John Borrows (2002, 94) asks, "How can lands possessed by Aboriginal peoples for centuries be undermined by another nation's assertion of sovereignty? What alchemy transmutes the base of Aboriginal possession into the golden bedrock of Crown title?" Law is often imbued with a kind of magical power, conjuring up things that were not there before, and property law is particularly rife with mythical constructions (Jessie Allen 2008). Law as magic, or as a magic trick, is reflected in a Nisga'a Tribal Council lawyer's explanation of the underlying title of the Crown:

> You know the old magician's trick of grabbing the tablecloth and yanking it out from underneath the fully set table while leaving the table settings intact. This is kind of like that only the film is being run backwards. So Crown sovereignty is the tablecloth and it goes whoosh, right in underneath the plates. And at that moment the relationship between the plates and the tablecloth gets called Aboriginal title.[40]

Does modification into fee simple mean that the Nisga'a have accepted Crown title as the underlying title? If fee simple is always a grant upon the underlying title of the sovereign, this would negate the temporal priority and source of Aboriginal title that Nisga'a and other Indigenous peoples in Canada have asserted as a pre-existing inherent right – as a right that they specifically do not receive from the Crown. Nisga'a negotiators addressed this in two ways. First, the fee simple estate that the Nisga'a secured in the treaty is more than what an individual property owner has in any BC town or city. In the latter, the Crown holds back certain conditions, reservations, provisos, and exceptions, such as subsurface mineral rights, leaving the property holder with ownership of what is in effect the surface of the soil. The Nisga'a estate in fee simple is the fullest fee simple available in law, without restrictions, and the Nisga'a possess the subsurface mineral rights. According to paragraph 3 of Chapter 3 (Lands) in the treaty,

> On the effective date, the Nisga'a Nation owns Nisga'a Lands in fee simple, being the largest estate known in law. This estate is not subject to any condition, proviso, restriction, exception, or reservation set out in the *Land Act,* or any comparable limitation under any federal or provincial law. No estate or interest in Nisga'a Lands can be expropriated except as permitted by law, and in accordance with, this Agreement. (Canada, British Columbia, Nisga'a Nation 1998, 31)

The second way in which Nisga'a negotiators addressed the problems posed by fee simple was by including a statement in paragraph 7 of the Lands chapter to prevent the escheat of any Nisga'a lands to the Crown. Lands escheat, or revert to, the Crown when an estate has no heirs. Escheat is one of the remaining primary functions of the doctrine of tenures. The idea that lands held under any estate revert to the Crown when there are no heirs flows from this notion of the underlying title of the Crown (McNeil 2018b; Sanderson 2018). Discussing the significance of the doctrine of tenures, Kent McNeil (2018b, 277) explains that "although the Crown has the underlying or radical title, in practical terms since the decline of feudalism all this means is that the land will escheat (go back) to the Crown if the fee simple owner dies intestate and without heirs."

I spoke to negotiators who asserted that the Nisga'a fee simple estate went all the way down into the earth, like radical title, and I suggest that the Nisga'a may have carved out a different kind of property interest through this treaty. As one negotiator put it, their fee simple includes "the ground as far as you can go under your feet and the sky as high as you can go above." Another said, "there is no Crown title, not on Nisg̲a'a lands." He added, "the Crown has nothing on Nisg̲a'a lands. That's the privilege of the estate ... We have down to the core of the earth and up to the sky." He and others involved in the treaty talks took fee simple, in its most expansive form, as the most appropriate container that existed in the common law to express their ownership. They also struggled to detach it from its feudal and colonial entanglements by severing their fee simple from the Crown's underlying title (Blomley 2014b, 169). Blomley (2014a) argues that Nisg̲a'a and other First Nations in the BC treaty process are expanding the category of fee simple in practice and in theory. And indeed, the Nisg̲a'a treaty does seem "to vest Crown-like entitlements in the Nisg̲a'a regarding the ultimate ownership of land" (Graben 2014, 435). Sari Graben (2014, 435) notes that the "perpetual right of the Nisg̲a'a Nation to repossession may reflect the creation of a new type of interest in law. Much as the Crown holds a radical or allodial title to all lands, making it the ultimate 'owner' of the land, so now do the Nisg̲a'a." Nisg̲a'a negotiators, faced with the constant demands to compromise and bend to the legibility of the state, pushed to create something different in the common law in respect of their ownership. The Nisg̲a'a have done this with other colonial belief systems and institutions, such as Christianity. There is more potential here, and necessity, for a legally innovative concept of an Aboriginal fee simple in which allodial title rests with the First Nation, to be negotiated more explicitly and confidently in future treaties.

For many people in the Nass Valley, the more important issue was how much land they would retain as a result of the treaty settlement and what they could do with it. Many felt that the amount of land was not enough. Under the treaty, the Nisg̲a'a Nation owns 1,992 square kilometres in fee simple,[41] and Nisg̲a'a Lisims Government has co-management responsibilities on the 27,000 square kilometres of the Nass Wildlife Area. The Lands chapter of the treaty does not mention the ango'oskw. They are referred to only in the preamble to the treaty, where it states that "the Parties acknowledge the ongoing importance to the Nisg̲a'a Nation of the *Simgigat* and *Sigidimhaanak* (hereditary chiefs and matriarchs) continuing to tell their *Adaawak* (oral histories) relating to their *Ango'oskw* (family hunting, fishing, and gathering territories) in accordance with the *Ayuuk* (Nisga'a traditional laws and practices)" (Canada, British Columbia, Nisga'a Nation 1998, 1). Of particular concern is that the ango'oskw of some families were not included in the core treaty lands. One interviewee declared that the ango'oskw were the biggest casualty of the land claim. He emphasized how central they were to a sim'oogit's identity and said that the chiefs, even before the treaty, had made "tremendous adjustments" to accommodate change. As he noted, because most ango'oskw lay beyond the core lands, the traditional system of land tenure and governance was no longer really applicable to them. Here, he said, it was essential to understand the common bowl.

The common bowl refers to the decision made by the chiefs and elders in the early twentieth century to put all Nisga'a territories together to most effectively pursue the land claim. This was the first accommodation made by the Nisga'a regarding how they organized themselves in relation to territories. The approach was not in effect in 1887, of course, when Commissioners Cornwall and Planta visited the Nass River. Their report refers to various Nisga'a chiefs who identified individual ango'oskw and requested papers recognizing their rights to such.[42] When the Nisga'a Land Committee was formed in 1907, it adopted the principle of tribal ownership encompassing all the ango'oskw to determine the boundaries of the land claim. It employed this strategy when it presented its claim to the British Privy Council in its 1913 petition, to the federal and provincial governments, and in the courts. For its part, the Nisga'a Tribal Council also adopted the common bowl philosophy, enshrining it in a preliminary statement that would be part of the Framework Agreement presented at the annual convention meeting in 1989 (Griffin and Spanjer 2008). A two-page statement of the common bowl approach to the land claim has been part of the agenda booklets for the tribal council's annual conventions since then, with the subtitle "A Statement to Reinforce Our Forefathers Agreement to Address the Nisga'a Land Question 'Collectively' Rather than 'Individually,' in Order to Avoid Dissension or Friction among Tribal Members."[43] The agreement in principle for the treaty states that on the effective date, "Nisga'a Lands will be owned communally by the Nisga'a Nation" and that "title to Nisga'a Lands will vest in Nisga'a Government" (Canada, British Columbia,

Nisga'a Tribal Council 1996, 9). In 1996, the Nisga'a Tribal Council held a special assembly from February 22 to 25 to explain the agreement in principle. Over 1,200 people attended. At the end of the assembly, they voted to empower the president of the tribal council to sign the initialled agreement in principle.

The imagery of the common bowl refers to the Nass River and its valley as a bowl that sustains the population. In Nisga'a, it is *sayt-k'ilhl wo'osihl Nisga'a* (all-one or same-bowl from which the Nisga'a share).[44] The use of the common bowl to organize the land claim, one interviewee explained, "came from a recognition that we needed to act as one," as *sayt-k'ilim-goot*, which means being of one heart and working together. It reflects the important value of sharing and prioritizing the collective over the individual: "You are not an individual unless you recognize certain obligations to your community. Through the years," he said, "it's what kept us unified." The emphasis on the collective is a common theme. Sim'oogit Minee'eskw, Rod Robinson, wondered how Nisga'a would maintain it when they were up against a society that puts so much emphasis on the individual. "It's a constant challenge," he said, "to remind people, yes you can be individuals, but you're not an isolated unit here." Discussing settlement feasts, he noted that they constitute collectiveness, belonging, and the common bowl all rolled into one. Passing on the name of the deceased ensures that continuity persists. At and through these feasts, "there is also the reminder that people aren't just individuals. They have obligations to their family, tribe, community and nation." The common bowl was a strategy for unity and strength. Now, he said, people whose property lies within the core lands "have to be prepared to share with those who have lost theirs."[45]

There are different levels of engagement with the idea of the common bowl. One person I talked with in Gingolx told me he had never heard of it. Others expressed frustration that that pact made by chiefs long ago was not being recognized or honoured. It would be difficult to have not heard of the concept, because it was promulgated in community meetings, annual conventions, and all documents leading up to the conclusion of the treaty. While it dates back to the strategizing that went into the petition of 1913, the use of the common bowl metaphor to reframe landholdings is relatively recent and was undertaken under pressure. People are experiencing the final achievement of the treaty quite differently depending on a range of factors including but not limited to age, gender, family position, relative income, and access to employment. I spoke with many who do not feel that all Nisga'a are benefitting equally from what is now supposed to be common property – the treaty lands belonging to their nation. "There is no common bowl," a Gingolx resident said to me, "there is no sharing."[46] She complained about income inequality in the villages and about the permits that the Nisga'a government now requires for gathering traditional foods. She and others complained about having to go to the central Nisga'a Lisims Government for permission to harvest in what was formerly their ango'oskw, or even formerly their reserve. These are two kinds of entitlements, one traditional and one not, both of which are set against the more recently established authority of the centralized Nisga'a Lisims Government on common lands.

Acquiring permits to harvest on common lands is a source of frustration for some Nisga'a citizens, who say that it contradicts traditional law and who are displeased that their government is exacting this kind of bureaucratic oversight.[47] When people ask why they must have a permit to hunt, harvest shellfish, or pick berries in locales where their families have done the same for decades, they are rejecting the notion of common lands and the jurisdiction of the Nisga'a Lisims Government as set out in the treaty. Nisga'a government employees were frustrated by this attitude, pointing out that the permits are necessary because they help them to keep track of harvesting numbers and thus to manage fish, wildlife, and things such as pine mushrooms.[48] The Nisga'a Lisims Government sets a number for a yearly moose hunt, for example, and in the larger Nass Wildlife Area Nisga'a citizens can shoot a moose as long as they have a hunting permit and a moose ticket issued by the Nisga'a government. Permits are also required for other harvesting in the Nass Wildlife Area, as they are on the core treaty lands.

Some Nisga'a said that ango'oskw of their family had been sacrificed and that they never expected the common bowl to have such an outcome. One negotiator recalled the negative reaction when, at a critical stage in the treaty talks, the communities were informed of the size of the settlement lands: "We brought it back to our people. It was a really sad day when that parcel was offered. People were furious. They were

A contemporary boundary marker delineating Nisga'a treaty lands.
Photograph by author.

saying, that's not why I put my name/territory in there. That's not why my ancestor did, to come to this." In the villages, the negotiators "were condemned. We were being pointed at by our hereditary chiefs, matriarchs."[49] Andrew Robinson (1999, 77), from Laxgalts'ap, describes being "so angry that my family's lands, my wilp lands, were not in Category 'A' lands, and the remainder of the territory outside was no longer a part of recognized Nisga'a lands." Another negotiator mentioned the difficulty of knowing what the chiefs really agreed to when they decided to put their lands together back in the early twentieth century, as they prepared their 1913 petition to send to the king. He said the common bowl was a strategic use of a cultural metaphor to deal with a practical issue, which was the encroachment of settlers. It made sense at the time and was a culturally appropriate strategy that strengthened the Nisga'a claim against the Crown. However, the chiefs probably did not imagine that when the land claim was finally resolved more than a hundred years later, some ango'oskw would not remain within the core lands. Some chiefs also thought that after a treaty was reached, they would receive a sort of allotment of their ango'oskw to manage and were disappointed when that did not occur (McNeary 1976).[50]

Dead Capital and the Landholding Transition Act

In 2012, Nisga'a Lisims Government implemented the Landholding Transition Act, which enables individual Nisga'a citizens to possess fee simple ownership of Nisga'a land. I heard Nisga'a government officials, treaty negotiators, and citizens talk about the possibility of private landownership even before the treaty came into effect. In Canada, the federal government holds reserves as "Lands reserved for the Indians," as stipulated in section 91(24) of the Constitution. Underlying title vests in the Crown. Reserve land cannot be seized for debt or sold to anyone other than the federal government. This provision reflects parts of the Royal Proclamation of 1763, and to some degree it has protected reserve lands from fragmentation and loss through property speculation. Band members who reside on reserves can have entitlements to the lots they occupy, known as certificates of possession, but they do not own the lots in the way that an off-reserve landowner would through fee simple title. On the whole, the banks have not recognized reserve land as a form of collateral that would secure a loan. Some First Nations have been working with the major banks to change this, but more commonly banks do not perceive reserve land in this way.

The Landholding Transition Act makes it possible for Nisga'a citizens to apply for and own certain plots of land in fee simple. It is supposed to help generate economic development in villages where unemployment is high and there are few local businesses. The Nisga'a government website, for example, states that the act will "support the prosperity of Nisga'a citizens by allowing them to own their homes in the same way that families own their homes everywhere in Canada – in fee simple." It also states that "with this change, Nisga'a citizens have the ability to sell, transfer, or will their land to anyone" and "to mortgage these lands in order to secure a loan." Most academic analyses of the act are critical of it, and the text on the website includes the comment that "the Nisga'a Nation is aware that unrestricted fee simple ownership of Nisga'a Lands is considered to be controversial in the academic community. We are certain, however, that the strength of our jurisdiction and the deep sense of commitment to the land that our citizens hold will serve to make a success of this initiative."[51]

In a 2013 interview for the CBC Radio news program *The Current*, Nisg̱a'a citizen Laurie Mercer spoke enthusiastically about how the Landholding Transition Act was finally enabling her to "become a landowner" in her village. Nisg̱a'a have a long history of saying that they have always owned their land, but Mercer's statement does signal a shift in thinking from collective to individual ownership, meditated through the period during which Indian Act regulations made any kind of ownership on reserves impossible. Mercer and her husband dreamed of owning a restaurant where they could serve traditional food, "and the land transition act would now allow us to borrow against our home and our land to start our restaurant. Before if I wanted to go to the bank, it would be very hard, because they knew the land was tied to the [federal] government." In the same interview, the president of the Nisg̱a'a Nation said that a real estate boom was not expected in the Nass Valley, but that was not what the act was about. Instead, it was "geared towards giving our citizens the opportunity to be able to access financing ... to be able to make decisions of their own."[52]

Currently under the act, the Nisg̱a'a Land Title Office can create no more than 10 square kilometres of privately owned fee simple land on Nisg̱a'a territory. The grants can be made only to a Nisg̱a'a citizen and must be for an area of no larger than 0.2 hectares, zoned for residential use, in any of the four Nisg̱a'a villages. At most, this would amount to 0.05 percent of all Nisg̱a'a lands. After acquiring fee simple title, a Nisg̱a'a citizen can sell his or her land to a purchaser who is not a citizen of the Nisg̱a'a Nation and who may also not be Indigenous. This is a significant change from the Indian Act restrictions regarding who can live on reserves and be entitled to housing there, and some people worried that it would alter their communities. However, the property remains within the Nisg̱a'a core land and is subject to the laws and regulations of the Nisg̱a'a government. It is not removed from lands held by the Nisg̱a'a Nation in a way that would produce the checkerboard effect that typifies some reservations in the United States. As of May 2018, fifty-seven parcels were registered in fee simple, with no foreclosures.[53]

In the United States and Canada, policy makers, politicians, and reformers have touted the civilizing effects of private property against the detrimental impact of communal landholding (Biolsi 1995). Speculators and developers supported arguments about the civilizing effects of land privatization policies because they wanted access to Indian land. In the United States, the Dawes Act of 1887 is one of the best-known federal land privatization initiatives. Introduced by Senator Henry Dawes of Massachusetts, it was designed to break up collectively held tribal lands by allotting private parcels of 160 acres to every head of family and 80 acres to individuals over the age of eighteen (Calloway 2013). After twenty-five years, this allotted land could be sold or mortgaged, with the result that it would be alienated from Indian ownership. The remaining unallotted lands were declared surplus and removed from tribal holdings. Even though not all reservations were allotted, the Dawes Act nevertheless resulted in the loss of approximately 90 million acres of tribal lands. The intent of assimilating projects and their outcomes are not always the same. Allotment did not assimilate Native Americans by changing them into individual property owners, but it did effectively transfer large amounts of tribal property to non-Indians (Biolsi 1995, 31).

Even as Nisga'a Lisims Government was developing the Landholding Transition Act, Ottawa was devoting renewed attention to the idea of creating private property rights on reserves. There are some overlaps in the logic of these two processes. By 2010, the Conservative government under Stephen Harper had developed the First Nations Property Ownership Act (FNPOA) as potential legislation. It drew heavily on proposals that were being formulated by the First Nations Tax Commission, a federally funded organization whose chief commissioner is appointed by Canada's Governor-in-Council. Manny Jules, former chief of the Secwépemc First Nation in the interior of British Columbia, is the current chief commissioner. Under the proposed FNPOA, legal title to reserve lands would be transferred from the Crown to those First Nations who decided to participate in the initiative. The First Nation could then transfer a fee simple interest in these lands to band members or others. It would then be possible "for First Nation individuals' fee simple interest to be transferred, mortgaged or sold to non-Aboriginal people and be seized under realization proceedings. All interests would be registered in a new national First Nations-controlled and administered Torrens land registry system."[54] The underlying title or reversionary right would stay with the First Nation regardless of who held the fee simple title. A few communities and their leaders supported the FNPOA, but most were either skeptical or very critical. In 2010, as it was being developed, the Assembly of First Nations passed a resolution to reject it (Fabris 2016, 8). In 2014, the Standing Committee on Aboriginal Affairs and Northern Development conducted a study on land management and sustainable economic development on reserves. Most of the First Nations leaders who spoke to the committee during the hearings phase of this study did not support the FNPOA.[55] In the end, the act did not make it into Parliament before the Conservatives were defeated by the Liberal Party in the 2015 election.

According to right-wing media outlets, as well as some academics and First Nations leaders, the Nisg̱a'a Landholding Transition Act is a move in the right direction and an example of what should be put in place if the FNPOA were implemented (Flanagan, Alcantara, and Le Dressay 2010). A major difference between the Nisg̱a'a Landholding Transition Act and the FNPOA, however, is that the Nisg̱a'a government was creating individual parcels out of lands that it already owned in fee simple as a result of the Nisg̱a'a Final Agreement. More specifically, it was taking this step after the establishment of a land claim and self-government agreement in which the Nisg̱a'a acquired a set of constitutionally protected rights that include self-government and harvesting rights on 27,000 square kilometres outside of the core lands. By contrast, the FNPOA would transfer fee simple title to a First Nation only on existing reserves. It would not restore ownership and jurisdiction to the larger traditional territories that are the focus of land claims agreements. The arguments for the economic benefits of the two pieces of legislation both rely on the value of private property, however, presuming that it is intrinsically related to the generation of wealth. For example, a reporter for the conservative *National Post* newspaper wrote that "for the Nisg̱a'a and the First Nations looking to follow their example, private ownership of aboriginal land will pull their people out of poverty and put Canadian First Nations on the road toward unprecedented levels of economic and political power."[56]

Nisga'a politicians and elected officials sometimes referred to the work of Hernando de Soto when praising the Landholding Transition Act and its potential benefits. Hernando de Soto is a Peruvian economist, millionaire, founder of the neoliberal Institute of Liberty and Democracy in Lima, and author of *The Mystery of Capital: Why Capitalism Triumphs in the West and Fails Everywhere Else* (de Soto 2000). He established the institute with the help of the Atlas Foundation, a key neoliberal think-tank near Washington, DC. He maintains that Third World poverty is largely due to the absence of regularized property rights among the urban poor. By this, he means the poor who generally live in the shantytowns, slums, and *favelas* on the edges of major cities, often squatting on land to which they do not have title. When they do possess some form of title, it is irregular, unrecorded, and not recognizable to any bank or financial institution. De Soto (2000) holds that the poor are not as poor as everyone thinks; their essential problem is that their assets are dead capital and are thus of little economic use to them. Dead capital is a potential asset that is trapped in forms that cannot enter the market (De Soto 2000, 47). Formal legal titling is supposed to enable the poor to release the latent value of their property, changing it from dead to live capital (Christophers 2009, 102). De Soto was the keynote speaker at the First Nations Property Ownership conference, which was organized by the First Nations Tax Commission in Vancouver in 2010 (Gutstein 2014).[57]

A fundamental tenet of neoliberal economics is that private property rights are essential to the flourishing of markets and economic development. The expectation is that when people have secure property rights, they have more incentive to work hard and use their assets efficiently; their entrepreneurial spirit is both stimulated and supported (Mitchell 2005; Verdery and Humphrey 2004, 3). David Harvey's (2005, 2) definition of neoliberalism foregrounds these aspects: "Neoliberalism is in the first instance a theory of political economic practices that proposes that human well-being can best be advanced by liberating individual entrepreneurial freedoms and skills within an institutional framework characterized by strong private property rights, free markets, and free trade." In their book on restoring property rights on First Nations reserves, Flanagan, Alcantara, and Le Dressay (2010, 181) state that "market economies are built on the exchange of property rights. The market cannot function without property rights that are secure, easily defined, enforced, and traded. This is especially true with respect to land. Land is the most fundamental type of property, and therefore property rights in land are the bedrock of the market economy." This logic naturalizes private property rights as the only kind of property relationship that can secure economic prosperity or produce wealth.

Critics suggest that turning Aboriginal title into private property is an "assault on Indigenous noncapitalist means of production and reproduction and communal Indigenous ontologies and epistemologies" (Hall 2015, 32). Certainly, to hear Nisga'a government leaders describe land as dead capital is unlike anything one would have expected from people who have traditionally referred to their land as an inalienable commodity that is not for sale. This is a significant transformation, from land as a behest from the supernatural that one is obligated to steward for future generations to land as an alienable commodity that is dead unless it is inserted into the legal regime of the state and capital. Many Nisga'a see the decision to create fee simple parcels differently, however. Indigenous people in Canada and elsewhere make all sorts of decisions with respect to the use of their lands and resources, including real estate development or other ventures. People reminded me that they had spent more than a hundred years living on reserves that Canadian law said belonged to the federal government, over which they had no control or decision-making power. Nisga'a experienced this as a form of tenancy on their own lands and as something that differentiated them from other Canadians. It was an acute form of disempowerment for people whose wealth and identity were particularly rooted in the land. In Gitwinksihlkw, a village councillor talked about the limitations enforced by the Indian Act. His frustration was palpable. He connected the Landholding Transition Act to self-government and the jurisdictional authority that the Nisga'a gained through the treaty. He also linked it to correcting their exclusion from some of the entitlements of other Canadian citizens. He asked, "Why can't we do this, have opportunities like other people to move forward?" He felt that the act would not produce any overnight change but defended their government's *ability* to create this kind of legislation. He and others expressed frustration about how upset people become when they feel that Indigenous people are behaving in a non-traditional manner or in ways that are inconsistent with their culture, and about how Indigenous people are constantly judged one way or the other by both non-Indigenous and Indigenous people alike. The Nisga'a frequently and unapologetically associate self-government with their ability to make decisions regarding their land. This is reflected in Ed Allen's assertion that "we have always reserved unto ourselves our right to make decisions in respect of our ownership and use of Nisga'a Lands" (Edward Allen 2004, 235; Scott 2012).

The economic impact of the Landholding Transition Act has yet to be determined. Assessing and measuring its effect in conjunction with other factors shaping the economy of the region and Nisga'a citizens falls to Nisga'a governments. The important thing here is to step back from broad claims about the wealth-generating effects of private property. Indigenous poverty in Canada has many causes, and the connection between the ability to get a mortgage and increased economic opportunities is often overstated (Palmater 2010). This poverty comes from centuries of colonization, dispossession, and federal government underfunding of essential services (Palmater 2011). It is disingenuous to replace the impact of dispossession and land loss "with a simplistic depiction of colonization as the denial of capitalism on reserve lands" (Pasternak 2014a, 2). During the 2014 hearings of the Standing Committee on Aboriginal Affairs and Northern Development into land management proposals and economic development on reserves, including the FNPOA, many leaders said that regional isolation and lack of infrastructure were more important than the absence of private property rights when it came to economic development for their communities.[58] Studies show that the land titling projects spearheaded by de Soto and the World Bank did not result in increased lending or capital available to the urban poor (Mitchell 2007).

Conclusion

The Nisga'a have spent a century and a half dealing with colonial, provincial, and federal governments and individual settlers, traders, and missionaries on the issue of their land. Throughout countless legal and political challenges and seeming dead ends, they have been strategic and persistent. Their work has resulted in groundbreaking accomplishments such as the ruling on Aboriginal title in the *Calder* case. They have also made enormous adjustments and borne considerable costs. The land claims and treaty negotiating process does not occur on a level playing field. Throughout, Nisga'a leaders have struggled to maintain the cultural link between governing authority – the right to self-government – and decision making over the land and its resources. In 1983, James Gosnell, the older brother of Joe Gosnell, delivered a blistering speech at a meeting of the Assembly of First Nations in Ontario where he connected self-government with the ability to control what was happening on Nisga'a lands. James Gosnell was a leader of strength and passion who pulled no punches. In this speech, he railed against the venality and ineptitude of the federal and provincial governments and defended Indigenous demands for a third order of government:

> We do not have a say in the commercial fishing industry on the coast where I come from. In the timber, the best timber in the world, we don't have a say in that. Today we're 95 percent unemployed in my territory ... That's why we are proposing self-government. We want to manage those trees, we want to manage the salmon, we want to have a say in the mining that's now going to go on in our areas, because we want a piece of the pie, and we want to have a say in the piece of the action in which decisions are made. That's what self-government is all about. (Quoted in Rose 2000, 88)[59]

Gosnell's statement is steeped in the expectation that the Nisga'a should be in charge of their territories, and his anger was that of a leader who was hamstrung by federal and provincial governments in his ability to govern and realize the benefits of the land to support Nisga'a communities in ways they chose for themselves. For most Indigenous communities, successful self-governance depends upon a sufficient land base and resources that they have the authority to make decisions about, according to their criteria and for their benefit (Ladner 2006). This could involve something like logging, as James Gosnell indicates, but on a completely different scale than industrial clear cuts. For Nisga'a, the land and its wealth have always been both a source of governing authority and a responsibility of that authority. Years later, Joe Gosnell addressed a Special Assembly in the community hall at Gitwinksihlkw. He spoke of the early days of denial of Aboriginal title in the province, when men such as Premier Smithe refused to acknowledge their rights, when "they told us that we didn't own the land." "And yet, we do," he said. "Each one of you here is a recipient to that. You own the land. You will tell people what to do on your land, not the other way around."[60]

Treaty Citizenship: Negotiating beyond Inclusion   **3**

The right of Indigenous peoples to determine the criteria of membership in their communities is recognized in article 33 of the United Nations Declaration on the Rights of Indigenous Peoples.[1] In addition, article 1, section 2, of the International Labour Organization's Indigenous and Tribal Peoples Convention states that self-identification as Indigenous or tribal is a fundamental right of groups to whom the convention applies (Merlan 2009, 305). The fact that both of these documents take such a stance points to the difficulties Indigenous people have experienced in being externally defined, sometimes out of existence, by the states in which they live. Historically, the Canadian government offered First Nations people the Faustian bargain of acquiring citizenship on the condition that they relinquish their separate rights, political status, and identity as "Indians" under the law. For Indigenous peoples, their status as members of "nations within," with rights of self-determination, distinguishes their demands from those of other minorities. It requires legal and political solutions that enable the existence within a state of rights in, and allegiances to, separate political communities. This entails multilevel, differentiated forms of citizenship that encompass separate and distinct rights and the separate political status of Indigenous communities within states (Lightfoot 2013).

In this chapter, I examine the political and cultural dimensions of the treaty citizenship that sprang from the Nisga'a Final Agreement. The ability to control citizenship is an important expression of sovereignty, but the criteria that communities choose – such as blood or ancestry – can pit self-government as a collective right against individual civil rights (Joanne Barker 2011). The question of who is a citizen is tied to another question: Do treaties transform state-Indigenous relations in a positive way, or do they consolidate historically problematic categories of differentiation and exclusion? The Nisga'a ground their definition of citizenship in matrilineal descent and perceive this as constituting a return to traditional practices and a rejection of patrilineal requirements of the Indian Act. More broadly, by insisting that they can be part of Canada only through the treaty, the Nisga'a assert an identity as a political collectivity that enjoys a special nation-to-nation relationship with the state.

Citizenship and Indigenous People: A History of Exclusion
For decades, First Nations people could attain Canadian citizenship only by giving up their legal and cultural identities as Indians under the Indian Act (Battiste and Semaganis 2002; Johnston 1993). After Canada became a country in 1867, federal Indian policy focused on assimilation, with policy makers firm in their position that First Nations must become "civilized" before they could take on the rights and responsibilities of citizenship, such as voting and the ability to own private property. The category of "status Indian" was created by the Gradual Enfranchisement Act in 1869 and then repeated in the Indian Act of 1876 (Lawrence 2003). It is here, in law, that the Canadian government created a category of people who were legally apart on the basis of a racial identity that was meaningless to them before colonization but that would eventually become an important axis of political identification, a category of rights, and a source of conflict between those who had status and those who did not (Lawrence 2003). Status Indians were entitled to certain benefits and services, including the ability to live on reserves, but were also made wards of the state and subjected to the paternalistic and restrictive legislative oversight of the federal government.[2] Policy makers justified wardship by arguing that Indian people had to be protected until they were assimilated into mainstream society, after which they would no

longer need special oversight from the government. The Indian Act also stipulated all the ways that people could lose their status and no longer be legally recognized as Indians. Among these was the gendered exclusion of status women who married non-status men, to which I will return below. Although assimilation was the stated goal of Indian policy, the Indian Act facilitated the separation and exclusion of First Nations people from the rights and duties of Canadian citizenship in a way that highlighted their legal and conceptual externality from the nation-state.

The emphasis on assimilation was a marked departure from earlier Imperial relations between the British Crown and Indigenous peoples in North America. Assimilation would eliminate Indigenous peoples as political entities who had a special relationship with the state that flowed from treaties, the Royal Proclamation of 1763, and the Canadian Constitution itself. Patrick Wolfe (2006) identifies the logic of elimination that undergirds settler colonialism and assimilation. Writing about the United States and Australia, both of whose policy trajectories resemble that of Canada, Wolfe (2006) shows that the physical destruction of Indigenous people shifted into state attempts to eliminate them through legislation and/or education. In Canada, Deputy Superintendent of Indian and Northern Affairs Duncan Campbell Scott notoriously characterized the goal of federal Indian legislation by saying, "Our objective is to continue until there is not a single Indian in Canada that has not been absorbed into the body politic, and there is no Indian question, and no Indian Department" (quoted in Palmater 2011, 28). To absorb Indians into the body politic was to include them through the elimination of their separate legal status, as well as their distinct cultural and political identities. In Canada and the United States, assimilation has also been a way of removing tribal lands from the collective ownership of Indigenous people and breaking up the reserve land base into individual pieces of private property under no special jurisdiction.

Civil and political rights such as the right to vote did eventually become available to First Nations individuals in Canada without the explicit condition that they give up their separate status; in 1960, for example, all status Indians were finally granted the federal franchise and could vote in federal elections. The attempt to assimilate First Nations by legislation peaked at the end of that decade when the Liberal government of Pierre Trudeau issued the infamous 1969 White Paper. Jean Chrétien was Indian Affairs minister at this time. The White Paper proposed to eliminate status Indians as a legal category, to repeal the Indian Act, to transform reserves into private property, and to delegate all program and service delivery carried out by the Department of Indian Affairs to mainstream provincial agencies (Dale Turner 2006). It also proposed that specific references to Indians be deleted from the Constitution so as "to end the legal distinction between Indians and other Canadians."[3] This would have meant removing section 91(24) of the Constitution, which sets out federal legislative authority over – but also *responsibility for* – Indians and lands reserved for Indians. Outraged by the White Paper, Indigenous people launched a counterattack (Cairns 2000).[4] The White Paper policy would have eliminated the political relationship that First Nations and other Indigenous people in this country expect to have with the Crown (Dale Turner 2016). In the view of the authors of the White Paper, the distinctions that the Indian Act created – in rights for and obligations to status Indians – were detrimental to equality, and status Indians would be better included in the social and economic fabric of Canada if their separate legal status were eliminated. The goal was to completely erase any legal distinction, including separate lands, for registered Indians so that they could be, as Duncan Campbell Scott had suggested, fully absorbed into the body politic. Trudeau officially withdrew the White Paper in 1970.

Debating Citizenship

After the Nisga'a and federal and provincial governments signed the Nisga'a Final Agreement, it had to be approved by a majority of Nisga'a voters and then ratified by the provincial and federal legislatures. This took two years. The political parties who supported the treaty held majorities in both governments. In Ottawa, the Liberals were in power under Jean Chrétien, and the NDP was still the government in Victoria. Both were opposed by other parties on the right of the political spectrum. In Ottawa, this was the Reform Party under Preston Manning; in British Columbia, the Liberals tried to undermine the treaty in every way possible. The Reform Party became the Canadian Alliance in 2000. The Alliance joined with the former Progressive Conservative Party in 2003 to "unite the right" and became the Conservative Party of Canada. In 2006, the Conservatives were elected, remaining in power for ten years. Back in 1999 and 2000, the BC Liberals and the Reform Party argued that the treaty threatened Canadian unity, cost too much in land and cash, and contradicted the democratic principle of equality before the law (Blackburn 2007).

Nisga'a jurisdiction over citizenship was an especially heated issue when the treaty was debated in the House of Commons and the Senate. During these debates, the issue of who would be a citizen of the political communities that resulted from land claims and self-government agreements was tied to another question: Did these agreements transform state-Indigenous relations into a more just distribution of rights, resources, and powers, or did they consolidate historically problematic racial categories of differentiation and exclusion? The treaty refers to Nisga'a "citizens," defines a Nisga'a citizen as "a citizen of the Nisga'a Nation as determined by Nisga'a law," and sets out enrolment criteria that are based on ancestry (Canada, British Columbia, Nisga'a Nation 1998, 10). In fact, it includes 157 references to "citizen" or "citizenship." This is a striking number, especially given that the next BC treaty – the Tsawwassen Final Agreement – uses "citizen" only 6 times. The Tsawwassen agreement was concluded in 2007 and came into effect in 2009. Of its 6 references to "citizen," 4 are to Canadian citizens or citizenship and 2 are to "other First Nations" citizens and citizenship. There is no mention of citizens of the Tsawwassen Nation. The Maa-nulth Final Agreement, concluded in 2011, gives "citizen" 31 times. Only in 2014, with the Tla'amin Final Agreement's 134 references, do we approach the same confident use of "citizen" to characterize enrolled members in a treaty. Presumably, this confidence sprang in part from the fading of political memory and the fact that Canadian sovereignty had not disintegrated after 2000. The opposition to the use of "citizen" and the criteria that determined who could and could not be a Nisga'a citizen did not prevent ratification of the Nisga'a Final Agreement. Nonetheless, it generated so much angst and so much criticism that anyone who negotiated a treaty in its immediate wake unsurprisingly avoided the use of such language.

I have described the arguments regarding Nisga'a citizenship elsewhere (Blackburn 2009). The main points of contention were that the word "citizen" evoked different or special rights that superseded those of other Canadians; that it created a form of dual citizenship in law that would harm the legal unity of the country; and that the language of citizen and nation (and really, the agreement itself) threatened the sense that all Canadians are part of the same polity with a common citizenship and a common cause. This ideal of a common citizenship across a shared and uniform national polity reflects the imagined communities described by Benedict Anderson (1991) in his analysis of the origins of nationalism. In Canada, tensions between English- and French-speaking Canada make this an impossible ideal to begin with, but it also means that the need to emphasize unity over separation is never far from the minds of federal politicians, contributing to their fear of words such as "sovereignty" and "nation" and "citizen" (Scott 2012, 144). The criticisms I discuss here came mainly from the conservative side of the political spectrum, whether from MPs and senators in the House and Senate or from their constituents and supporters outside of politics, in the media and the general population.

In pursuing these different rights and using "citizen" to label themselves, the Nisga'a challenged the deeply entrenched view that citizenship means the same and equal rights in a state that is organized around one sovereignty and one political identity. The fact is, however, that Nisga'a and all Indigenous people in Canada have rights that other Canadians do not. The Constitution recognizes that Aboriginal and treaty rights exist, separately, and protects those rights; this is part of the constitutional fabric of the country. These rights are inherent and were in play before the rights of non-Indigenous Canadians came into being; their source is not the state. When Canada became a country in 1867, Indigenous people, and specifically those referred to as Indians under the Indian Act, were defined differently, in law, with different rights, entitlements, and restrictions. Section 91(24) of the BNA Act and the legal differentiation established through the Indian Act are imperfect expressions of a Crown-Indigenous relationship that was forged well before Canada became a country, through the royal proclamation and treaties. The relationship between the Crown and Indigenous peoples differs from that between the Crown and non-Indigenous Canadians, and it includes different rights, obligations, and responsibilities. I will return to this point in the next chapter.

The Nisga'a defended their use of "citizen" in a few ways. For example, they stated that it was the best choice to signal their affiliation with the political community that is the Nisga'a Nation. A Nisga'a negotiator told the Standing Senate Committee on Aboriginal Peoples,

> We do not understand why anyone would object to the use of the term "citizen" to refer to the members of the Nisga'a nation. No doubt, if we had agreed to describe ourselves merely as members there would have been little or no objection. We believe that the correct word to describe someone who belongs to a nation is "citizen." We wish to affirm, not deny, our existence as the Nisga'a nation, a nation that is within Canada.[5]

Indeed, "citizenship" rattled critics of the agreement because it suggested a certain type of political community. It sounds like something that states should have the authority to determine; it brings with it the concepts of sovereignty and territorial borders. It is, as Paul Nadasdy (2017, 142) points out, "so loaded with conceptual baggage that its use in an Indigenous context is fraught with both theoretical and practical dangers." The Nisga'a insisted that they were a political community, not a political community seeking separation from Canada but a political community that should have a nation-to-nation relationship with Canada, and that therefore "citizen" and "citizenship" were the appropriate terms. They were perfectly clear on their refusal to accept "member" as an alternative word. Members belong to voluntary organizations, such as clubs, and to be a member of something does not signal a political identity in the way that being a citizen does. The Indian Act also identifies First Nations as "members" of bands, and the Nisga'a refused to repeat this terminology and the memory of state control that went with it. "Band member," one former negotiator told me, "meant there was no such thing as self-definition. You were defined by legislation, which was the Indian Act. It relegated you to status as a member of a band in a confined reserve."[6]

By using "citizen," the Nisga'a were drawing on the linkage in Western political theory between citizenship and the modern nation-state to say that they were a political community and self-governing before settlers arrived in their territory. They were also investing the word with content drawn from Indigenous political theory and principles, particularly around the significance of the relationship between their rights and their territory (Dale Turner 2006). These are difficult things to do simultaneously because "citizen" is not an Indigenous word, as I discuss below, but to identify oneself as a member of a nation is generally to locate oneself in a territory. Another former negotiator complained that "citizen" incensed the right-wingers but said that "the self-description as citizens is really a declaration that we've always had this inherent connection to our land." There was no other term "to make that connection."[7] He noted that the wilp and the pdeek are based on ancestral rights to territory, a system that differs markedly from Western forms of property ownership. In New Aiyansh, a resident who had returned to Nisga'a territory after some years away affirmed this relationship to the land: "I'm a Nisga'a citizen first before I'm a Canadian citizen. We've known all along that we belong here, in this place. If they want to call this country where we are Canada, then I'm also a Canadian citizen."[8] John Borrows (1999a, 80) uses the concept of "landed citizenship" to capture the importance of land, territory, and relationships to non-human persons in Indigenous forms of citizenship. This concept refers to a very different kind of citizen than the rights-bearing individual of liberal political theory.

Citizenship, nationhood, and sovereignty are deeply intertwined but also subject to rearticulation. Whereas the Nisga'a link their right to call themselves citizens with their status as a nation, the politicians who debated the treaty wondered whether the presence of a group of people with separate rights who called themselves "citizens of the Nisga'a Nation" would challenge Canada's sovereignty in some way. Treaty negotiators reassured everyone who asked that the treaty did not weaken Ottawa's authority over Canadian citizenship or create an uncontrollable legal duality in the state. One told the Senate committee that "citizen" was nothing to worry about, "because of the way in which it is defined in the treaty and the fact that all of the rights that accrue to such a person are specifically stated in the treaty and nothing exists outside of it."[9] He insisted that the power of the Nisga'a to determine their citizenship had nothing to do with the power to grant Canadian citizenship and that nothing about Nisga'a citizenship produced dual citizenship in Canada. As he said, "If someone comes to Canada legally and goes onto Nisga'a lands and is made a citizen, whatever the federal law is with respect to that person's ability to remain in Canada remains the law under which he or she is governed. That person has no special rights with respect to Canadian citizenship as a result of that." Nisga'a citizenship "relates to their lands, their assets, and living within their territory."[10]

A federal negotiator likewise told me that opting for "member" would have saved a lot of trouble but that "citizen" did not mean much more than that. In relation to citizenship, the lawmaking authority of the Nisga'a carried limitations:

> They can't grant passports or entry into or out of Canada or create citizens or take citizenship away from anybody – Canadian citizenship. They can't do any of that. The word that's used in the Indian Act is member, and that's one significant reason why the Nisga'a, and why we accepted, moving to a different language ... And so citizen was used. And I don't know if it was a good use or bad use, I suppose it's academic at this point because that's what it is. But it doesn't mean more than if we had used the word member ... It's used in a way that does not in any way imply sovereignty.[11]

Nisga'a negotiators did not intend that "citizen" would imply sovereignty either – as they tried to explain to critics in the Senate – but they did insist on using the word to convey an identity as a political community with self-governing jurisdiction within Canada. They accepted limitations to their governance, as explained in Chapter 1, but fought for control over citizenship as one of their areas of paramount jurisdiction. This is because they saw such control and their ability to describe it as they pleased as essential parts of their political stature and of the nation-to-nation, government-to-government relationship they expect to have with the state. It is also because they wanted to make culturally relevant citizenship criteria.

In liberal political theory, citizenship involves "a political identity, an expression of one's membership in a political community," and a set of rights (Kymlicka and Norman 1995, 301). The Nisga'a are using citizenship to signal all of these things, contending that they have rights as citizens of the Nisga'a Nation not because of the racialized difference generated by the state and linked, formerly, with their exclusion but because they belong to a previously existing political community that holds inherent and extra-constitutional rights (Wilkins and Lomawaima 2001). They are not using it to label, in direct translation, a pre-contact term or a pre-contact form of political subjectivity, a point to which I return below. Their insistence on these rights and the ability to decide who gets access to them challenges hegemonic practices that locate citizenship in rights that are granted or denied by the state. The opposite argument, that all Canadians should have the same rights and be governed by the same laws, presumes that Canadians have rights that flow only from their status as citizens of Canada.

Tribe, Kin, and Contract: These Are Not Race-Based Rights

For decades, Indigenous people have been defined by the states in which they live. State categorizations of who is and is not Indigenous have determined the boundaries of "Indianness" as a racial identity for the purposes of "structuring race relations and controlling the distribution of resources" (Klopotek 2011, 5). Indigenous people's ability to define and control membership in their communities is fundamental to processes of self-determination and decolonization, but they occur against or in the midst of these prior and ongoing state definitions. In Canada, land claims and self-government agreements all include criteria for who can be a beneficiary of the agreement, with varying language. In the case of the Nisga'a, the treaty establishes criteria for enrolment as a Nisga'a citizen. As I have shown, the word "citizen" was a lightning rod for criticism and concerns about what sort of polity with what sorts of powers the treaty created. The actual citizenship criteria were also attacked as illiberal and leading to a set of race-based rights. This allegation is commonly made against the collective rights of Indigenous communities in Canada. Race haunts all definitional criteria of Indigenous people in this country. Any Indigenous community that attempts to establish criteria of inclusion in a modern treaty or under reformed Indian Act legislation is faced with the task of protecting its rights, honouring community norms of membership, and "the long and immensely convoluted history of relations between Indigenous peoples and settler governments" (Gover 2010, 9).

In setting their citizenship criteria, the Nisg̱a'a chose to return to reckoning by matrilineal kinship, broadly defined. Thus, a person whose mother was a Nisga'a who belonged to one of the four pdeeḵ, or tribes, can be enrolled as a citizen. For enrolment purposes, a person's qualifying Nisg̱a'a female relation can be on either the maternal or paternal side and as far back as four generations. Individuals may also be enrolled if they were adopted by a Nisga'a as children, even if they themselves are not Indigenous. A descendant of either of these categories is also eligible for enrolment. Lastly, a person may qualify for enrolment if he or she marries a Nisg̱a'a person, is Indigenous, and has been culturally adopted according to Nisga'a protocols. Non-Indigenous individuals who marry a Nisga'a person and are culturally adopted do not qualify for enrolment and citizenship; they cannot vote and have no access to the treaty rights. Non-Indigenous people who live on Nisga'a lands for short periods, such as schoolteachers or police officers, cannot become citizens and cannot vote in Nisg̱a'a elections. Only citizens are entitled to the rights in the treaty and to participate in self-government by voting in Nisg̱a'a elections. Nisga'a Lisims Government has the legal jurisdiction to alter these rules if it feels that any change is necessary.

The enrolment criteria came about after years of community consultation and input from elders. When the treaty was up for debate in the House and the Senate, though, many MPs, senators, and their allies argued that the focus on ancestry made the treaty a set of race-based rights and contradicted democratic principles of universal citizenship. The fact that residents on Nisga'a lands who were not Nisga'a and not Indigenous could not become citizens or vote in Nisg̱a'a elections also provoked a great deal of outrage. Some senators were unwilling to sanction the formation of a government where membership and voting rights were based on ancestry. Others declared that genealogical definitions contradicted the ideals of universal citizenship. Some compared the Nisg̱a'a use of ancestral or "birthright" criteria with Ottawa's use of blood to define who was an Indian under the Indian Act. The Indian

Act did not employ a blood quantum rule but instead linked blood to parentage; until 1951, a status Indian was "any male person of Indian blood reputed to belong to a particular band," "any child of such person," and "any woman who is or was lawfully married to such person" (Jamieson 1978, 43). Pointing out that the Indian Act initiated "a racial blood definition," one senator lamented "this unbelievable paradox that the reprehensible notion of blood in the definition of the Indian Act, which was European and foreign to the aboriginals, may somehow continue on in this treaty."[12]

Blood has long been used as a signifier of essence in the racialization of Indigenous people in North America (Rifkin 2010, 38; Audra Simpson 2014; Sturm 2002, 2014; TallBear 2013). Some First Nations in Canada employ blood quantum to define their membership criteria, but they more commonly rely on forms of ancestral reckoning (Gover 2010; Audra Simpson 2014). Blood is not a criterion for citizenship in the Nisga'a Nation. Enrolment in the nation and access to treaty rights depends on matrilineal ancestry. The Nisga'a defended this link between matrilineal descent and citizenship as culturally appropriate and a positive act of self-governance. A former tribal council employee who worked closely on the enrolment criteria told me that these provisions came about through the efforts of a committee composed of elders and in consultation with community members during many annual conventions. The criteria were formulated to reflect Nisga'a cultural practices and to be as distinct from Indian Act definitions as possible. Until 1985, First Nations women lost their Indian status if they married a man who was not a status Indian, and their children would not be entitled to status. By contrast, a non-Indigenous woman who married a status Indian acquired status herself (Jamieson 1978). The former employee explained that the Nisga'a criterion for enrolment "*begins* with a person's mother," so even if the mother married a non-Nisga'a man, her children could still enroll. This, he said, "corrects some hardships" but "also ... make[s] sure that what happened with the Indian Act never happens again."[13] By going through female lines, the Nisga'a rejected the patrilineal methods of descent reckoning and legal membership that were formerly used by the state. These criteria are also an example of how the treaty enables an exercise of Nisga'a jurisdiction and lawmaking that refers to Nisga'a culture.

In her work on tribal sovereignty, Joanne Barker (2005, 16) argues that "the making ethnic or ethnicization of indigenous peoples has been a political strategy of the nation state to erase the sovereign from the indigenous." To put this another way, the "erasure of the sovereign is the racialization of the 'Indian'" (Joanne Barker 2005, 17). Indigenous peoples in Canada and the United States are asserting political rights as political communities; they are not asserting race-based rights as members of a race. Writing about whether US senator Elizabeth Warren should have taken a DNA test to prove her Native American ancestry, Circe Sturm (2017, 345) refers to the "tendency in the United States and Canada to minoritize indigeneity and take what should be debates about sovereignty, citizenship, political authority, and territorial jurisdiction, among other issues, and turn instead to questions of racial and cultural authenticity, or even genetic descent." She maintains that what is lost in such controversies "is attention to American Indian identity as a political status, that rests on tribal sovereignty and the premise that tribes have the sovereign right to determine their own citizenry" (Sturm 2017, 345). Communities get to decide their criteria of inclusion and belonging regardless of whatever anyone's DNA test results might happen to be.

When critics say that a matrilineal criterion is "like the reprehensible notion of blood," they are suggesting that it is racist and thus should not be approved by the federal government. Another implication of this claim is that Indigenous peoples who use such criteria are losing their moral authority. For example, Circe Sturm (2002, 2014) shows that critics accused the Cherokee of adopting the racial categories and racism of their colonizers, a decision that compromised their authentic Indianness and overturned the symbolic moral capital that Indigenous peoples are supposed to possess in most disagreements with the state. This perpetuates a racial logic more than any genealogical reckoning; that is, the criticism itself is embedded in a logic of race. These charges of racism also work against Indigenous peoples' assertions of rights and sovereignty.

The genealogical reckoning used by Nisga'a and other Indigenous peoples is embedded in Indigenous epistemologies that foreground relationships between people and the land (Kauanui 2008, 194). The ancestral criteria used for enrolment in the Nisga'a Final Agreement are not about identifying some blood quantum or the right kind of DNA markers: they are about finding relations. The head of the committee that oversaw enrolment for the first several years after the treaty came into effect told me that people start with saying who their mother is. Before the treaty, it was all in people's memories, as she put it, but now the enrolment committee meets and all this knowledge of genealogy comes out in their discussions. The committee consists of eight people, two from each pdeek, all of whom must reside in a Nisga'a village and must be knowledgeable in Nisga'a culture, ancestry, the ayuukhl, tribes, and community institutions.[14] One committee member described its work as difficult. "You have to really know people," she said, "where they married," and "where they came from."[15] Eventually, however, as another person close to the work of the committee told me, they recall the stories and relationships. The process here is one of locating applicants within genealogies and family histories, of recovering and remembering relationships between people within a historical community. Some aspects of this are exclusive, to a degree, and unlike the principle of universal citizenship. This suggests that the term "citizenship" must be rethought to accommodate the kinds of political communities and memberships that are produced by treaties such as the Nisga'a Final Agreement (Nadasdy 2017).

Politicians in the House and Senate and witnesses who spoke to the Standing Senate Committee on Aboriginal Peoples also worried that the ancestral linkage in the Nisga'a citizenship criteria precluded the universality of rights within the Nisga'a Nation. This concern about blood and ancestry prompted a discussion about whether the Nisga'a truly grasped the commitment to equality, minority rights, and democratic principles that citizenship is supposed to entail. One commentator argued that the "closed membership society" desired by the Nisga'a went against the grain of the last two centuries of evolution in Western political thought.[16] A representative from the conservative Fraser Institute cited "the evidence of history and all logic and reason and the development of western political thought" to critique the treaty's membership criteria.[17] Some senators linked universal citizenship rights with the principles of modern democracy in a way that questioned the Nisga'a commitment to both democracy and modernity. One asked the Nisga'a negotiators why they did not provide "something that we consider to be important in so-called European style of governance, and that is to establish or entrench minority rights within the institutions."[18] He raised the twin spectres of tribalism and ethnic primordialism, asking if non-universal citizenship is "the vision we want for a united Canada with the globe shrinking in the twenty-first century? We have yet to learn the bitter lessons of the twentieth century respecting the clash between ethnicity on the one hand and open citizenship on the other."[19] He said the Nisga'a seemed to prefer a move from a purely "tribal system" to a democratic one but that, when it came to minority rights, they did not go all the way.[20] "A citizen," he declared, "should be a person, without qualification. If he meets an objective standard, he is entitled to vote ... That is what citizenship is ... In the Nisga'a treaty," however, "people are excluded. You cannot become a Nisga'a citizen ... unless you are born into the tribe. This sets up ... a conflicting notion of citizenship."[21]

In Europe, some citizenship codes are built on *jus sanguis* (right of the blood), or *jus solis* (right of the soil), or some combination of the two (Nadasdy 2017). The senator should have known that. The truth is, non-Indigenous people living on Nisga'a lands are not actually governed very much by the Nisga'a government. Its lawmaking authority pertains mostly to Nisga'a citizens, and it does not tax non-Nisga'a residents.[22] More particularly, the enrolment criteria were crafted to safeguard the treaty assets – the land, the cash, the fish, and the jurisdictional authorities – for the benefit of Nisga'a citizens. If non-Indigenous people could enroll in the treaty and be Nisga'a citizens, they would have access to the treaty rights of the Nisga'a people. If they could vote in Nisga'a elections, they could influence the management and distribution of these rights and resources. This would be one more mechanism of dispossession in a long history of dispossession (Audra Simpson 2014). Additionally, the treaty rights are a subset of the Aboriginal rights that are recognized and protected in section 35 of the Constitution. These rights arise from Indigenous peoples' presence as organized political communities before Canada became a country; they are not the universal entitlements of all Canadians (Borrows 2001). As mentioned, they are a different set of rights. Indigenous governments are differently constituted but no less legitimate. In 1983, the Penner Report on Indian self-government in Canada explained this dilemma, which I quote in full here:

> The combination of collective ownership by the First Nation and the jurisdiction of the Indian First Nation government leads to a unique situation. Indian First Nation governments serve not only in governmental matters but, in some ways, also represent their members' interests in assets owned in common. In this way, Indian First Nation governments are different from municipal and provincial governments. This poses a special problem in regard to non-Indians living on Indian lands, who might feel that, as residents, they have a right to participate in the government of the community. Yet, as non-members, they do not share in the ownership of the assets administered by that government and have no right to a voice in such matters. (Canada, House of Commons Special Committee on Indian Self-Government, 1983, 110)

To talk about Indigenous government and rights within settler states is inevitably to talk about something other than universal rights, and this requires us to think of multiple forms of citizenship in overlapping political communities.

The president of the Nisga'a Tribal Council, Joseph Gosnell, defended the particularity of Nisga'a rights by saying that the treaty rights and assets are the ancestral inheritance of the Nisga'a people. He used a kinship analogy to defend Nisga'a citizenship entitlements:

> By way of comparison, would any one of you seated across the table in this room allow strangers or individuals who stay with you temporarily to decide how your family's internal assets would be handled? Would you do that? That is the problem that faces us: people who come into our communities maybe for a year, two years or three years and then they are gone ... Would you allow someone to handle your family's personal assets? I do not think so.[23]

One senator's response to this comment is illustrative. "These are not family assets," he stated:

These are public assets that are held in trust as fiduciaries. What I am talking about here is the right of a citizen to fully participate and vote on matters affecting his life and the area in which he chooses to reside ... The right to vote goes to the heart of any right to participate in a civic society.[24]

He wondered why, "having accepted the European notion that you get nationhood or sovereignty and, with that, you get citizenship, then why would you not take the next step which is, under the European thesis, the minority rights entailed in citizenship? In other words, why ... take two-thirds of the package and not the last third of the package?"[25] In the House of Commons, one MP objected to Nisga'a citizenship requirements with a statement whose references to racial exclusion and entitlement were no doubt intended to appeal to a conservative base but that also presented the Nisga'a government as regressive:

The Nisga'a treaty is a giant step backwards into a world where status and power is defined by one's race and position and where national unity is divided into fiefdoms of privilege. With the passage of the Nisga'a treaty, we are embracing a regressive social system that could easily have been designed in the middle ages. To begin with, all the residents on Nisga'a land will not have the right to vote for their local governments under the Nisga'a treaty. Only the Nisga'a peoples will be allowed to vote. Non-Nisga'a residents are excluded on the basis of race.[26]

Preston Manning, leader of the Reform Party, added to this emphasis on the backwardness of the treaty by saying, "Is it really the federal government's vision for the future of aboriginal government across B.C. and the rest of Canada that racially specific enclaves would exist in which one's bloodlines determine one's right to vote? It is stunning that any government on the threshold of the 21st century would even sign such an agreement."[27]

Marisol De la Cadena (2010, 360) writes of the fear that Indigenous politics are "traditional and archaic and therefore dangerous as they can evolve into antidemocratic fundamentalism." The comments quoted above evoke exactly this kind of fear. The Nisga'a were characterized as being insufficiently evolved politically and as being stuck in some pre-modern, pre-democratic tribal slot. In addition, the government negotiators and the politicians who supported the treaty were accused of pandering to this inappropriateness out of political correctness and general weakness. They were not seen as guided by legal imperatives stemming from Canadian jurisprudence on Aboriginal rights, the treaty-making obligations flowing from the Royal Proclamation of 1763, the Constitution, or even precedents protecting minority rights. The standard narrative of modernization contains an evolution up and away from social groupings and relationships built around kin, custom, or tribe toward autonomy, individualism, and relationships based on modern legal forms, of which contract is pre-eminent (Richard Ford 1999; Perry 1995). The reference to the "tribal system" and the exhortation that the Nisga'a take the "next step" into the modern world reveal these distinctions. In this trajectory, the modern citizen emerges out of pre-modern political systems as an individual political subject, "no longer formally confined by the particularities of birth, ethnicity or gender," or tribe (Bryan Turner 1990, 194). Political theorists have traditionally viewed status relationships as antithetical to liberal society (Richard Ford 1999). Attachments based on blood, language, or religion are replaced by an Enlightenment model of modern political participation based "on the idea of an educated, post-ethnic, calculating individual, subsisting on the workings of the free market and participating in a genuine civil society" (Appadurai 1996, 142–43).

This placement of the Nisga'a and other Indigenous people on the margins of modernity is nothing new. It has long been made in conjunction with the criteria of citizenship and belonging for Indigenous people in Canada. Indeed, it has corresponded with their previous exclusion from citizenship. The debate about citizenship criteria in this treaty was another instance in the lengthy conversation about their suitability as Canadian citizens. It took the form it did because, in their defence of ancestral membership criteria, the Nisga'a seemed to be showing that they had not relinquished the kinds of tribal affiliations that originally marked them as not modern, not yet ready for Canadian citizenship, and in need of assimilation.

Cultural Belonging/National Belonging

During the Senate committee hearings, one senator asked if the Nisga'a language possessed a word for "citizen" that could be used instead of the symbolically loaded English one. The senator suggested that if this word existed, a set of rights must presumably accompany it. There was some whispering on the sidelines among the Nisga'a delegation, to the effect that yes there was such a word – it was "Nisga'a." This is not entirely accurate, though, because there is no Nisga'a word for a "citizen" of the broader collective known as the Nisga'a Nation.[28] President Joe Gosnell replied to the senator's question:

> It is important for the committee and the rest of the honorable senators who are not present to recognize very clearly that every citizen of our nation today belongs to one of the four major crests that we hold. There is no Nisga'a today that is born who does not belong to one of these four groupings of clans. Everyone fits into our structure. There is no individual standing off to one side who has nowhere to go. You belong. You are born into a lineage. You are born into our nation.[29]

This answer is not about individual rights in a political community but about belonging tied to kinship and birth. All Nisga'a are members of one of four exogamous pdeek, or tribes – the Ganada (Raven–Frog), Laxgibuu (Wolf–Bear), Gisk'aast (Killer whale–Owl), and Laxsgiik (Eagle–Beaver). Identified by their two major crests, the pdeek constitute the four corner posts of the Nisga'a Nation. Each one is composed of matrilineally defined huwilp, or Houses. Members of a pdeek are descended from a common ancestor but cannot trace their descent to one woman; members of a wilp, however, can. Children belong to their mother's wilp and have access to ango'oskw through this matrilineal affiliation. They also have rights to ango'oskw through their father, who belongs to a different wilp and pdeek. The wilp of a person's father is his or her *wilksilaks*. People in the same wilksilaks perform specific services for one another throughout their lives and make important contributions to feasts at each other's marriage and death (Nyce 2010).[30] Historically, your kinship kept you alive because your maternal and paternal relationships gave you access to resources. In the past, people who had no relatives and did not know their origins were *wa'aayin*, meaning "not whole" or "never healed" (Boston and Morven 1996, 55). Wa'aayin was the lowest level in Nisga'a society. It included illegitimate children and freed slaves, but high-ranking people could be demoted to *wa'aayin* by their relatives if they brought shame on the wilp through bad behaviour (Halpin 1973, 105; Boston and Morven 1996, 55).

The Nisga'a continue to value a way of life that emphasizes kin-based social obligations and collective responsibilities (Robinson 2008, 58). This remains the case despite more than a century of assimilation efforts on the part of church and state. The missionary James McCullagh, who worked in Old Aiyansh at the turn of the century, is known for wanting to get people out of their "Houses" and into "houses" – independent family dwellings that reduced the bonds of collective living. Nisga'a individuals told me that fulfilling their social obligations involved hard work, but the support of the collective compared positively to the more individualistic non-Indigenous world. "It's harder to be a white person," one man said to me. "The support is not there." Ultimately, as he explained,

> what it comes down to is, I'm not by myself. I saw this especially when my uncle died. There was a lot of fear when he passed away, because all his responsibilities were ours now ... But when I went to our tribal feast and I saw the strength of our house, I knew I wasn't by myself. Halfway through, I knew it was going to be okay. We had lost a significant member but what he taught us was there.[31]

Sometimes, non-Indigenous people are culturally adopted into a wilp and given a Nisga'a name so that they can participate in community life. This is also referred to as being "taken in." Once taken in, "you are part of an extended family. You have obligations to them and share the good times and the sad times. You have to be there for the feasts, doing your part."[32] People who have been taken in but who do not keep up with their obligations can be publicly censured, and I certainly heard some grumbling about the failure of outsiders to understand the difficulties of fulfilling the duties of this kind of citizenship.

Kinship-based social organization positions people within a framework of cross-cutting obligations, responsibilities, and support. It creates belonging and identity, but not everyone had or has the same rights, entitlements, or obligations; these are differentiated according to wilp, pdeek̲, and rank. In contrast, the treaty – like other land claims agreements – creates a set of uniform rights for Nisg̲a'a citizens in relation to a centralized government. All Nisg̲a'a citizens have the same entitlement to Nisg̲a'a lands, resources, programs, and services, and Nisg̲a'a Lisims Government is required to regulate access to them. This political arrangement requires a reorientation between individual Nisg̲a'a and their government because formerly there was no such thing as universal citizenship across a centrally organized Nisg̲a'a Nation.

Permits illustrate some of the challenges of this reorientation. As mentioned in Chapter 2, people complained about having to acquire permits from a centralized government before they could fish or gather mushrooms. The tensions around the implementation of the common bowl also show the strains of the transformation away from ango'oskws to commonly held public lands. Paul Nadasdy (2017) describes a similar issue among the Kluane First Nation in Yukon in the wake of a land claims agreement that identifies Kluane territory and authorizes Kluane government to regulate hunting. Family hunting territories are now part of common lands managed by that government. Nadasdy (2017, 176) writes that "the category of Kluane First Nation citizen steamrolls the complex particularities of local social relations and land use practices, and erects in their place a simplified and universal set of relations among Kluane citizens and between them and the environment." In discussing the Gitxsan Nation, which lies adjacent to the Nisg̲a'a, Valerie Napoleon (2009) likewise notes that its citizenship obligations and entitlements were not to and from a centralized state but were refracted through a kinship system. This is why Nadasdy (2017, 140) argues that "First Nation citizenship is not simply the recognition in law of an already existing form of political subjectivity" but is instead a "new category of political belonging." This is an important and difficult transformation, one that potentially but not inevitably takes First Nations into new realms of individualizing subjectivity.

Nisga'a continue to live within and meet the obligations of kinship across huwilp and pdeek̲ in villages and between the villages and towns throughout British Columbia. At the same time, they talk of needing to become entrepreneurial and to engage with economic development opportunities, including tourism and resource extraction. Residents of the Nass Valley have juggled these differing values for a century and a half in various ways and would continue to do so even if the treaty did not exist. Now that it does exist, people feel pressure to make it work in a way that can be measured, especially given that they fought so hard to attain it. But they also need to make a living, which can be a struggle in an area that is currently experiencing the decline of a resource-based economy. When I visited the Nass Valley shortly after the treaty came into effect, my landlady assured me that things were going well, that the Nisga'a were well into self-government, and that the young people were learning to be entrepreneurs. Nothing much had changed in the village, and in fact a couple of businesses had closed since my last visit. On my next trip, I found the same; even Nass Camp, where I had waited for the treaty to come into effect on the night of May 10, 2000, and that formerly had a restaurant and gas station, had closed after being bought by Nisga'a Lisims Government. A store in Gitwinksihlkw that sold sandwiches, chips, and some souvenirs had also shut its doors. Increasingly, in personal conversations, in speeches given by Nisga'a elected officials, in what people talk about at the biennial special assemblies, in various initiatives to bring business and resource development into the valley that are publicly promoted by the Nisga'a government, Nisga'a express the need to become more entrepreneurial and to stimulate economic development. They talk about the absence of economic opportunities in the valley and of needing training and workshops to address this gap.

In all these conversations and meetings and assemblies, they also note that the individualism of entrepreneurialism is inconsistent with the obligations of good citizenship from a Nisga'a cultural perspective. One interviewee spoke at length about the need to define prosperity differently to capture culturally relevant indicators, such as access to fish and other wild foods, cultural knowledge, and community support. At an Open for Business forum held by the Nisga'a Lisims Government in 2018, one speaker explained that many people could not attend because several deaths had occurred in the communities; they stayed away because they were grieving but also because they were involved in the settlement feasts and other family duties that are required at such times. He said that the business world did not understand this situation and did not stop for feasts, and that Nisga'a always needed to balance the demands of their employment environment with those of Nisga'a culture. Others spoke about the need to engage with economic opportunities such as tourism and mining while maintaining Nisga'a culture and values, including protecting the environment.

At the same time, people stated that self-reliance, thrift, and hard work were always important cultural values for the Nisga'a and suggested that they should be revived. In discussing their parents' and grandparents' generations, many people described lives of hard work and social responsibility within the framework of the wilp and pdeek̲. Elders frequently took up this theme about how hard people worked in the past, how frugal and independent they were, but also how strong the communities were collectively. People linked this way of life with their former practice of self-government and complained that the younger generations had become too dependent on government assistance. This is perhaps a common criticism that older generations make against the younger. More particularly, many people blamed the Indian Act and the introduction of welfare in the 1950s for their loss of self-reliance, saying that when welfare was initiated the elders warned them that people would forget how to work. Many reserved their most contemptuous comments for the Indian Act, which they saw as suffocating and oppressive. "Over time," one woman said, "we became helpless," so that "when the treaty came about and the reality was there for us to be self-governing, lo and behold, our people are a dependent people." She and others referred to being stuck in an Indian Act mentality and of needing to deprogram themselves so they could become "healthy, thinking people" again.[33]

Historically, the goal of state assimilation projects was to dismantle Indigenous people's attachments to kin, community, and territory, and to transform them into the individualized, landless subjects that are best suited to a certain rung of capitalism (Lightfoot 2013, 129). In her analysis of citizenship, Aihwa Ong (1996, 738) asks "if a minority group

116   *Beyond Rights*

can escape the cultural inscription of state power and other forms of regulation that define modes of belonging within states." She contends that citizenship is a category through which people are disciplined into the individualized rights-bearing subjects of a modern liberal state, even as they struggle with these terms of belonging and often fail to achieve them (Ong 1996, 2006). In their failures, they are seen as bad subjects who are unworthy of citizenship. Within the dominant ideology of neoliberalism, good citizenship is increasingly defined as the duty "to reduce [our] burden on society," to maximize our individual capital, and to be entrepreneurs of ourselves (Ong 1996, 739). Dependency is generally cast as antithetical to the responsibilities of citizenship in capitalist societies (Fraser and Gordon 1997). This is true, but though people's talk about their loss of self-reliance brings them into proximity with neoliberal norms of citizenship – standards by which they continue to be negatively judged – they are not merely recapitulating a neoliberal rationality in their self-critique. They are commenting on the dilemmas they encounter as they seek to restore culturally meaningful modes of citizenship in the face of these individualistic market-oriented ideals. This process generates deep ambivalence but does not stop people from working to fuse their cultural values and political aspirations into contemporary expressions of Nisga'a citizenship.

Conclusion

Anthropologists have defined citizenship as a status whose criteria are challenged and contested by subaltern people as they demand full, rather than second-class, membership in the states that encompass them (Ramirez 2004; Rosaldo 1997). They have also theorized citizenship as a category through which people are disciplined into particular kinds of subjects in the course of their struggle to belong or to access state services and goods (Ong 1996). However, Indigenous people are engaged in a unique struggle with citizenship. Although they have long histories of exclusion from citizenship in settler states, their political status and goals have always been about more than equal access to the rights of other citizens. For many, the "gift" of settler citizenship was little more than a form of coercive inclusion (Audra Simpson 2014). Their status as members of nations that possess rights of self-determination distinguishes their demands from those of other minorities. This fact requires wholly different political configurations, ones that enable the existence within a state of distinct political communities with separate rights and jurisdictions. As revealed in this chapter, politicians who reviewed the treaty bill in the Senate found this political dilemma extremely challenging. It remains unresolved within Canadian political culture today, and anyone reading about any Indigenous issue in the mainstream news will encounter all of these arguments about rights, equality, difference, and deservedness.

In addition, the Nisga'a challenged the hegemonic norms of citizenship for Indigenous people in Canada, seeking a treaty citizenship on the basis of rights that flow from their status as a political community, not a racial group, with a special relationship to their land. In doing so, they disrupted the state as the sole source of rights and realigned the relationship between their rights as Indigenous people and their relationship with the Canadian state. Treaties are mechanisms that embody the differing kinds of relationships that Indigenous people seek with the state, through which they can participate as citizens in what should, ideally, be the shared political community of Canada. Historically, treaties also created citizenship for settlers. As Aaron Mills (2017, 225) puts it, "they're how we constitute ourselves as communities of communities, across our difference."

The Treaty Relationship: Reconciliation and Its Discontents

4

When the final report of the Truth and Reconciliation Commission (2015, 33) was released in 2015, its authors emphasized the significance of treaties: "It is important for all Canadians to understand that without Treaties, Canada would have no legitimacy as a nation. Treaties between Indigenous nations and the Crown established the legal and constitutional foundation of this country." Indeed, though many Canadians might think of treaties as outdated historical relics, nothing could be further from the truth. Treaties are foundational to the Canadian state (Asch 2014; Miller 2009). Treaty rights are acknowledged and protected by section 35 of the Constitution. Many Indigenous people hold that treaties created Canada through their consent. What this means is that Indigenous involvement through treaty making was critical for this country to take the shape it now possesses (Borrows 2010). The Truth and Reconciliation Commission report also stated that treaties have an important role to play in the present: "Treaties are a model for how Canadians, as diverse peoples, can live respectfully and peacefully together on these lands we now share." In its calls to action, the report included renewing or establishing "treaty relationships based on principles of mutual recognition, mutual respect, and shared responsibility for maintaining those relationships into the future" (Truth and Reconciliation Commission 2015, 230).

In this chapter, I examine the significance of treaties as a mechanism of reconciliation. The political, legal, and economic nature of treaties, as well as their historic significance, makes them an essential component in the relationship between Indigenous people and other Canadians, and we must understand that reconciliation needs to embrace elements of the treaty relationship. Thus, treaties must be implemented in good faith, and all signatories must understand both their specific requirements and their broader spirit and intent. Also, treaties can contribute to reconciliation only if and when the nation-to-nation vision of a treaty becomes a realistic possibility. To talk about treaties as a form of reconciliation in the absence of meaningful political change is no more than empty rhetoric.

The Challenge of Implementation

The implementation of a treaty occurs after it is signed, the relevant legislation is ratified, and the press puts its cameras away. Modern-day treaties are complex agreements that cover multiple areas of governance, resource management, and service delivery to their beneficiaries. Implementing them requires cooperation and coordination between Indigenous, federal, and provincial or territorial governments. Whereas most modern treaties are accompanied by long implementation plans, these documents are not legally binding and do not provide an adequate framework for making the treaties work. The Nisga'a were not naive about entering into their treaty but are now quite critical of the federal government's approach to implementation. This has a direct bearing on whatever potential any treaty may hold as a component of reconciliation. In the past, and today, Indigenous peoples expect a treaty to establish a relationship between themselves and the rest of Canada. Prior to the arrival of Europeans, treaty making was a well-established mechanism in intertribal relations. For the Nisga'a, as with other Indigenous peoples in Canada and the United States, treaties are covenants that bind the parties in long-term associations of mutual support and obligation (Craft 2013; Miller 2009; Leanne Simpson 2008). This was the vision that Indigenous peoples brought to treaty making between each other and then in their dealings with the European newcomers (Williams 1999). It remains their vision today.

What they find instead is that the ink is barely dry before the federal government stops all talk of the broad objectives of the treaty, such as reconciliation, inclusion, and improving the lives of the signatories, and looks only to fulfill the narrow legal obligations set out in the document. In many instances, Ottawa fails to understand even those obligations. Nisga'a complain that when they approach the relevant government department concerning lands or fisheries or program delivery to their citizens, they are typically shunted to what was formerly known as the Department of Indian Affairs and Northern Development (DIAND). In 2011, the Harper government changed the name of the department to Aboriginal Affairs and Northern Development. In 2015, it was rechristened Indigenous and Northern Affairs Canada (INAC) by the recently elected Liberal government. Readers will know that the name has been altered again and that INAC has been split into two departments, to which I will return later in this chapter. The Nisga'a and representatives of other treaty nations say, however, that treaties are made with the Crown in right of Canada, not with DIAND or INAC or whatever the name of the department currently happens to be. They are nation-to-nation/government-to-government agreements, not agreements with a particular federal department, especially not the department that is charged with administering the Indian Act.

In 2003, the Nisga'a and more than a dozen other Indigenous signatories of modern treaties founded the Land Claims Agreements Coalition (Fenge 2015).[1] Based in Ottawa, the coalition brings modern-treaty nations together to share knowledge and to advance implementation and recognition of the importance of treaties to the constitutional structure of Canada.[2] It also provides a platform from which to lobby the federal government on matters of implementation. The reasoning here is that a unified coalition will have a stronger voice and potentially a greater impact than if each nation lobbied independently around the same issues. The coalition also made two submissions to the United Nations Human Rights Council, Universal Periodic Review of Canada, in 2007 and 2012. In its 2012 report to the United Nations, the coalition stated that "the treaty rights arising from modern land claims agreements express the mutual desire of the Crown and Aboriginal peoples to reconcile through sharing the lands, resources and natural wealth of this subcontinent in a manner that is equitable and just, in contrast to the discriminatory and assimilationist approaches that have characterized their historical relations."[3]

The Nisg̱a'a are one of several coalition members who have gone to court in an attempt to get their federal and provincial treaty partners to fulfill their treaty obligations. The issues at stake in these cases include environmental assessment processes, co-management arrangements, consultation, and financing (Graben and Mehaffey 2017; Promislow and Verrier 2019, 52). In 2013, the Nisg̱a'a launched legal proceedings against the Government of British Columbia regarding its decision to issue an environmental assessment certificate to Avanti Kitsault Mine. Avanti had proposed to reopen a molybdenum mine in Alice Arm, forty kilometres north of Gingolx. Molybdenum is used to make steel alloy. Alice Arm is the eastern arm of Observatory Inlet, which is itself an arm of Portland Inlet. It lies in the Nass Wildlife Area, where Nisg̱a'a citizens have treaty rights to hunt, fish, and collect seafood. The BC government granted Avanti its environmental assessment certificate in March 2013, before the environmental assessment requirements set out in the treaty had been met, thus breaching the treaty. Chapter 10 of the treaty stipulates that any project on or off Nisg̱a'a lands that may have adverse environmental effects on residents of Nisg̱a'a land, the land itself, or Nisg̱a'a treaty interests requires environmental assessment involving the Nisg̱a'a government and Nisg̱a'a communities. Among other things, it specifies that the assessment must examine the impact of any project on the existing and future economic, social, and cultural well-being of the Nisg̱a'a citizens who may be affected. Nisg̱a'a Lisims Government filed a petition in the BC Supreme Court in response. At a December 2015 Land Claims Agreements Coalition meeting in Ottawa, Jim Aldridge, legal counsel for Nisg̱a'a government, outlined these developments and noted that federal, provincial, and territorial governments do not cope well with the specificity of land claims agreements. Speaking to the challenges of implementing modern treaties, he stated that governments default to a cookie cutter, one-size-fits-all approach to things like environmental consultation rather than really understanding the specific details of treaty agreements.[4]

When the Nisga'a negotiated the Chapter 10 environmental assessment and protection clauses, the history of the Alice Arm molybdenum mine and the lack of sufficient environmental safeguards were at the top of their mind. The mine has been operated on and off since the early twentieth century but most recently between 1980 and 1982 by a Canadian subsidiary of Connecticut-based AMAX Corporation. It has a murky history of environmental approval (Raunet 1996). The environmental certificates issued by Ottawa at the time did not conform to existing standards, permitting AMAX to dump mine tailings directly into Alice Arm, an area that the Nisga'a and especially Gingolx residents rely on for fish, shellfish, and other seafood products. The tailings contained heavy metals, including arsenic, zinc, cadmium, mercury, radium-226, and uranium (Raunet 1996).[5] Their negative effects on the marine and freshwater environments in Alice Arm and nearby Lime Creek are still present. The Nisga'a protested the dumping and even travelled to New York to confront the company shareholders (Raunet 1996, 209). In 1980, before the dumping began, Nisga'a Tribal Council president James Gosnell and Nelson Leeson appeared on a popular TV talk show hosted by media personality Jack Webster to air their concerns. They explained that AMAX was proposing to dump the tailings into Alice Arm, on the premise that they would be contained within the inlet. Gosnell suggested that the waste would escape and thus damage commercial fishing on the Northwest Coast. To make their point, they asked if tailings of this sort would ever be dumped into Burrard Inlet.[6] The mine was shut down in 1982 but only because the world market for molybdenum made it no longer profitable.

This is the mine that Avanti, the new owner, intended to reopen in 2013.[7] Working with the provincial and federal governments, Avanti did not fully engage the Chapter 10 requirements of the treaty – a chapter written by Nisga'a whose formative experience of environmental assessment was its utter lack at the AMAX mine. After the Nisga'a government launched the lawsuit, the senior management of Avanti changed and the company took a more open and conciliatory approach to dealing with the concerns. Avanti addressed the weaknesses in the initial environmental assessment and protection report, bringing the proposed mine operation into compliance with Chapter 10. The Nisga'a withdrew from the court proceedings. In July 2014, Nisga'a Lisims Government and Avanti concluded a benefits agreement with stronger environmental protections in place. As a result of this agreement, the BC government will share a percentage of the net mineral tax revenue it collects from the mine with the Nisga'a Nation. The agreement states that the Nisga'a will use these monies "in pursuit of matters over which they have jurisdiction and control as provided for under the Nisga'a Final Agreement, including, among other things, the delivery of programs and services."[8] "Net mineral tax revenue" means the total amount of tax, penalty, and interest paid by an operator under the Mineral Tax Act for a BC fiscal year, minus the total amount of tax, penalty, and interest refunded and interest paid to the operator of the mine under the Mineral Tax Act for that fiscal year. Mitchell Stevens, president of Nisga'a Lisims Government, said,

> We are pleased to have finally reached an agreement with Avanti that will enable the project to proceed while ensuring that our treaty rights are respected, and our Nation's environment is protected ... This demonstrates that when proponents take the Nisga'a Nation's interests and concerns seriously, practical agreements can be reached in a timely manner. We are now counting on the provincial and federal governments to fulfill their responsibilities under our Treaty in respect of this and other projects in our area.[9]

In 1975, the James Bay Cree were the first to make a modern land claims agreement after the Quebec government, headed by Premier Robert Bourassa, announced plans to dam huge portions of their territory. The James Bay and Northern Quebec Agreement was negotiated in two years, as the bulldozers waited, and the Cree then struggled for more than thirty years to get their treaty implemented in any meaningful way, finally taking the provincial government to court (Coon Come 2015; Feit 2010; Papillon 2008). As a result of the court action, the "Agreement concerning a New Relationship between the Government of Canada and the Cree of Eeyou Istchee" was concluded in 2008. It addressed all outstanding implementation issues and included a $1.4 billion payment from Canada to settle related litigation and its costs and to fund implementation for twenty years (Eyford 2015, 77). At a 2015

Land Claims Agreements Coalition event in Ottawa, I listened as Matthew Coon Come, then grand chief of the Grand Council of the Crees, spoke about how much hope the Cree initially had around the James Bay Agreement. They expected to enact self-governance in a meaningful way in their territory and to provide culturally relevant programs and services. He warned that if treaties are "not properly implemented, they also have the potential to perpetuate great harms. They can become a tool of dispossession. They can be used to disenfranchise and marginalize us."[10] He was speaking directly to the decades-long struggle of the Cree to get governments to honour their obligations after the Cree had agreed to extinguish their title on parts of their territory in exchange for the rights and benefits set out in the James Bay Agreement, thereby enabling the hydroelectric development to take place.

Nunavut Tunngavik, the organization representing the Nunavummiut residents of Nunavut, also sued the federal and Northwest Territories governments over lack of implementation of their agreement. The territory of Nunavut came into being in 1993, when Ottawa and representatives of central and eastern Inuit of the Northwest Territories concluded the Nunavut Land Claims Agreement. It is the largest land claim settlement in Canadian history, covering approximately 350,000 square kilometres. In 2006, Nunavut Tunngavik began legal proceedings against Canada for contractual breaches in sixteen areas of the agreement (Campbell, Fenge, and Hanson 2011, 47).[11] Two of these areas concerned increasing the levels of government employment of Inuit within the settlement area to a representative level and providing assistance to Inuit firms that were competing for government contracts, as promised in articles 23 and 24 of the agreement. Nunavut Tunngavik and Canada settled this lawsuit out of court in 2015. As a condition of the settlement, Canada is required to pay Nunavut Tunngavik $255 million to facilitate implementation. Nunavut Tunngavik committed to using part of this money to provide training for Inuit employment.

More recently, in the Yukon Peel Watershed case, the Na-Cho Nyak Dun, the Tr'ondëk Hwëch'in, and the Vuntut Gwitchin took legal action against the Yukon government for repeatedly failing to honour its obligations under the Yukon Umbrella Final Agreement with respect to the management of the Peel River Watershed. This watershed has been the subject of various management plans, but the Yukon First Nations who brought the litigation argued that the Yukon government failed to act in keeping with the requirements of Chapter 11 of the umbrella agreement. In December 2017, the Supreme Court of Canada ruled in favour of the First Nations and their treaty rights, as given in the umbrella agreement, with respect to management and decision making in the Peel Watershed. This ruling has been seen as a vindication of modern treaty rights, but it emerged only through litigation. Going to court is expensive, stressful, and time consuming; it drains resources from communities and governments and should not be what First Nations have to resort to to make governments deliver on their treaty obligations. It is contrary to the kind of relationship that treaties should establish between partners, and it distracts Indigenous governments from the more important issues of nation building, cultural revitalization, and economic development.[12] Graben and Mehaffey (2017, 177) make the point that this deep investment "in lobbying, lawyering, and legislating is key to the efficacy of Aboriginal governments under contemporary treaties ... While exhausting and expensive, contemporary treaties require Aboriginal governments to vigilantly and strategically defend what legal rights they believe they obtained through the agreements."

One reason for Ottawa's failure to implement treaties in any meaningful way is that it has no organizational structure to oversee and coordinate the process. Until recently, the structure of government was basically unchanged. In 2007, the Report of the Auditor General of Canada made this point in its chapter on the Inuvialuit Final Agreement. The Inuit of the Western Arctic signed the agreement in 1984 after ten years of negotiation and are now a member of the Land Claims Agreements Coalition. In a withering assessment of government implementation, the auditor general concluded,

> Twenty-three years after the Agreement came into effect, INAC still has not developed a strategy for implementing it. INAC has never formally identified federal obligations under the Agreement or determined which federal departments were responsible for which obligations. It has not developed a plan to ensure that federal

obligations are met. The Department does not have a strategic approach to identify and implement Canada's obligations, nor does it monitor how Canada fulfills them.[13]

In 2007 and 2008, the Standing Senate Committee on Aboriginal Peoples met to examine and report on the implementation of federal government treaty obligations. Witnesses included representatives from the auditor general's office, officials from federal departments including DIAND (as it was then called), and members of the Land Claims Agreements Coalition. The committee report observed that the federal government was more concerned with concluding agreements than with implementing them. The deputy minister of DIAND confirmed this during the hearings: "The tendency is that once the announcement ... is finished and the cameras have been shut off and we are on to implementation that people do not spend as much time on implementation issues. That is something that happens in government."[14] The turnover rate of senior officials, including ministers and deputy ministers, is high. This means that short-term initiatives and newsworthy photo opportunities become the order of the day rather than sustained management attention and policy follow-through.[15] More particularly, there is no organized effort on the part of the federal government, outside of the department charged with Indigenous affairs, to oversee and coordinate implementation (Papillon 2008, 5). Time and again, people complained about the lack of government coordination of its treaty obligations. Before its most recent round of restructuring, INAC was tasked with implementing treaties and had within it an Implementation Branch, but it had no authority to compel other government departments to comply with their particular responsibilities. In some instances, officials and staff in these departments were unaware that they had such responsibilities.

Testifying before the Senate committee, Nisga'a Lisims Government CEO Kevin McKay described this situation:

> Even when the department is trying ... to bring about the objectives of the agreement it is often frustrated to arrive at other departments to find that it has insufficient clout with those other departments. The other departments consider it [the treaty] to be the Department

of Indian and Northern Affairs' agreement and not theirs. In this way, they fail to acknowledge our nation-to-nation relationship with Canada, something we fought so hard to achieve through the negotiation of our Treaty.[16]

The deputy minister of DIAND said much the same thing:

> A challenge that our department faces ... is that ... we are not solely responsible for implementation or in possession of all the levers and tools related to implementation. We have had difficulty in the past fully engaging other government departments ... More often than not, these agreements are presumed by our colleagues to be the responsibility of our department.[17]

The Senate committee recommended "that the Government of Canada, in collaboration with the Land Claims Agreements Coalition and its present and future members, take immediate steps to establish an independent body, through legislation, such as a Modern Treaty Commission, to oversee the implementation of comprehensive land claims agreements, including financial matters."[18] The committee also recommended that the mandate of this commission be developed with the Land Claims Agreements Coalition and its members. The coalition continues to push for the creation of a Modern Treaties Implementation Review Commission as a "legislatively established independent review body" that would report "directly to Parliament on the effectiveness of government in meeting the terms of modern treaties in Canada" (Cameron and Campbell 2019). In January 2019, coalition members met with Prime Minister Justin Trudeau and discussed the establishment of the commission, but no progress has been made. Crown-Indigenous Relations and Northern Affairs Canada (CIRNAC), the latest incarnation of Indian Affairs, possesses a Modern Treaty Implementation Office. At a coalition conference in February 2020, speakers continued to emphasize the importance of establishing a Modern Treaties Implementation Review Commission as an independent oversight body outside of CIRNAC.

Treaty implementation requires working across all federal departments, as well as coordinating various tasks and initiatives. Administrative responsibilities written into the treaties are often joint in their structure and financing. A 2013 internal audit report on the implementation of modern treaty obligations, produced by Aboriginal Affairs and Northern Development Canada, confirms that "the implementation of modern treaties is a whole-of-government responsibility. Over 30 federal departments and agencies have specific legal obligations pursuant to these agreements, and over 400 obligations apply to all departments and agencies."[19] The Nisga'a treaty includes provisions on fisheries management, wildlife harvesting, roads and rights of way, lands, programs and services to citizens, and environmental assessment, to name a few, all of which entail working with provincial and federal governments. The Fisheries chapter establishes a Joint Fisheries Management Board, which involves the Nisga'a, the Province, and Ottawa. The Wildlife and Migratory Birds chapter establishes a Wildlife Committee and involves the Nisga'a in decision making around wildlife harvesting and monitoring. Indeed, virtually every federal organization's mandate will intersect with established treaty rights at some point.[20]

The problem that modern-treaty nations encounter is the failure of these ministries to understand that treaty obligations bind the Government of Canada as a whole, not simply the department responsible for Indigenous affairs. Nor do officials and employees in these ministries sufficiently understand the constitutional nature of treaty obligations. Too often, they approach treaty implementation as a discretionary policy matter – as something that is added to the pile of what is affordable this year in the usual budget and decision-making processes. Too often, departments "see the implementation of treaty provisions as an aspect of ... policy," which can "vary according to budgetary and other considerations. So the act of implementing treaty provisions is seen as essentially similar to other policy-making, priority-setting and program-management functions of the government" (Cree-Naskapi Commission 1986, 6). This is a fundamental misunderstanding of the nature of treaty obligations.

Between 2013 and 2015, members of the Land Claims Agreements Coalition were able to work with Bernard Valcourt, Conservative minister of Aboriginal Affairs and Northern Development, to formulate a "whole-of-government" Cabinet directive on treaty implementation.

The relationship between the Harper government, the coalition, and Indigenous people in Canada was not a good one, but Minister Valcourt did secure his government's commitment to the directive in 2015. It sets out "an operational framework for the management of the Crown's modern treaty obligations" and directs all federal departments and agencies to "ensure that they are aware of, understand, and fulfill their departments' obligations pursuant to all modern treaties in effect."[21] The directive also established a Deputy Ministers Oversight Committee and a Modern Treaty Implementation Office (Cameron and Campbell 2019). The oversight committee includes deputy ministers of all federal departments whose mandates intersect with treaty rights.[22] Shortly after the Cabinet directive was announced, the Conservative government lost the election and Justin Trudeau's Liberal Party came to power. The directive and the Deputy Ministers Oversight Committee are still in place. After the election, Trudeau undertook a different set of restructurings and policy initiatives geared toward establishing a new relationship with Indigenous people, to which I return below.

There is another conceptual barrier to implementation, which is that governments read treaty provisions literally and with a view to keeping their responsibilities small. To put it another way, governments have sought to satisfy their contractual obligations in isolation from each other and often sparingly. Obligations are important, but fulfilling them does not fulfill the broader objectives of treaties. This has long been an issue in the interpretation of historic treaties, which are typically just a few pages long. It remains a problem with their modern-day counterparts, which cover more than two hundred pages. For example, a clause in the James Bay Agreement states that Canada and Quebec will assist and promote the efforts of the Cree concerning economic development (Peters 1991, 193).[23] This was one of the disputed issues in the lawsuit brought by the Cree against the two governments; they argued that under the terms of the clause, Quebec and Canada were required to promote economic development beyond what they might normally have done anyway according to existing programs for First Nations.

Writing about historic treaties, Aimee Craft (2013, 11) maintains that "in order to interpret and implement a treaty, we look to its spirit and intent, and consider what was contemplated by the parties at the time the treaty was negotiated." Indigenous signatories saw their treaties as creating a social contract between treaty partners that bound them in relationships of mutual support. Aaron Mills (2017, 225) describes historic treaties as "frameworks for right relationships: the total relational means by which we orient and reorient ourselves to each other through time, to live well together and with all our relations within creation. They have a legal quality in the sense that they constrain behavior and they are at once political, social, economic, spiritual, and ecological." There is evidence that in the early period of treaty making, Crown representatives understood the long-term relationship aspects of the agreements and willingly entered into the Indigenous protocols that affirmed them (Asch 2014). The Supreme Court of Canada has produced guidelines for the interpretation of historic treaties that state they are not to be interpreted strictly on the basis of the written texts.

Modern treaties are more likely than historic treaties to be interpreted contractually (Newman 2011). This is not to say that treaties are not contractual agreements – they are. The contractual nature of modern treaties means that they are legally binding and can be relied on by the parties. Treaties also have the force of law, which makes them more than contracts. Contracts are mutually binding only on whoever is in the contract. Because treaties have the force of law, other parties, such as a mining company, for example, or mushroom pickers who want to enter Nisga'a lands and gather pine mushrooms, must abide by the treaty. Beyond this, treaties are social and political compacts. A strictly contractual approach to their implementation and interpretation is inconsistent with a more holistic and relational approach. Time and again, the Nisga'a and other treaty nations say that the Crown does not respect the spirit and intent of treaty making, that it does not see or understand the broader objectives of treaties, and that it does not perceive them as nation-to-nation agreements that have the force of law. One Nisga'a Nation employee in Gitlaxt'aamiks complained to me that governments think of treaties as a divorce, when in fact they should be more like a marriage. He was referring first-hand to a sense that federal and provincial governments saw the Nisga'a treaty as a finished deal that relieved them of further dealings with the Nisga'a – and that was the end of it. In his opinion, treaties were charters for a more equitable political relationship, and only when this was achieved could something resembling reconciliation ensue. Sloan Morgan, Castleden, and Huu-ay-aht First Nations (2018, 319) similarly mention a feeling of "divorce" among members of the Huu-ay-aht First Nations after they finalized the Maa-nulth treaty in 2011. Huu-ay-aht members had expected the relationship between themselves and the federal and provincial governments to be far different after the treaty than it is turning out to be.

Reconciliation, Aboriginal Rights, and Section 35
When the Standing Senate Committee on Aboriginal Peoples released its report on land claims implementation in 2008, it echoed this criticism, saying that "the government's focus ... has largely been to discharge its obligations in a narrow sense, rather than working to achieve the full breadth of reconciliation promised by treaties."[24] Reconciliation entered into political discourse in descriptions of Indigenous-Crown relationships during the 1990s. I first encountered it when I worked as a research associate at the Royal Commission on Aboriginal Peoples between 1993 and 1996. Part of the commission's mandate was to find paths to reconciliation. By the time I began research on the Nisga'a treaty, politicians, negotiators, and commentators were all calling it a form of reconciliation. I heard the treaty referred to variously as signifying a "new era of reconciliation," a "historic reconciliation," an "important step toward reconciliation and the dream of true equality," and a "balanced and sensible reconciliation of issues that have frustrated and divided British Columbians for more than a century."[25] Recent annual reports of the BC Treaty Commission designate BC treaties as absolutely critical to forging reconciliation and to implementing the rights of Indigenous peoples as expressed in the United Nations Declaration.[26]

Globally, the 1990s were characterized by a proliferation of transitional justice mechanisms that connected their mandates with reconciliation and repair (Huyssen 2000; Teitel 2003). Truth commissions, trials, state inquiries, apologies, financial reparations, and other forms of redress multiplied in what scholars of transitional justice have called the age of apology and reparations. Transitional justice is used in states that are undergoing political transitions, such as that from white minority rule and apartheid to democratic rule and free elections in South Africa.

The South African Truth and Reconciliation Commission is one of the best-known examples, but transitional justice mechanisms have also been instrumental in changeovers to democracy in Eastern Europe, South America, and Latin America. In these contexts, reconciliation is linked with regime change and structural alterations in the state, where the conditions that fostered political oppression and violence are supposed to be eradicated. These transitions are always imperfect. Apologies and truth and reconciliation commissions often prove disappointing for those who participate in them but are instrumental in the restoration or renewal of state legitimacy (Bur 2001; Laplante and Theidon 2007; Trouillot 2000; Wilson 2001). Many have criticized the South African Truth and Reconciliation Commission for its emphasis on forgiveness and its mechanism of offering amnesty in exchange for testimony from certain perpetrators (Soyinka 1999). Justice, accountability, and reconciliation are uneasily conjoined, and many would say that you cannot arrive at reconciliation without justice and accountability. Canada is distinct among states that are appealing to reconciliation because it has used a transitional justice mechanism – the Truth and Reconciliation Commission on Indian residential schools – in the absence of any actual political transition. No regime change will occur, and the nature of the Canadian state will not be fundamentally transformed. As a result, many structural inequalities, and structurally based injustices, remain current and very much part of Indigenous people's everyday lives.

In Canada, reconciliation has a specific legal meaning that can be understood only in relation to the way in which Aboriginal and treaty rights are framed in the Constitution and interpreted by the courts. This legal meaning determines why governments negotiate treaties and why reconciliation has been brought in to describe a political situation that is not characterized by any actual transition. As John Borrows (2017, 20) argues, reconciliation dominates "the jurisprudence dealing with Indigenous issues and is a flawed metaphor" in this context.

The Nisga'a treaty transforms all of the section 35 Aboriginal rights of the Nisga'a people into a set of known and defined, carefully delineated treaty rights and jurisdictional authorities. Other treaties achieve the same thing for the various Indigenous nations that enter into them. Section 35(1) of the Constitution recognizes the existence of Aboriginal rights, including treaty rights, and has done so since the Constitution was repatriated in 1982. Although repatriation involved Ottawa in debates with provincial governments and particularly Quebec, Indigenous people quickly realized that their interests and the small protection of their status vis-à-vis the Crown through section 91(24) of the BNA Act were at risk of being eclipsed. They lobbied to have Indigenous nationhood recognized as an explicit element of the Canadian constitutional structure as a third order of government. Recall that one criticism of the Nisga'a treaty's self-government provisions – discussed in Chapter 1 – was that it created a third order of government without amending the Constitution. The lobbying of Indigenous groups did not result in constitutional recognition of Indigenous nationhood, but it did result in the creation of section 35, which states,

> 35.(1) The existing aboriginal and treaty rights of the aboriginal peoples of Canada are hereby recognized and affirmed.
>
> (2) In this Act, "aboriginal peoples of Canada" includes the Indian, Inuit and Métis peoples of Canada.
>
> (3) For greater certainty, in subsection (1) "treaty rights" includes rights that now exist by way of land claims agreements or may be so acquired.
>
> (4) Notwithstanding any other provision of this Act, the aboriginal and treaty rights referred to in subsection (1) are guaranteed equally to male and female persons.[27]

Section 35 refers to treaty rights that already exist, which includes all such rights set out in treaties prior to 1982. These are identifiable, although the courts are often called upon to interpret their meaning. Both *R. v Marshall* and *R. v Sioui* are prominent cases wherein the Supreme Court of Canada was asked to interpret early pre-Confederation treaties.[28] In *Marshall*, Donald Marshall Jr., a Mi'kmaq of the Membertou First Nation in Nova Scotia, was charged with fishing for eels out of season and selling them. Marshall went to court, claiming that he was exercising a treaty right held by the Mi'kmaq and Maliseet First Nations since the peace and friendship treaties of 1760 and 1761. These treaties promised the Mi'kmaq and Maliseet an ongoing right to fish, hunt, and gather to earn a moderate livelihood. In 1999, the Supreme Court ruled that Marshall did have a treaty right to fish for a moderate livelihood outside of seasonal regulations established by the Department of Fisheries and Oceans. As I completed this book, Mi'kmaq lobster fishers were attempting to exercise this right in Nova Scotia while being violently harassed by non-Indigenous fishers. In *R. v Sioui*, the Supreme Court found in favour of four members of the Huron-Wendat Nation who argued that the 1760 Huron-British Treaty secured their ability to hunt and camp in their territories off reserve, including in what is now Jacques Cartier provincial park in Quebec. Dating from September 5, 1760, the Huron-British Treaty guaranteed the Huron-Wendat safe passage and rights to practise their religion and customs in the wake of the French defeat by the British at Quebec (Morin 2018). Charged under provincial laws for camping, fishing, and hunting in the park, the four Huron-Wendat men cited this treaty in their defence.

Unlike the rights documented in treaties, the Aboriginal rights referred to in section 35 are left unspecified. There is no list, and in this the section differs from the UN Declaration on the Rights of Indigenous Peoples, which is very specific. Many critics thus suggested that section 35 was an empty box – that it contained nothing. The federal government held a series of first ministers conferences involving provincial premiers, territorial leaders, and Indigenous organizations to discuss the content of section 35 Aboriginal rights. The Nisga'a Tribal Council attended these conferences, as did many other Indigenous organizations. Three conferences were held in Ottawa between 1983 and 1987 but with no positive result. The provincial politicians and Indigenous leaders who attended them could not agree on what section 35 rights would be. Provincial premiers such as Bill Bennett of British Columbia expressed the most concern about Aboriginal title and the right to self-government, whereas Indigenous leaders wanted to expand the possibilities inherent in both of these things. The worry around the size and scope of Aboriginal rights – in the minds of the non-Indigenous politicians – was suggested by a series of questions from Prime Minister Pierre Trudeau. "What is it you are talking about?" he asked. "Is it the deer that are roaming, or the gold under the ground? What is it you want in a nutshell?" James Gosnell, then president of the Nisga'a Tribal Council, replied that "aboriginal title is our ownership of this land and if you want me to put it like, lock, stock and barrel or total ownership, whether it is the mountains, inside the mountains, up in the air, the snow, the sea, you name it, subsurface rights and everything that there is in that land was given to us by God for our use to survive."[29]

In the wake of the failed first ministers conferences, section 35 Aboriginal rights must now be politically negotiated, as they were in the Nisga'a treaty, or interpreted by the courts. The courts occasionally rule on the nature of an Aboriginal right, in cases involving fishing or hunting, for example, but these decisions involve single rights in isolation. The first Supreme Court ruling on a section 35 Aboriginal right was *R. v Sparrow*.[30] In this 1990 case, the court agreed with Ron Sparrow of the Musqueam First Nation that he had an Aboriginal right to fish for food and that correspondingly this right did not originate from the Department of Fisheries and Oceans. One reason that the Nisga'a treaty took so long to negotiate was the fact that it entailed defining everything that could be counted as an Aboriginal right of the Nisga'a people. Their Aboriginal rights have now been turned into treaty rights; protected by section 35, they represent the final settlement of Nisga'a Aboriginal rights. This is why these agreements are referred to as "comprehensive" land claims.

It is here with section 35 that we find the legal meaning of reconciliation as applied to Aboriginal rights and by extension to treaty making. The legal concept of reconciliation "originated with recognition and affirmation of Aboriginal and treaty rights by s. 35(1) of the Constitution Act, 1983" (McNeil 2003, 2). After 1983, the Supreme Court of Canada repeatedly asserted that the rights protected in section 35 must be understood in such a way as to reconcile the prior presence of Indigenous people with the sovereignty of the Crown. In *R. v Van der Peet*, for example, Justice Lamer of the Supreme Court wrote that the purpose of section 35(1) was to provide

> the constitutional framework through which the fact that aboriginals lived on the land in distinctive societies, with their own practices, traditions and cultures, is acknowledged and reconciled with the sovereignty of the Crown. The substantive rights which fall within the provision must be defined in light of this purpose; the Aboriginal

> rights recognized and affirmed by s. 35(1) must be directed towards
> *the reconciliation of the pre-existence of Aboriginal societies with the*
> *sovereignty of the Crown.*[31]

Lamer repeated this in *Delgamuukw*, writing that "it is through negotiated settlements, with good faith and give and take on all sides, reinforced by the judgments of this Court, that we will achieve what I stated in *Van der Peet* ... to be a basic purpose of s. 35(1) – 'the reconciliation of the pre-existence of aboriginal societies with the sovereignty of the Crown.'"[32] This goal and the meaning of reconciliation were rearticulated by the Supreme Court in 2005, when Justice Binnie wrote in *Mikisew Cree First Nation* that "the fundamental objective of the modern law of aboriginal and treaty rights is the reconciliation of aboriginal peoples and non-aboriginal peoples and their respective claims, interests and ambitions."[33] In *Haida Nation*, the Supreme Court referred to treaties – past, present, and future – saying that they "serve to reconcile pre-existing Aboriginal sovereignty with assumed Crown sovereignty, and to define Aboriginal rights guaranteed by s. 35 of the *Constitution Act, 1982*."[34] Treaty negotiations do not reconstruct the rights that an Indigenous nation held before colonization. Instead, they transform the constitutionally recognized but technically unknown Aboriginal rights of the First Nation into a set of knowable treaty rights that works in the present. This process makes the rights fit within the framework of the contemporary Canadian political order; this is the crux of section 35 as a vehicle for the reconciliation of previously existing Aboriginal society with the sovereignty of the Crown. Reconciliation requires that the rights laid out in the treaty be oriented to what one Nisga'a politician referred to as the "reality of a modern Canada."[35] Negotiators stressed that the Nisga'a were negotiating their way into Canada, not out of it, and referred to creating a modern set of rights as a positive act of inclusion.

Treaties cannot be a means of reconciliation if Aboriginal rights bear all the burden of legal and cultural accommodation in a process that is more about legal reconciliation than restructuring the relationship between the Crown and Indigenous people. If the Supreme Court's vision demands that Aboriginal rights always be made compatible with Crown legal and political orders, meaningful reconciliation will never happen

(Ladner 2018, 247). Requiring Aboriginal rights to be reconciled *with* the sovereignty of the Crown runs the risk that they must be defined in ways that do not challenge the sovereignty of the Crown (Asch 1999; McNeil 2003). The nature of the right to self-government is important here; it needs to be given content in treaties in ways that truly enable Indigenous governance. This could be as a third order of government, but it certainly requires a more expansive approach to section 35 and treaty making. Anishinaabe scholar Dale Turner (2013, 108) points out that reconciliation

> is not possible as long as Aboriginal legal and political thought remains marginalized in the normative conversations about the meaning and content of s. 35(1). The main problem with interpreting section 35(1) of the constitution is ... how we ought to reconcile aboriginal ways of knowing with a legal and political context that is premised on the supremacy of Crown sovereignty.

Nisga'a negotiators worked incredibly hard for gains around self-government and the refusal to surrender Aboriginal title, but these were won at great expense and always against the expectation that they would inevitably compromise. The Truth and Reconciliation Commission report (2015, 25) notes that the "Government of Canada appears to believe that reconciliation entails Aboriginal peoples accepting the reality and validity of Crown sovereignty and parliamentary supremacy in order to allow the government to get on with business. Aboriginal people ... see reconciliation as an opportunity to affirm their own sovereignty and return to the partnership ambitions they held after Confederation." The closure assumed in the word "reconciliation" is problematic. We need to understand that reconciliation is not a fixed point, with a before and an after, but that it is always in the process of being and becoming (Blackburn 2007; Ladner 2018).

The Treaty Relationship: Moving beyond Reconciliation
The final report of the Truth and Reconciliation Commission (2015, 230) recommends that Canada "reconcile Aboriginal and Crown constitutional and legal orders to ensure that Aboriginal peoples are full

partners in confederation, including the recognition and integration of Indigenous laws and legal traditions in negotiation and implementation processes involving Treaties, land claims, and other constructive agreements." Treaties have the potential to enable Indigenous legal orders and governments to coexist with their non-Indigenous counterparts; this is what Nisga'a negotiators fought for. Such coexistence is in keeping with the original spirit and intent of treaty making. Discussing pre-Confederation treaties that followed the Royal Proclamation of 1763, James Tully (1995, 111) characterizes the relationship they created as "treaty constitutionalism," involving the mutual recognition and accommodation of the Indigenous peoples and the British Crown as equal, self-governing nations. In the early treaty-making era, treaties facilitated coexistence in a dynamic inter-societal context (Macklem 2016). The treaty relationship continues to hold this potential. John Borrows (2010, 21) suggests that treaties could build Canada on more solid ground, creating an inter-societal framework in which Indigenous laws intermingle with Imperial laws "to foster peace and order across communities." This is one reason the treaty arrangements to protect Indigenous law-making abilities on a sufficient land base are so important. Without this, treaty making amounts to a containment of Indigenous rights and a subordination of Indigenous jurisdiction (Coulthard 2014, 67).

The difficulties of implementation show us that the federal government has no mechanism for dealing with Indigenous peoples as equal partners who hold constitutionally protected rights. No actual political transition accompanies the talk of reconciliation and a new relationship. The federal bureaucracy can make changes for dealing with Indigenous peoples, but these – like declarations about new relationships and reconciliation – occur outside of deeper structural and ideological change. In late August 2017, Prime Minister Justin Trudeau announced that INAC would be divided into two ministries – Crown-Indigenous Relations and Northern Affairs Canada (CIRNAC) and Indigenous Services Canada. CIRNAC has a broad mandate, which includes fulfilling Ottawa's treaty obligations. Indigenous Services is responsible for service delivery in areas such as health, housing, and education. In announcing the change, Trudeau said that bureaucrats and the Indigenous peoples whom they serve "deserve an updated structure that is much more in keeping with the true spirit of reconciliation."[36] CIRNAC Minister Carolyn Bennett said in a press conference that the move was "about de-colonizing. It's about getting back to the original relationship that was the spirit and intent of the treaties. It's about getting rid of paternalism."[37] A statement on the INAC website at the time asserted that

> through dissolving Indigenous and Northern Affairs Canada, we are taking a significant step forward in advancing self-determination for all Indigenous peoples. A Department of Crown-Indigenous Relations and Northern Affairs and a Department of Indigenous Services, will work with Indigenous partners to ensure we close the socio-economic gaps that exist and to advance the recognition of rights, resolving long-standing disputes through negotiations, and support self-determination. INAC's dissolution is an important step in a broader agenda to make our national journey of reconciliation a reality.[38]

This development came as quite a surprise to everyone, even those in the federal government. No Indigenous leaders had been consulted on its merits or given advance information about it (King and Pasternak 2018). Reactions were quite mixed; some commentators were cautiously optimistic, whereas others suspected that the bureaucratic burdens of a colonial relationship would simply be doubled, adding "another layer of bureaucracy and twice as much obfuscation."[39] Six months later, in February 2018, the Liberals announced a new initiative whereby they would develop an Indigenous Rights Recognition and Implementation Framework. A worrisome aspect of this initiative is that it is currently the magnet for all federal energy, at the expense of other commitments and treaty rights that have been in place for decades or longer.

For the Nis̱ga'a and other modern-treaty nations, the main concern about the split of INAC is whether it will help or hinder the implementation of their treaties. The Deputy Ministers Oversight Committee is chaired by CIRNAC and meets several times a year; progress has been made in consolidating a whole-of-government approach to treaty implementation that includes processes for monitoring and measuring across federal departments. The actual implementation of modern treaties, however, does not seem to have improved in the wake of this restructuring and the accompanying statements about returning to the spirit and intent of the original treaties. Disputes and litigation between modern-treaty nations and federal, provincial, and territorial governments are proliferating, and there is a sense that attention to treaty implementation is being set aside in favour of Ottawa's proposed Rights Recognition Framework (King and Pasternak 2018). There is a marked lack of transparency regarding what the framework will entail, but many commentators feel that it is moving the government's focus away from treaty rights and obligations (King and Pasternak 2018). In their report for the Yellowhead Institute, Hayden King and Shiri Pasternak write that "there is much confusion over the content of the Rights Framework legislation, not only because of the speed at which it is being deployed, the lack of transparency, and the overwhelming amount of new policy, but because many of the pieces are not publicly available." At the most recent Land Claims Agreements Coalition conference, in February 2020, Jim Aldridge, legal counsel for the Nisg̱a'a Nation, echoed these concerns and worried that the Crown's attention was being diverted from treaty implementation just when the coalition was starting to get some traction. The five-page 2019 mandate letter for the CIRNAC minister mentions "treaty obligations" only once, and CIRNAC's Modern Treaty Implementation Office is to be replaced with a more generically titled National Treaty Commissioner's Office.[40] Aldridge said that whatever the Rights Recognition Framework might encompass – and again, this is not clear – it should not be at the "expense of fulfilling ... the obligations that were made to groups" who were required to negotiate everything because that was the government policy at the time. The Nisg̱a'a and others who made modern treaties through the federal comprehensive claims process or the BC treaty process did so at great cost and with enormous sacrifices, in the interest of securing a constitutionally protected agreement, and have no desire to be "moved to the back of the bus because there is a new fashion in town."[41]

Conclusion

In 2018, the biennial special assembly of the Nisg̱a'a Nation concluded with the signing of a revenue-sharing agreement between British Columbia and Nisg̱a'a Lisims Government concerning revenue generated by the Brucejack Gold Mine. This signing is a significant bookend for the analysis I offer here, coming as it did eighteen years after the treaty had been ushered into effect with other ceremonial signings involving other politicians and other speeches filled with talk of the future. Owned by Pretium Resources, Brucejack Gold Mine lies approximately 65 kilometres north of the town of Stewart and about 200 kilometres north of Gitlax̱t'aamiks. It sits within the Nass Wildlife Area, where Nisg̱a'a citizens have treaty rights. This part of the province is also known as the Golden Triangle because it contains some of the richest gold ore bodies in the world, as well as deposits of silver, nickel, and copper.[42] In 2015, Nisg̱a'a Lisims Government concluded a community benefits agreement with Pretium that will provide education and training of Nisg̱a'a workers for employment in the mine. It has made benefits agreements with other mining companies in the Nass Wildlife Area, including Avanti, as mentioned above, and KSM Seabridge Gold. Under the terms of the 2018 revenue-sharing agreement with the Province, the Nisg̱a'a Nation will receive a share of the net mineral tax revenue collected by the Province from Pretium Resources as long as Pretium operates the mine. At the special assembly, Nisg̱a'a president Eva Clayton said that the nation could receive up to $8 million per year from the agreement. This revenue is to be used for things over which the Nisg̱a'a have jurisdiction, including the delivery of programs and services.

Scott Fraser, minister of Indigenous Relations and Reconciliation, was present to sign on behalf of the Province. In his speech, he described the Nisg̱a'a treaty as an "ideal in reconciliation" and the revenue sharing agreement as proof that the Nisg̱a'a and Victoria were partners in a treaty relationship that would bring certainty and ensure sharing of wealth. He stated that

> agreements like this are important demonstrations of our commitment to government-to-government relationships, to sharing in our collective wealth and to honouring our treaty partnership, the spirit and intent and the words of that treaty. Your partnership approach not only with us but with Pretium Resources on the Brucejack mine project shows how treaties bring certainty for all of us. Economic development agreements support a strong economy, and share the

> wealth in ways that respect your treaty rights ... This revenue sharing agreement is an example of how we work together to support prosperity, health and self-determination of Nisga'a communities. As a treaty partner we recognize the importance for the Nisga'a Lisims Government to have the revenue you need to run your government and deliver the services that the people need. It just makes sense that you realize the benefits from resources developed in the Nass Area.

The minister went on to talk about how Victoria and the Nisga'a Nation worked as partners on the same side of the table during the environmental assessment that preceded the opening of the mine. "This is not a relationship that's about the bottom line," he said, "it's about a relationship that respects our mutual decision making ... We want to recognize the partnership-based approach created by Nisga'a and Pretium that benefits Nisga'a people and all British Columbians."[43]

Fraser's comments are an example of how reconciliation bleeds into all sorts of political talk, including talk of economic initiatives and agreements and the nature of the treaty relationship. Six years have passed since the Truth and Reconciliation Commission released its final report on residential schools, and reconciliation is a fixture in Canadian political discourse on Indigenous issues. Yet, Ottawa needs to do much more to meet the recommendations of that report, including implementing and honouring the objectives of historic and modern treaties. The really hard work around reconciliation will require addressing the reality that Indigenous people have separate and distinct rights and are seeking to exercise jurisdictional authority over land and resources in relationship with the rest of Canada. Treaties provide an avenue for this, but they must be negotiated in ways that enable Indigenous governance and territorial jurisdiction, and they must be implemented. At a conference to mark the 250th anniversary of the Royal Proclamation of 1763, Nisga'a Lisims Government CEO Kevin McKay said, "Modern treaties are not the silver bullet, they are not a magic wand. Modern treaties are a book of opportunities, but these opportunities need to be seriously considered and worked on, by all parties to the modern treaties."[44]

Conclusion

> Treaty making is an important stage in the long process of reconciliation, but it is only a stage.
>
> — *Mikisew Cree First Nation v Canada*, 2005[1]

Twenty-five comprehensive land claims agreements have been made in Canada since 1975. Since 2000, eighteen of these have included self-government. As modern treaties, they create constitutionally protected rights and take their place in an established inter-societal practice of treaty making between Indigenous peoples and representatives of the Crown in what is now Canada. Modern treaties are complex and multifaceted legal documents. They are contracts, they are statutes, and they have the force of law. They are also social and political compacts that should create lasting reciprocal associations between the partners. In its calls to action, the final report of the Truth and Reconciliation Commission (2015, 230) included renewing treaty relationships "based on principles of mutual recognition, mutual respect, and shared responsibility." This recommendation speaks to the fact that federal and provincial government implementation of both historic and modern treaties has not been grounded in mutual recognition and shared responsibility but instead has been a piecemeal and too often flawed approach.

Ratified in 2000, the Nisga'a treaty is now in its twenty-first year of implementation. When I began research on this agreement, it was celebrated by its supporters as a just resolution to the long-standing claims of the Nisga'a Nation. It was linked with reconciliation in a broad moral sense and the more specific legal sense of reconciling the Aboriginal rights and title of the Nisga'a Nation with the sovereignty of the Crown, as spelled out by the Supreme Court (Blackburn 2007). Some who opposed it argued that the treaty was a collection of race-based rights, that it would make British Columbia ungovernable, that it was an unauthorized creation of a third order of government, and that any form of separate rights was a violation of the democratic principle of equal rights for all. Other critics of the treaty argued that it was a new form of assimilation for Indigenous people that did not provide enough governing autonomy and land, and that it infringed on the territory of the neighbouring Gitxsan Nation. In this book, I have focused on three core rights that are brought into the treaty – the right to self-government, the right of Aboriginal title, and the right of the Nisga'a to control their citizenship. Rights mean little unless you have the ability to exercise them, and like other modern treaties, the Nisga'a Final Agreement involved lengthy negotiations about the application, nature, limitations to, and protection of these rights. In various ways, these provisions of the treaty challenged how federal and provincial governments had previously dealt with Indigenous peoples in this country. The treaty is not perfect, but negotiating the right of self-government into its pages was a milestone in Canada. The constitutional status of treaties means that the Nisga'a agreement does not just distribute delegated state power but instead establishes a constitutionally protected Indigenous government. Some scholars propose that the treaty did in fact create a third order of government (Poelzer and Coates 2015). The possibility of a third order of government hovers around the edges of this treaty, even if it is not entirely a manifestation of one. More significant is the assertion by Justice Williamson, in the *Campbell* case that challenged the constitutional validity of the treaty, that an Aboriginal right to self-government survived the BNA Act and the Constitutional renewal of 1982 and remains, waiting, unresolved in the margins of Canadian federalism. Modern treaties could be the instruments for the protection and expression of this right – bringing it out of the margins – and the jurisdictional authorities that should go with it.

The Nisga'a blazed the trail in winning Supreme Court recognition of unextinguished Aboriginal title. I have tried to show both the groundbreaking nature of this and the difficulty of translating title into a modern land claims agreement. It would be even more groundbreaking if First Nations or Inuit were not obliged to translate their Aboriginal title into fee simple. Aboriginal title has the potential, as a *sui generis* right in the common law that is already the product of the relationship between Indigenous peoples and the Crown, to serve as a container for an Indigenous system of land tenure in a treaty. Treaty making in Canada is currently on the wane. It could be partly reinvigorated if governments were to replace the overwhelming need to fix a form of property tenure on Indigenous lands that conforms with non-Indigenous legal and political orders and economic systems with a more expansive approach.

When the Nisga'a negotiated their treaty, they were not the first to demand that they control their membership criteria. They were the first, however, to apply the word "citizen" to those who could enroll in their treaty. Nisga'a insisted on using this word to signify their status as a political community with a government-to-government, nation-to-nation relationship with other governments in Canada. They also insisted on their ability to set their own citizenship criteria as the right of a political community and asserted it as an area of paramount jurisdiction. In this book, I have argued that the Nisga'a agreement combines what is essentially a new principle of universal citizenship across the Nisga'a Nation, to be exercised on what the treaty creates as common property, with culturally relevant criteria of belonging. The Nisga'a treaty and others like it were and continue to be criticized as forms of special rights. Aboriginal rights in Canada are distinct. This is a fact and a legal reality – one that needs further elaboration in actual political practice – but railing about them being special or race based ignores legal precedents underlying the formation of this country. Treaty agreements should protect and give expression to sets of distinct rights that reflect the historic relationship between Indigenous peoples and the Crown. The treaty creates a form of treaty citizenship for Nisga'a citizens that mediates their relationship with the rest of Canada, but Indigenous signatories to treaties are not the only ones whose belonging and rights in Canada are set in place by the social, legal, political, and economic compact that is a treaty (Mills 2017).

Treaties are an essential component in the relationship between Indigenous people and other Canadians, and are an important element in any framework for reconciliation. Although the federal and provincial governments have taken some positive steps to adopt a whole-of-government approach – moving away from a strictly contractual understanding of treaties – they do not do enough to implement historic and modern treaties. This simply intensifies the cynicism around the whole project of reconciliation, and for good reason. It is also likely that fewer agreements like the Nisga'a treaty will be made in the near future. One reason is that Ottawa's current policy on Aboriginal rights is shifting toward the as yet not well-defined Rights Recognition Framework. For its part, the provincial government of British Columbia is placing its emphasis on the United Nations Declaration on the Rights of Indigenous Peoples. In November 2019, it passed legislation that required all provincial laws to be brought into alignment with the declaration. These steps are clearly the new fashion in town, and First Nations and Inuit communities who have made modern treaties are right to be concerned that their implementation will cease to be a priority. Federal and provincial governments are also increasingly negotiating bilateral agreements with Indigenous communities that take the place of modern treaty negotiations and agreements. These include revenue-sharing agreements, impact benefit agreements, community benefit agreements, and sectoral governance agreements that deal with one aspect of government administration. The Tahltan First Nation, which lies to the north and east of the Nisga'a Nation, has made impact benefit and revenue-sharing agreements with the mining company Pretium and the provincial government concerning Brucejack Gold Mine that are similar to those made by the Nisga'a Nation. The Tahltan have no treaty with the provincial and federal governments, and indeed a treaty is not necessary for this kind of agreement. At the time of writing, over 140 BC First Nations have made forestry agreements that involve them in economic benefits from logging on their traditional territories; approximately 50 have made natural gas benefit agreements or other agreements related to liquefied natural gas; and 20 have made economic and community development agreements like those made by the Nisga'a and the Tahltan that give them a share of mineral tax revenue on new mines and mine expansions. In British Columbia, the provincial government has also made reconciliation agreements with over a dozen First Nations that include funding for economic development, capacity building, and closing "socioeconomic gaps" (Papillon 2014).[2]

For many Indigenous communities, negotiating agreements like these is much easier than obtaining a treaty. They consume less time and do not require going into debt to finance years of talks with federal and provincial governments. Communities see that not only do treaties take a long time to negotiate but that their social and economic benefits are slow to materialize (Papillon 2008). Bilateral agreements are also easier to make because less is at stake (Alcantara 2007). The First Nation is not asked to define or modify any of its rights, and no rights are extinguished. These agreements deal with a single issue at a time and do not come with the burden of negotiating everything – governance, lands, citizenship, wildlife entitlements, fisheries, fiscal financing, environmental regulation, and more – in the model of a full and final settlement required by comprehensive treaty negotiations.

At the same time, because they are not treaties, they are not constitutionally protected. Nor do they share in the status of treaties as binding compacts between peoples who need to figure out how to coexist. They do not create the scale of jurisdictional authority that a self-government agreement, negotiated as part of a modern treaty, does, and they need to be understood as both temporary and subject to changes in policy and financing (Papillon 2014). Treaties are not perfect. Modern treaties need to be easier to negotiate, and federal and provincial government mandates need to be more flexible and less focused on the containment of Aboriginal rights (Egan 2012). Ottawa in particular needs to commit to treaty implementation through a Modern Treaties Implementation Review Commission. Nevertheless, treaties remain one of the best and time-honoured means of establishing and providing for multifaceted relationships between Indigenous and non-Indigenous peoples in North America. The components of a treaty relationship are social, legal, economic, political, and spiritual. Treaties establish, or have the potential to establish, relationships between political communities – nation-to-nation, government-to-government – that also take into account our responsibilities to the environment around us (Noble 2018). Thus, it is fitting that the Truth and Reconciliation Commission (2015, 196) argued that "treaties are a model for how Canadians, as diverse peoples, can live respectfully and peacefully together on these lands we now share" and urged all Canadians to consider themselves treaty people.

Notes

Introduction

1 Quoted in British Columbia (1888), 432.

2 Land Claims Agreements Coalition, "What Is a Modern Treaty?" http://landclaim scoalition.ca/modern-treaty/.

3 Throughout this book I use the terms "Aboriginal," "Indigenous," "First Nation," and "Inuit." "Aboriginal" appears in section 35 of the Constitution and thus has a legal significance. Section 35 refers to Aboriginal peoples and Aboriginal rights, and the Canadian courts have now devoted four decades to jurisprudence on the content of these rights. It is in this context that I refer to Aboriginal rights. Section 35 also specifies that "Aboriginal" encompasses First Nations, Metis, and Inuit peoples. "First Nations" gained momentum during the 1970s, replacing "Indian" and "Native," but it does not include the Inuit or the Metis. It is now used in general discourse, though "Indian" continues to have legal meaning in the Indian Act. In international human rights law and discourse, "Indigenous" is the preferred choice.

4 Janna Promislow (2014, 1107) notes that "treaty making has arguably been central to Indigenous-Crown relations in North America from first contact and continuing on today. It is one of the most persistent features of both colonial and Canadian state relations with Indigenous peoples. Beyond that summary statements about treaty histories should be made cautiously. There was after all no uniform experience of colonization in the geographic expanse that became Canada."

5 *Calder et al. v Attorney-General of British Columbia*, [1973] S.C.R. 313.

6 House of Commons, *Debates* (October 26, 1999), 679.

7 Government of Canada, Department of Justice, "Principles Respecting the Government of Canada's Relationship with Indigenous Peoples," http://www.justice.gc.ca/eng/csj-sjc/principles-principes.html.

150 *Notes to pages 13–19*

8   Rod Robinson, interview with author, June 13, 2000.

9   Nisga'a Lisims Government, "Nisga'a Settlement Trust," https://www.nisgaanation.ca/nisgaa-settlement-trust.

10 Sterritt et al. (1998, 251) argue that the core area overlaps the traditional territory of the Gitxsan and the Gitanyow. Nisga'a government representatives and treaty negotiators had different things to say on this issue and it remains unresolved.

11 For the text of the petition, see Nisga'a Lisims Government, "1913 Petition," https://www.nisgaanation.ca/1913-petition. The petition exists in multiple archives.

12 Frank Calder was born at Naas Harbour Cannery near Gingolx in 1915. He was adopted and raised by Arthur Calder (Chief Nagwa'un) and Louisa Calder. Frank Calder was elected to the Legislative Assembly of British Columbia in 1949 in the riding of Atlin as a representative of the Co-operative Commonwealth Federation, which later became the New Democratic Party. Calder served in this capacity until 1979. He passed away in 2006. Nisga'a Lisims Government, "Honouring Our Past – Dr. Frank Calder," https://www.nisgaanation.ca/news/honouring-our-past-dr-frank-calder.

13 The bylaws, constitution, and goals of the Nisga'a Tribal Council state that, among other things, it should "negotiate and settle the Nisga'a Comprehensive land claims which is based on the Nisga'a aboriginal title." From 1955 onward, the council held annual conventions during which the elected representatives reported on the progress of this work. These conventions ran on a rotating basis in the four villages, as well as in Terrace and Prince Rupert. As the treaty negotiations became more detailed and complex, the conventions became increasingly important as places to deliver information about the state of negotiations to the people and get feedback. For example, the 1998 convention included presentations from committees dealing with eligibility and enrolment, ratification, implementation, the Nisga'a constitution, fiscal financing, lands and resources, Nisga'a government, and cultural artifacts.

14 Rod Robinson also mentioned the poor roads and health facilities in the valley, the latter amounting to a few aspirin being given out from someone's house. He said that the council worked to prevent the export of children to residential schools and to bring educational institutions to the reserves. Rod Robinson, interview with author, June 13, 2000.

15 *Calder* at 410.

16 The technicality was the matter of Crown immunity in British Columbia. Under the doctrine of Crown immunity, litigants were required to get consent from the attorney general before they could sue the Province. In Latin, this consent is called a "fiat." The Nisga'a Tribal Council had not obtained a fiat (Godlewska and Webber 2007, 5). At the thirtieth anniversary celebration of the *Calder* case, lawyer Thomas Berger explained the government policy: "Where you were suing the estate of the Crown – that is, you wanted Crown land or Crown resources – they would not issue a fiat. They would in tort cases but not in contract and not in cases where

Notes to pages 20–31   151

you were trying to ... 'impeach the estate of the Crown.'" He said his tactic was to argue that the Nisga'a were not impeaching the estate of the Crown, because all they wanted was a declaration that Aboriginal title had never been extinguished. They did not sue for damages or for the return of the Nass Valley, but rather for the declaration on Aboriginal title (Berger 2007, 48). In abstaining, Justice Pigeon referred to this requirement and declined to consider the issues of either Aboriginal title or extinguishment. Crown immunity was removed from the books in British Columbia in 1974 (Godlewska and Webber 2007, 6).

17 Indian and Northern Affairs Canada and Price Waterhouse, "Economic Value of Uncertainty Associated with Native Claims in BC," 1990, http://www.publications. gc.ca/site/eng/9.848644/publication.html.

18 BC Treaty Commission, "Negotiations Update," http://www.bctreaty.ca/ negotiation-update.

19 Nisga'a Nation, 41st Annual Convention Booklet, April 27–May 1, 1998, New Aiyansh, BC.

Chapter 1: We Have Always Made Laws

1 These were Nisga'a Effective Date Procedures Act, Nisga'a Lisims Government Act, Nisga'a Interpretation Act, Nisga'a Administrative Decisions Review Act, Nisga'a Citizenship Act, Nisga'a Offence Act, Nisga'a Elections Act, Nisga'a Financial Administration Act, Nisga'a Capital Finance Commission Act, Nisga'a Programs and Services Delivery Act, Nisga'a Personnel Administration Act, Nisga'a Land Act, Nisga'a Nation Entitlement Act, Nisga'a Village Entitlement Act, Nisga'a Lands Designation Act, Nisga'a Land Title Act, Nisga'a Fisheries and Wildlife Act, and Nisga'a Forest Act.

2 A negotiator explained to me that if the court challenge occurred during a phase-in period, the Nisga'a would be much more vulnerable than if the treaty were fully in play. Once that occurred and money had changed hands, the court could potentially be striking down a government, which would be much harder than striking down a treaty.

3 Author's fieldnotes, May 11, 2000.

4 Interview with author, May 15, 2000.

5 John Borrows (2010, 43) notes that he has "known many *Indian Act* elected chiefs and councilors who reference their own First Nations legal values in debating and making decisions under its structures. Furthermore, many so-called Indian bands pre-existed the Indian Act and find their inherent governmental power in their pre-Confederation authority. In that respect, they are not a product of the *Indian Act*. In fact, in my own family, my great-grandfather was both a hereditary chief and an elected chief under the *Indian Act*."

6 Clement Cornwall was appointed to represent the federal government, and Joseph Planta represented the Province (Fisher 1977).

7 The Anglican missionaries on the Northwest Coast favoured cooperation with the federal government and its policies, including the establishment of reserves and

152 Notes to pages 31–35

the implementation of the Indian Act (Patterson 1983). At Laxgalts'ap the Reverend Green, a Methodist, followed the lead of the more radical William Duncan of the Church Missionary Society. Duncan is well known as the missionary who worked with the Tsimshian at the Christian village of Metlakatla. Green supported the Nisga'a's attempts to get their land title recognized and urged them to keep the federal government at arm's length. Present-day residents of Laxgalts'ap remark on Green's role in supporting people in the village to fight for their lands.

8 Anglicized spellings of Gints'aadax are Kinsada and Kinzadah (Patterson 1989). Gints'aadax moved to Gingolx from the village of Ank'idaa in 1878. Active in trade with the British at Port Simpson, he took the missionary William Duncan on an introductory tour up the Nass River in 1860 (Patterson 1989).

9 Historian Carol Ann Cooper (1993, 381) writes that after the Gingolx village council was in place, the chiefs "patrolled the river using guns, and informed the Department of Marine and Fisheries officials that a portion of the licensing fees on the Nass should remain with their village council as they were the acknowledged owners of the river."

10 Referring to sections of the Indian Act, Kiera Ladner (2006, 13) shows that the Department of Indian Affairs "is able to influence and interfere in a multiplicity of ways including through its control of all band funds, departmental administrative and accountability requirements, the use of third party management, its ability to override election results and thus call elections or appoint new band councils (sections 74–79), its local law making capacity (section 73 allows the Minister of Indian Affairs to make regulations for such matters as compulsory hospitalization and the treatment of infectious disease, dog control, fish and wildlife, and the borrowing of monies for housing and band projects) and its ability to override all by-laws made by the band council (as outlined in section 82)."

11 *Campbell v British Columbia (Attorney General)*, 2000 BCSC 1123, https://www.ceaa. gc.ca/050/documents_staticpost/cearref_21799/89911/04.pdf.

12 I thank Emma Feltes for discussion of this point.

13 Written Argument of the Nisga'a Tribal Council, In the Supreme Court of British Columbia, Between Gordon M. Campbell, Michael G. de Jong and P. Geoffrey Plant, and Attorney General of British Columbia and Attorney General of Canada and Nisga'a Tribal Council. Copy in author's possession.

14 Ibid.

15 The trader left his Cree wife and married another woman in a Christian ceremony under Quebec law (Slattery 2000, 202). The court not only ruled that his first marriage had been legally valid but that the children of it were entitled to inherit half of their deceased father's estate. As the trial judge wrote, it may "be contended that the ... laws and usages of the Indian tribes, were abrogated; that they ceased to exist" when the English and French began to trade with them, but "in my opinion it is beyond controversy that they did not, that so far from being abolished, they were left in full force, and were not even modified in the slightest degree, in

Notes to pages 36–41   153

regard to the civil rights of the natives." *Connolly v Woolrich and Johnson et al.* (1867), 17 R.J.R.Q. 75 at 84.

16 Author's field notes, August 21, 2007.

17 House of Commons, "Evidence," Standing Committee on Aboriginal Affairs, November 18, 1999, https://www.ourcommons.ca/DocumentViewer/en/36-2/AAND/meeting-12/evidence.

18 Written Argument of the Nisga'a Tribal Council.

19 In 1983, the Penner Report on Indian self-government (written by Keith Penner, Liberal MP and chair of the Standing Committee on Indian Affairs), actually recommended that Ottawa recognize Aboriginal government as a constitutionally protected third order of government. Penner acknowledged that this would require a constitutional amendment, which would be difficult if not impossible for any federal government to achieve. In place of that, he offered some alternatives, one of which was a bilateral process of treaty making wherein Ottawa and First Nations would negotiate on jurisdictional arrangements. The Nisga'a treaty negotiations are an example of just this, except that they were trilateral because the provincial government of British Columbia was involved. The Penner Report also acknowledged that Aboriginal people have a special place in the constitutional framework of Canada (Canada, House of Commons Special Committee on Indian Self-Government).

20 *Campbell* at para. 179.

21 *Haida Nation v British Columbia (Minister of Forests)*, [2004] 3 S.C.R. 511; *Taku River Tlingit First Nation v British Columbia*, [2004] 3 S.C.R. 550.

22 Gordon Campbell became more supportive of Aboriginal rights and treaty making in British Columbia after spending several years in government. See Justine Hunter, "How Campbell Changed His View," *Globe and Mail*, October 13, 2007, https://www.theglobeandmail.com/news/national/how-campbell-changed-his-view/article695589/. The Liberals reconciled themselves to the inclusion of self-government in BC treaties, but the pace of treaty making remains impossibly slow.

23 Canadian Constitution Foundation, "Media Advisory: Nisga'a Agreement Challenge at BC Court of Appeal," September 19, 2012, https://theccf.ca/media-advisory-nisgaa-agreement-challenge-at-bc-court-of-appeal/.

24 *Sga'Nisim Sim'Augit v HMTQ* (25 September 2001) Vancouver L000808 (BCSC) at para. 8.

25 *Sga'Nisim Sim'Augit (Chief Mountain) v Canada (Attorney General)*, 2013 BCCA 49 at paras. 86, 48.

26 Contributing factors in the Chief Mountain case include the history of Christian missions on the Northwest Coast, the transformation of Nisga'a settlements into Indian reserves, each under band councils that were sometimes in competition with each other, the lack of understanding of the treaty and what it does, and the treaty negotiating process itself. The 1888 *Papers Relating to the Commission Appointed to Enquire into the Condition of the Indians of the North-West Coast* gives

154 *Notes to pages 43–49*

hints of differences in strategy on how to deal with the pressures of colonization among the villages. Commissioners Cornwall and Planta wrote that the assertion of Indian title "was not shared in by the Kincolith branch of the Nish-kar nation, while it was strongly pressed by the people of Greenville and some of the chiefs from farther up the river. So with regard to the acceptance of the Indian Act, and of the presence of an Indian Agent amongst them, the Kincoliths were ready for both; the Greenville party was averse to both" (British Columbia 1888, 5).

27 Writing about the early-nineteenth-century fur trade along the Mackenzie River, Janna Promislow (2013, 46) notes that "in trading contexts, indigenous legal and political systems were not just left intact, but provided the operative norms for Indigenous-newcomer relations."

28 The list of powers encompasses membership in the Nisga'a Nation; administration of Nisga'a Lisims Government institutions, including marriage, social services, health services, child and family services, child custody, adoption, and education; management of Nisga'a lands; and management of resources on Nisga'a lands, including forests, fisheries, wildlife, and resources.

29 Senate, "Evidence," Standing Senate Committee on Aboriginal Affairs, March 21, 2000.

30 House of Commons, "Evidence," Standing Committee on Aboriginal Affairs, November 3, 1999.

31 Senate, *Debates* (February 9, 2000), 593.

32 Canadian Constitution Foundation, "Media Advisory."

33 Uniform jurisdiction creates the homogeneous spaces that are ideal for capital accumulation and is a spatial strategy that states employ through administration, repression, domination, and centralized power for this very reason (Brenner and Elden 2009, 356). Canada does not have this kind of uniform jurisdiction, regardless of agreements such as the Nisga'a treaty, because provincial and federal jurisdiction are separate on matters of land use and resource development.

34 House of Commons, *Debates*, November 1, 1999.

35 Joe Gosnell and Nelson Leeson, interview with author, December 1, 1999.

36 Interview with author, July 16, 2006.

37 Land Claims Agreements Coalition Conference, Gatineau, QC, February 11, 2020, author's notes.

38 In 2012, Aboriginal Affairs and Northern Development released a report titled "Community Well-Being and Treaties." Using educational achievement, labour force activity, income, and housing to measure community well-being, the report found that the scores for Aboriginal communities were twenty points lower than those for non-Aboriginal communities. It also found that between 1981 and 2006, the well-being of modern treaty First Nations improved twice as fast as that of historic treaty First Nations. There were strong regional variations, however, and the study was limited in its ability to make a causal connection between improved community well-being and modern treaties. Aboriginal Affairs and Northern

Development, "Community Well-Being and Treaties," https://www.aadnc-aandc.gc.ca/DAM/DAM-INTER-HQ-AI/STAGING/texte-text/rs_re_pubs_cwb-treaties_PDF_1358355905129_eng.pdf.

39 For a flow chart representation of this, see Nisga'a Lisims Government, https://www.nisgaanation.ca/sites/default/files/Structure%20of%20Nisga%27a%20Lisims%20Government_0.pdf.

40 I draw these insights from conversations with elders and from statements made by Nisga'a community members.

41 Author's copy of the constitution. Also see Nisga'a Lisims Government, "Constitution of the Nisga'a Nation," 1998, 8, http://www.nisgaanation.ca/legislation/constitution-nisgaa-nation.

42 "Modern Treaty Implementation and Indigenous Law: An Exploratory Workshop, September 21–22, 2018" (summary report prepared by David Gill and Janna Promislow, February 11, 2019).

43 "Nisga'a Ayuuk̲: Laws, Customs and Traditions of the Nisga'a" (report prepared by Nita Morven, Ayuuk̲hl Nisga'a Department, Nisga'a Lisims Government, n.d.), 1.

44 Interview with author, July 25, 2011.

Chapter 2: Aboriginal Title, Fee Simple, and Dead Capital

1 "Report of Conferences between the Provincial Government and Indian Delegates from Fort Simpson and Nass River," *BC Sessional Papers*, 1887, 257.

2 Ibid.

3 *Calder et al. v Attorney-General of British Columbia*, [1973] S.C.R. 313 at 361.

4 "Report of Conferences," *BC Sessional Papers*, 1887, 257.

5 Ibid., 256.

6 Ibid., 256–57.

7 At this time, the Nisga'a were not yet appealing to the requirements of the Royal Proclamation of 1763, at least not directly. In the meeting with Smithe, they referred to having read about treaty making requirements in a law book. Hamar Foster (1995, 47–48) suggests that they had access to a copy of *The Treaties of Canada with the Indians of Manitoba and the North-West Territories*, by Alexander Morris, and that missionary William Duncan was the conduit through which this and other "law books" reached the Northwest Coast.

8 "Report of Conferences," *BC Sessional Papers*, 1887, 255.

9 Ibid., 261.

10 Migrations occurred in and out of the valley over the centuries. Some were undertaken in response to changes in the sea level. See Nisga'a Tribal Council (1984b).

11 Nisga'a Nation, 41st Annual Convention Booklet, April 27–May 1, 1998, New Aiyansh, BC, 86.

12 Joe Gosnell, speech given at the Special Assembly of the Nisga'a Nation. Gitwinksihlkw, May 7, 2014. Transcript in author's possession.

156 Notes to pages 62–79

13 Interview with author, August 21, 2007.
14 "Royal Proclamation, 1763," University of Toronto Libraries, https://exhibits.library. utoronto.ca/items/show/2470.
15 *St. Catharines Milling and Lumber Co. v R.* (1887) 13 S.C.R. 577, https://scc-csc.lexum. com/scc-csc/scc-csc/en/item/3769/index.do [*St. Catharines*].
16 *St. Catharines* at 55.
17 *Calder* at 404.
18 Ibid. at 328.
19 Ibid. at 375.
20 *Delgamuukw v British Columbia*, [1997] 3 S.C.R. 1010.
21 Ibid. at paras. 112, 113.
22 Ibid. at para. 158.
23 Ibid. at paras. 128, 126.
24 *Tsilhqot'in Nation v British Columbia*, [2014] 2 S.C.R. 257.
25 Ibid. at para. 73.
26 Canada, British Columbia, Nisga'a Nation (1998), 20.
27 "Treaty No. 8 Made June 21, 1899 and Adhesions, Reports, Etc.," https://www. rcaanc-cirnac.gc.ca/eng/1100100028813/1581293624572#chp4.
28 For the full text, see *The James Bay and Northern Quebec Agreement*, http://www. naskapi.ca/documents/documents/JBNQA.pdf.
29 For the full text, see *Umbrella Final Agreement between the Government of Canada, the Council for Yukon Indians, and the Government of the Yukon*, https://cyfn.ca/wp -content/uploads/2013/08/umbrella-final-agreement.pdf.
30 British Columbia (1888), 20.
31 Ibid.
32 Interview with author, March 17, 2000.
33 Joe Gosnell, interview with author, December 1, 1999.
34 Negotiator, interview with author, March 3, 2000.
35 Sanderson (2018, 333) suggests that the story at the base of feudal land law is a creation story "about property and the nature of land holdings." Indigenous creation stories, he argues, similarly "set out a normative conception of people and their relationship to each other and to the lands on which they reside" (337). Sanderson suggests that it is essential that different creation stories, and the social and legal orders they invoke, have room to coexist.
36 Interview with author, March 3, 2000.
37 *R. v Sparrow*, [1990] 1 S.C.R. 1075 at 1103.
38 *Delgamuukw* at para. 145.
39 *Tsilhqot'in Nation* at para. 69.
40 Negotiator, interview with author, March 7, 2000.
41 The scope of the Nisga'a territorial claim is disputed. In *Tribal Boundaries in the Nass Watershed*, Sterritt et al. (1998) argue that the Nisga'a reached into Gitxsan territory when articulating their territorial boundaries and that the treaty currently

infringes on Gitxsan territory. Lawyer Peter Grant argues that certain features of the BC treaty process contributed to the enduring problem of overlapping territories among First Nations in the province. When the process launched during the early 1990s, provincial politicians made it clear that First Nations could not expect to get more than 5 percent of their claimed traditional territory. The treaty process did not require First Nations to substantiate the territorial maps they submitted with their Statements of Intent, unlike in the federal comprehensive claims process. Grant suggests that this situation encouraged First Nations to draw their traditional boundaries as large as possible, knowing that they would have to negotiate for a small part of it as settlement lands. Grant links the overlap problem in BC treaty negotiations to these two factors. Peter Grant, "The Legacy of Treaty Making: Reconciliation or a New Era of Divide and Conquer," https://web.archive.org/web/20170226125934/http://grantnativelaw.com/wordpress/wp-content/uploads/2015/08/The_Legacy_of_Treaty_Making.pdf.

42 Cornwall and Planta's report is full of examples of chiefs identifying their territories and requesting protection for them, individually. At Naas Harbour on October 18, 1887, Chief David Mackay (Sim'oogit Axdii Wil Luu Gooda) from Greenville said, "Now I wish to speak about a piece of hunting ground that belonged to my forefathers on Observatory Inlet, a stream called Hoos-chat-ko. I want a paper securing me the right to it – not that I shall object to others hunting on it, with my leave. I have a house and get my salmon and furs there. There is also a trail there. I have made it into a valley where I hunt, I don't want to sell it to any white people; I want it for myself and my people." Similarly, Frederick Allen of Gingolx told the commissioners on October 20 that "we want to refer again to what we said before about Portland Inlet and Canal. There are three chiefs here, two nephews and the other a brother of Mountain's, living here, and they wish to have the reservation made so that the right will descend to them when he dies. They will not object to other Indians going there. They are: George Quck-soo, Alfred Walls, Henry Alfred. Paul Kledach claims Alice Arm as his hunting ground; he wants that. Chief Clubux owns Hastings Arm as his hunting ground. When he dies his brother, Patrick O'Brien, wishes it to descend to him." British Columbia (1888), 436–37, 444.

43 Nisga'a Nation, 41st Annual Convention Booklet, April 27–May 1, 1998, New Aiyansh, BC, 86.

44 "Nisga'a Ayuuḵ: Laws, Customs and Traditions of the Nisga'a" (report prepared by Nita Morven, Ayuuḵhl Nisga'a Department, Nisga'a Lisims Government, n.d.), 25.

45 Rod Robinson, interview with author, June 13, 2000.

46 Interview with author, July 16, 2006.

47 I spoke with an elder who complained about the permits and remarked that her son defended them by saying that was the way it had to be. She said he sounded like a white man.

48 An employee in the Fisheries and Wildlife Department of Nisga'a Lisims Government highlighted some of the tensions involved. He said that families can fish in an ango'oskw outside the core lands, but they must show their Nisga'a citizenship card and must acquire a permit from federal fisheries. The point here was that the Nisga'a government must distinguish between treaty Nisga'a and other First Nations who claim the area. It had to know who was who. Some Nisga'a resisted this, feeling that they were over-governed. He defended the regulations, though, saying that now that the Nisga'a had settled on the treaty, they were obligated "to account for the harvest" and data must be calculated each year. He talked about how older people could have difficulty with the notion of reporting in such a manner, but that Nisga'a had agreed to harvest certain numbers, and issuing permits was a better tool to manage resources.

49 Interview with author, December 1, 1999.

50 Katherine Verdery (1994, 1073) writes about the transformations in property that occurred in Romania during the shift to socialism and then back again in a way that highlights the challenges of property transformations in multiple directions. Family farms that had been passed on through the generations were turned over for collectivization under the socialist regime. One challenge of this kind of collectivization was erasing the memories of a landscape with edges and owners. Verdery shows that decollectivization contributed further to overlapping "fuzzy" layers of property entitlements.

51 Nisga'a Lisims Government, "Nisga'a Landholding Transition Act," https://www.nisgaanation.ca/nisgaa-landholding-transition-act.

52 CBC Radio, "Nisga'a First Nation: This Land Is My Land," The Current, November 4, 2013. A real estate agent from the nearby town of Terrace said that it would be "difficult to establish any kind of value" for the Nisga'a properties, "as it is uncharted territory. There isn't very much to compare it to." In her opinion, "the ideal purchasers would be businesses that are interested in the ecotourism. As far as individual homeowners, it's quite isolated, and so wouldn't be too desirable for the average person, and so that again brings difficulty into establishing any kind of a value to these properties."

53 Statement made by Dianne Cragg, Registrar of Land Titles, Special Assembly of the Nisga'a Nation, Gingolx, May 8, 2018.

54 House of Commons, "Study of Land Management and Sustainable Economic Development on First Nations Reserve Lands: Report of the Standing Committee on Aboriginal Affairs and Northern Development," March 2014, 30, http://publications.gc.ca/collections/collection_2014/parl/xc35–1/XC35–1–1–412–4-eng.pdf.

55 Ibid.

56 Tristin Hopper, "B.C. First Nation Leads Historic and Controversial Move toward Aboriginal Private Home Ownership," National Post, January 25, 2015, https://nationalpost.com/news/canada/b-c-first-nation-leads-historic-and-controversial-move-toward-aboriginal-private-home-ownership.

Notes to pages 88–94   159

57 See Donald Gutstein (2014) for a discussion of the role of the Harper government and Indian and Northern Affairs Canada in supporting this conference as well as the work of Manny Jules and the First Nations Tax Commission.

58 At these hearings, Chief Robert Louie of the Westbank First Nation (WFN) stated that the existing Indian Act system through which bands could lease land was enough for the purposes of economic development. Chief Louie is known for having a pro-business approach to self-government, so it is interesting that in 2014 he argued that private property rights were not necessary because leases are a legal tool that investors can relate to. He said many critics thought "we could not develop on section 91(24) lands but we have – 91(24) works. WFN has the highest activity of permits and leases. We do not want fee simple lands." The five reserves of the Westbank First Nation are located in the Okanagan, a wine- and fruit-growing resort region of the BC interior. The reserves currently have nine thousand non-member residents. House of Commons, "Study of Land Management," 49.

59 Seeking participation in a resource extractive economy can put Indigenous communities in positions that some outside observers do not expect. Gosnell's statement here points to managing the resources, and is consistent with expectations of management and stewardship over territory. In the early 2000s, Nisga'a Lisims Government sought ways to continue small-scale logging operations and was counting on some financial benefit from this kind of activity. It also sought ways to salvage the enormous waste left behind by the large-scale logging that had taken place on Nisga'a lands. In 2006, I met a logging contractor in Gitlaxt'aamiks who had been hired to try to salvage this waste so it could be milled. We spent several evenings driving old logging roads looking at abandoned clear cuts. Much of the wood left behind was not salvageable because of rot.

60 Joe Gosnell, speech given at the Special Assembly of the Nisga'a Nation, Gitwinksihlkw, May 7, 2014. Transcript in author's possession.

Chapter 3: Treaty Citizenship

1 Article 33 states, "Indigenous peoples have the right to determine their own identity or membership in accordance with their customs and traditions. This does not impair the right of indigenous individuals to obtain citizenship of the States in which they live." United Nations, "United Nations Declaration on the Rights of Indigenous Peoples," art. 33, https://www.un.org/esa/socdev/unpfii/documents/DRIPS_en.pdf.

2 The Indian Act does not apply to Inuit, Metis, or non-status Indians. Many First Nations people in Canada do not possess status and so are not governed under the Indian Act. The term "Aboriginal," as used in section 35 of the Constitution, refers to Metis, Inuit, and First Nations people. In section 91(24) of the Constitution, "Indians" referred only to First Nations throughout most of Canada's history. The Supreme Court of Canada changed that in April 2016, when it ruled that Inuit and Metis should be classified as Indians for the purposes of section 91(24).

160 *Notes to pages 96–107*

3 Statement of the Government of Canada on Indian Policy, 1969, Presented to the First Session of the Twenty-Eighth Parliament by the Honourable Jean Chrétien, Minister of Indian Affairs and Northern Development.

4 In 1966, the Hawthorn Report had recommended the opposite approach to Aboriginal-state relations in Canada. Funded by the federal government, it was "the first major post-Second World War, Canada wide inquiry to assert that assimilation was neither an unquestioned goal nor an appropriate policy" (Cairns 2000, 162). Its lead author, UBC anthropologist Harry Hawthorn, introduced the notion of citizens plus to describe the ideal place of Indigenous people within the Canadian framework. He used "citizens plus" to refer to Indigenous people as holding a distinct set of rights and cultural identities, along with the full complement of rights available to other Canadian citizens. The Hawthorn Report was forward thinking for its time in advancing the notion that Indigenous people should keep all of their Aboriginal rights and have the general rights of Canadian citizenship. However, it did not bring this forward as an aspect of renewed treaty relationships or self-government.

5 Senate, "Evidence," Standing Senate Committee on Aboriginal Peoples, February 22, 2000, https://sencanada.ca/en/Content/Sen/committee/362/abor/04eva-e.

6 Interview with author, May 17, 2000.

7 Interview with author, May 17, 2000.

8 Interview with author, July 12, 2006. This does not mean that Nisga'a citizenship can be experienced only on treaty lands, but the programs and services provided by the Nisga'a government and the village governments are primarily for those who live on them.

9 Tom Molloy, quoted in Senate, "Evidence," Standing Senate Committee on Aboriginal Peoples, February 16, 2000.

10 Ibid.

11 Federal negotiator, interview with author, January 25, 2000.

12 Senate, *Debates* (February 10, 2000), 611.

13 Interview with author, June 12, 2000.

14 This composition is stipulated in Chapter 20, paragraph 8, of the treaty, which states, "The Enrolment Committee comprises eight Nisga'a individuals, as follows: two members from the Laxsgiik (Eagle) tribe, as selected by that tribe; two members from the Gisk̲'aast (Killer whale) tribe, as selected by that tribe; two members from the G̲anada (Raven) tribe, as selected by that tribe; two members from the Laxgibuu (Wolf) tribe, as selected by that tribe."

15 Interview with author, July 11, 2006.

16 Senate, "Evidence," Standing Senate Committee on Aboriginal Peoples, March 21, 2000.

17 Senate, "Evidence," Standing Senate Committee on Aboriginal Peoples, February 23, 2000.

18 Senate, "Evidence," Standing Senate Committee on Aboriginal Peoples, February 22, 2000.

Notes to pages 107–21   161

19 Senate, "Evidence," Standing Senate Committee on Aboriginal Peoples, February 16, 2000.
20 Senate, "Evidence," Standing Senate Committee on Aboriginal Peoples, February 22, 2000.
21 Senate, "Evidence," Standing Senate Committee on Aboriginal Peoples, February 16, 2000.
22 Reform Party members and other political critics of the treaty repeatedly asserted that the Nisga'a government would establish taxation without representation on Nisga'a lands. This was not true. The treaty does not allow Nisga'a government to tax non-Nisga'a people who live on Nisga'a lands.
23 Senate, "Evidence," Standing Senate Committee on Aboriginal Peoples, March 23, 2000.
24 Senate, *Debates* (April 6, 2000), 1014.
25 Senate, "Evidence," Standing Senate Committee on Aboriginal Peoples, February 22, 2000.
26 House of Commons, *Debates* (December 2, 1999), 2088.
27 House of Commons, *Debates* (October 26, 1999), 665.
28 The Nisga'a language has no direct translation for "citizen." A Nisga'a language teacher suggested that *hli gadihl Nisga'a* – meaning "the people of the Nisga'a," or "the Nisga'a people" – might work, but she could not think of anything "that says citizen." Historically, what people were called depended on where they lived on the Nass River. Names for villages begin with the prefix "Git" for that reason because "Git" translates as "people of."
29 Senate, "Evidence," Standing Senate Committee on Aboriginal Peoples, March 23, 2000.
30 For a comprehensive discussion of the role of the wilksilaks, see Allison Nyce, "Wilksilaks Transfer of Knowledge: A Working Model for Maintaining Tradition" (master's thesis, University of Northern British Columbia, 2010).
31 Interview with author, July 6, 2006.
32 Interview with author, May 21, 2000.
33 Interview with author, July 12, 2006.

Chapter 4: The Treaty Relationship

1 The coalition currently includes, in alphabetical order, Carcross/Tagish First Nation, Council of Yukon First Nations, Gwich'in Tribal Council, Ka:'yu:'K't'h'/Che:k'tles7et'h' First Nations, Kwanlin Dun First Nation, Maa-nulth First Nations, the Makivik Corporation, Nisga'a Nation, Nunavut Tunngavik Incorporated, Sahtu Secretariat Incorporated, Tla'amin Nation, Tlicho Government, Tsawwassen First Nation, and the Vuntut Gwitchin.
2 The coalition website contains a full record of documents and information. See https://landclaimscoalition.ca.
3 Land Claims Agreements Coalition, "Second Universal Periodic Review of Canada: Submission of the Land Claims Agreements Coalition, United Nations Human

162   *Notes to pages 121–25*

Rights Council, October 9, 2012," 3, http://www.landclaimscoalition.ca/assets/121009-LCAC-Submission-to-UPR.pdf.

4 Land Claims Agreements Coalition Conference, Ottawa, December 7, 2015, author's notes.

5 Canadian Press, "Kitsault Mine Lawsuit by Nisga'a Nation Targets Province," February 10, 2013, http://www.huffingtonpost.ca/2013/08/02/kitsault-mine_n_3696131.html.

6 James Gosnell and Nelson Leeson gave a very informative interview on the popular BC talk show "Webster!," available at https://www.youtube.com/watch?v=ClgrkfbjBI4. Gosnell and Leeson did a brilliant job in calling attention to the double standards of the environmental assessment. They suggested that a public inquiry was needed to uncover how the mine had received environmental approval. They also stated that if such a mine were to be in place in their territory, they wanted jobs and benefits for Nisga'a people. This interview occurred long before any corporation was legally required to consult with a First Nation and seek informed consent. Nelson Leeson explains that when the Nisga'a Tribal Council asked AMAX representatives what they were prepared to offer the Nisga'a, the representatives could only reply that the road the company would build to the mine site would give Nisga'a "access to the sea." As if Nisga'a needed a road to give them access to the sea.

7 Avanti Kitsault Mine is wholly owned by Alloycorp Mining of Toronto. The previous owner of the mine, AMAX Corporation, was registered in Connecticut and held worldwide mining interests.

8 "Nisga'a Nation–British Columbia Kitsault Economic and Community Development Agreement," July 31, 2014, https://www2.gov.bc.ca/assets/gov/environment/natural-resource-stewardship/consulting-with-first-nations/agreements/ecda_nisgaa_kitsault.pdf.

9 "Avanti Mining and the Nisga'a Nation Conclude Kitsault Mine Benefits Agreement," Keith Powell, Canadian Mining and Energy, June 17, 2014, https://www.miningandenergy.ca/mininginsider/article/avanti_mining_and_the_nisgaa_nation_conclude/.

10 Land Claims Agreements Coalition Conference, Ottawa, December 7, 2015, author's notes.

11 The Statement of Claim is available at https://www.tunngavik.com/publication_categories/litigation/.

12 In 1999, Billy Diamond, former grand chief of the Cree and lead negotiator for the James Bay Agreement, spoke to this very problem when he testified before the House of Commons Standing Committee as it reviewed the Nisga'a treaty bill. Diamond said, "the Crees of northern Quebec are currently suing the federal and provincial governments to the tune of billions of dollars for non-implementation of the James Bay and Northern Quebec Agreement. We are locked in a struggle that is costing both sides millions in court costs and lawyers' fees. The tragic part

is that what we need we cannot get from the courts. The courts will not tell me that I have a forestry sawmill, or that I have certain obligations. Courts are limited to damages and cannot take the place of the legislature." House of Commons, "Evidence," Standing Committee on Aboriginal Affairs, November 24, 1999, https://www.ourcommons.ca/Content/Committee/362/AAND/Evidence/EV1039871/aandev17-e.htm.

13 Office of the Auditor General of Canada, *2007 October Report of the Auditor General of Canada to the House of Commons*, https://www.oag-bvg.gc.ca/internet/English/parl_oag_200710_03_e_23827.html.

14 Senate, "Evidence," Standing Senate Committee on Aboriginal Peoples, February 12, 2008.

15 Standing Senate Committee on Aboriginal Peoples, *Honouring the Spirit of Modern Treaties: Closing the Loopholes: Interim Report, Special Study on the Implementation of Comprehensive Land Claims Agreements in Canada* (Ottawa: The Committee, 2008), 14.

16 Senate, "Evidence," Standing Senate Committee on Aboriginal Peoples, February 27, 2008.

17 Ibid., February 12, 2008.

18 Standing Senate Committee on Aboriginal Peoples, *Honouring the Spirit of Modern Treaties*, 49.

19 Aboriginal Affairs and Northern Development Canada, "Internal Audit Report: Audit of the Implementation of Modern Treaty Obligations" (prepared by Audit and Assurance Services Branch, September 2013), 1, https://www.rcaanc-cirnac.gc.ca/DAM/DAM-CIRNAC-RCAANC/DAM-AEV/STAGING/texte-text/au_mto_1390221240364_eng.pdf.

20 Aboriginal Affairs and Northern Development Canada, "Modern Treaty Implementation: Implications for Federal Departments and Agencies: Modern Treaty Training for Federal Officials," February 26, 2014, http://www.landclaimscoalition.ca/assets/Implications-of-Modern-Treaties-Alan-MacDonald.pdf.

21 For the full text of the Cabinet directive, see Government of Canada, "Cabinet Directive on the Federal Approach to Modern Treaty Implementation," https://www.rcaanc-cirnac.gc.ca/eng/1436450503766/1544714947616.

22 These include Canadian Heritage, Canadian Environmental Assessment Agency, Employment and Social Development Canada, Environment and Climate Change Canada, Finance Canada, Fisheries and Oceans Canada, Global Affairs, Health Canada, Indigenous Services Canada, Justice Canada, Department of National Defence and the Canadian Armed Forces, Natural Resources Canada, Parks Canada, Privy Council Office, Public Safety Canada, Public Services and Procurement, Transport Canada, and Treasury Board of Canada Secretariat. CIRNAC chairs the committee. See Government of Canada, "Implementation of Modern Treaties and Self-Government Agreements: Provisional Annual Report, July 2015–March 2018," https://www.rcaanc-cirnac.gc.ca/eng/1573225148041/1573225175098.

164 *Notes to pages 129–40*

23 More specifically, article 28.1.2 of the agreement states that "Canada and Quebec shall continue to assist and promote the efforts of the James Bay Crees and more specifically undertake, within the terms of such programs and services as are established and in operation from time to time, to assist the James Bay Crees in pursuing the objectives set forth herein in Sub-Sections 28.4 to 28.16." http://www.naskapi.ca/documents/documents/JBNQA.pdf.

24 Standing Senate Committee on Aboriginal Peoples, *Honouring the Spirit of Modern Treaties*, 29.

25 House of Commons, *Debates* (October 26, 1999), 657, 716, 679; House of Commons, "Evidence," Standing Committee on Aboriginal Affairs and Northern Development, November 4, 1999, 10:05.

26 British Columbia Treaty Commission, "Treaty Commission Annual Report 2016," http://www.bctreaty.ca/sites/default/files/BCTC-AR2016-WEB.pdf.

27 *Constitution Act, 1982*, being Schedule B to the *Canada Act 1982* (UK), 1982, c. 11, s. 35.

28 *R. v Marshall*, [1999] 3 S.C.R. 456; *R. v Sioui*, [1990] 1 S.C.R. 1025. There are many more such cases; I use *Marshall* and *Sioui* here as examples.

29 Federal-Provincial Conference of First Ministers on Aboriginal Constitutional Matters, Ottawa, March 16, 1983.

30 *R. v Sparrow*, [1990] 1 S.C.R. 1075.

31 *R. v Van der Peet*, [1996] 2 S.C.R. 507 at para. 31 (emphasis in original).

32 *Delgamuukw v British Columbia*, [1997] 3 S.C.R. 1010 at para. 186.

33 *Mikisew Cree First Nation* at para. 1.

34 *Haida Nation v British Columbia (Minister of Forests)*, [2004] 3 S.C.R. 511 at para. 20.

35 House of Commons, "Evidence," Standing Committee on Aboriginal Affairs and Northern Development, November 4, 1999.

36 Government of Canada, "Ministers Bennett, Philpott and Wilson-Raybould Recognize the 10th Anniversary of Adoption of the United Nations Declaration on the Rights of Indigenous Peoples," https://www.canada.ca/en/indigenous-northern -affairs/news/2017/09/ministers_bennettphilpottandwilson-raybouldrecognize the10thanniv.html.

37 Ibid.

38 Ibid.

39 Hayden King, quoted in John Paul Tasker, "'I Worry about This': Trudeau's Move to Dissolve Indigenous Affairs Department Prompts Concern," CBC News, August 29, 2017, http://www.cbc.ca/news/politics/trudeau-dissolve-indigenous-affairs -worried-1.4265842.

40 Office of the Prime Minister, "Minister of Crown–Indigenous Relations Mandate Letter," December 13, 2019, https://pm.gc.ca/en/mandate-letters/2019/12/13/ minister-crown-indigenous-relations-mandate-letter.

41 Jim Aldridge, Land Claims Agreements Coalition Conference, Gatineau, QC, February 12, 2020, author's notes.

42 BC Business, "Enter the Golden Triangle," https://www.bcbusiness.ca/Enter-the-Golden-Triangle.

43 Special Assembly of the Nisga'a Nation, Gingolx, May 11, 2018, author's notes.

44 Kevin McKay, Land Claims Agreements Coalition, Creating Canada Symposium, Gatineau, QC, October 7, 2013, author's notes.

Conclusion

1 *Mikisew Cree First Nation v Canada,* [2005] 3 S.C.R. 388, 2005 SCC 69 at para. 54.

2 British Columbia, "Reconciliation and Other Agreements," https://www2.gov.bc.ca/gov/content/environment/natural-resource-stewardship/consulting-with-first-nations/first-nations-negotiations/reconciliation-other-agreements.

References

Alcantara, Christopher. 2007. "To Treaty or Not to Treaty? Aboriginal Peoples and Comprehensive Land Claims Negotiations in Canada." *Publius: The Journal of Federalism* 38(2): 343–69. https://doi.org/10.1093/publius/pjm036.

–. 2013. *Negotiating the Deal: Comprehensive Land Claims Agreements in Canada.* Toronto: University of Toronto Press.

Alfred, Taiaiake. 2005. "Sovereignty." In *Sovereignty Matters: Locations of Contestation and Possibility in Indigenous Struggles for Self-Determination*, ed. Joanne Barker, 33–50. Lincoln: University of Nebraska Press.

–. 2009. *Peace, Power, Righteousness: An Indigenous Manifesto.* Oxford: Oxford University Press.

Allen, Edward. 2004. "Our Treaty, Our Inherent Right to Self-Government: An Overview of the Nisga'a Final Agreement." *International Journal on Minority and Group Rights* 11(3): 233–49. https://doi.org/10.1163/1571811042802019.

Allen, Jessie. 2008. "A Theory of Adjudication: Law as Magic." *Suffolk University Law Review* 41(4): 773–831.

Anderson, Benedict. 1991. *Imagined Communities.* London: Verso.

Appadurai, Arjun. 1996. *Modernity at Large: Cultural Dimensions of Globalization.* Minneapolis: University of Minnesota Press.

Asch, Michael. 1999. "From Calder to Van der Peet: Aboriginal Rights and Canadian Law, 1973–96." In *Indigenous Peoples' Rights in Australia, Canada and New Zealand*, ed. Paul Havemann, 428–46. Oxford: Oxford University Press.

–. 2014. *On Being Here to Stay: Treaties and Aboriginal Rights in Canada.* Toronto: University of Toronto Press.

–. 2018. "Confederation Treaties and Reconciliation: Stepping Back into the Future." In *Resurgence and Reconciliation: Indigenous-Settler Relations and Earth*

Teachings, ed. Michael Asch, John Borrows, and James Tully, 29–48. Toronto: University of Toronto Press.

Asch, Michael, and Norman Zlotkin. 1997. "Affirming Aboriginal Title: A New Basis for Comprehensive Claims Negotiations." In *Aboriginal and Treaty Rights in Canada: Essays on Law, Equality and Respect for Difference*, ed. Michael Asch, 208–29. Vancouver: UBC Press.

Barakat, Rana. 2018. "Writing/Righting Palestine Studies: Settler Colonialism, Indigenous Sovereignty and Resisting the Ghost(s) of History." *Settler Colonial Studies* 8(3): 349–63. https://doi.org/10.1080/2201473X.2017.1300048.

Barker, Joanne. 2005. "For Whom Sovereignty Matters." In *Sovereignty Matters: Locations of Contestation and Possibility in Indigenous Struggles for Self-Determination*, ed. Joanne Barker, 1–31. Lincoln: University of Nebraska Press.

–. 2011. *Native Acts: Law, Recognition and Cultural Authenticity*. Durham: Duke University Press.

Barker, John. 1998. "Tangled Reconciliations: The Anglican Church and the Nisga'a of British Columbia." *American Ethnologist* 25(3): 433–51. https://doi.org/10.1525/ae.1998.25.3.433.

Battiste, Marie, and Helen Semaganis. 2002. "First Thoughts on First Nations Citizenship: Issues in Education." In *Citizenship in Transformation in Canada*, ed. Yvonne M. Hebert, 93–111. Toronto: University of Toronto Press.

Berger, Thomas. 2007. "Frank Calder and Thomas Berger: A Conversation." In *Let Right Be Done: Aboriginal Title, the Calder Case, and the Future of Indigenous Rights*, ed. Hamar Foster, Heather Raven, and Jeremy Webber, 37–53. Vancouver: UBC Press.

Biolsi, Thomas. 1995. "The Birth of the Reservation: Making the Modern Individual among the Lakota." *American Ethnologist* 22(1): 28–54.

–. 2005. "Imagined Geographies: Sovereignty, Indigenous Space, and American Indian Struggle." *American Ethnologist* 32(2): 239–59.

Blackburn, Carole. 2005. "Searching for Guarantees in the Midst of Uncertainty: Negotiating Aboriginal Rights and Title in British Columbia." *American Anthropologist* 107(4): 586–96. https://doi.org/10.1525/aa.2005.107.4.586.

–. 2007. "Producing Legitimacy: Reconciliation and the Negotiation of Aboriginal Rights in Canada." *Journal of the Royal Anthropological Institute* 13(3): 621–37. https://doi.org/10.1111/j.1467-9655.2007.00447.x.

–. 2009. "Differentiating Indigenous Citizenship: Seeking Multiplicity in Rights, Identity and Sovereignty in Canada." *American Ethnologist* 36(1): 49–61. https://doi.org/10.1111/j.1548-1425.2008.01103.x.

Blomley, Nicholas. 1996. "'Shut the Province Down': First Nations Blockades in British Columbia, 1984–1995." *BC Studies* 3: 5–35. https://doi.org/10.14288/bcs.v0i111.1361.

–. 2014a. "Making Space for Property." *Annals of the Association of American Geographers* 104(6): 1291–1306. https://doi.org/10.1080/00045608.2014.941738.

–. 2014b. "The Ties That Blind: Making Fee Simple in the British Columbia Treaty Process." *Transactions of the Institute of British Geographers* 40(2): 168–79.

Borrows, John. 1999a. "'Landed' Citizenship: Narratives of Aboriginal Political Participation." In *Citizenship, Diversity, and Pluralism: Canadian and Comparative Perspectives*, ed. Alan C. Cairns, 72–86. Montreal and Kingston: McGill-Queen's University Press.

–. 1999b. "Sovereignty's Alchemy: An Analysis of *Delgamuukw v. British Columbia*." *Osgoode Hall Law Journal* 37(3): 537–96.

–. 2001. "Uncertain Citizens: Aboriginal Peoples and the Supreme Court." *Canadian Bar Review* 80(1–2): 15–41.

–. 2002. *Recovering Canada: The Resurgence of Indigenous Law*. Toronto: University of Toronto Press.

–. 2007. "Let Obligations Be Done." In *Let Right Be Done: Aboriginal Title, the Calder Case, and the Future of Indigenous Rights*, ed. Hamar Foster, Heather Raven, and Jeremy Webber, 201–15. Vancouver: UBC Press.

–. 2010. *Canada's Indigenous Constitution*. Toronto: University of Toronto Press.

–. 2016. *Freedom and Indigenous Constitutionalism*. Toronto: University of Toronto Press.

–. 2017. "Canada's Colonial Constitution." In *The Right Relationship: Reimagining the Implementation of Historical Treaties*, ed. John Borrows and Michael Coyle, 17–38. Toronto: University of Toronto Press.

Boston, Thomas, and Shirley Morven. 1996. *From Time before Memory: The People of Ḵamligihahlhaahl*. New Aiyansh, BC: School District No. 92 (Nisga'a).

Bouchard, Karen, Adam Perry, Bobby Clark, and Thierry Rodon. 2019. "Measuring Well-Being in the Context of Modern Treaties: Challenges and Opportunities." *Northern Public Affairs* 6(2): 66–69.

Brenner, Neil, and Stuart Elden. 2009. "Henri Lefebvre on State, Space, Territory." *International Political Sociology* 3(4): 353–77. https://doi.org/10.1111/j.1749-5687 .2009.00081.x.

British Columbia. 1888. *Papers Relating to the Commission Appointed to Enquire into the Condition of the Indians of the North-West Coast*. Victoria: Government Printer. http://www.llbc.leg.bc.ca/public/pubdocs/bcdocs_rc/464035/464035_ commission_indians_northwest_coast_bc.pdf.

Bruyneel, Kevin. 2007. *The Third Space of Sovereignty: The Postcolonial Politics of U.S. Indigenous Relations*. Minneapolis: University of Minnesota Press.

Bur, Lars. 2001. "The South African Truth and Reconciliation Commission: A Technique of Nation-State Formation." In *States of Imagination: Ethnographic Explorations of the Postcolonial State*, ed. Thomas Blum Hansen and Finn Stepputat, 149–81. Durham: Duke University Press.

Cairns, Alan. 2000. *Citizens Plus: Aboriginal Peoples and the Canadian State*. Vancouver: UBC Press.

References

Calloway, Colin G. 2013. *Pen and Ink Witchcraft: Treaties and Treaty Making in American Indian History*. Oxford: Oxford University Press.

Cameron, Kirk, and Alastair Campbell. 2019. "Towards a Modern Treaties Implementation Review Commission." *Northern Public Affairs* 6(2): 47–51. https://www.northernpublicaffairs.ca/index/towards-a-modern-treaties-implementation-review-commission/.

Campbell, Alastair, Terry Fenge, and Udloriak Hanson. 2011. "Implementing the 1993 Nunavut Land Claims Agreement." *Arctic Review on Law and Politics* 2(1): 25–51.

Canada, British Columbia, Nisga'a Nation. 1998. *The Nisga'a Final Agreement*. Ottawa: Queen's Printer.

Canada, British Columbia, Nisga'a Tribal Council. 1996. *Nisga'a Treaty Negotiations: Agreement in Principle*. Ottawa: Queen's Printer.

Canada, House of Commons Special Committee on Indian Self-Government. 1983. *Indian Self-Government in Canada: Report of the Special Committee*, 32nd Parl, 1st Sess, No 40 (12 October 1983 and 20 October 1983) (Chair: Keith Penner).

Cardinal, Harold, and Walter Hildebrandt. 2000. *Treaty Elders of Saskatchewan: Our Dream Is That Our Peoples Will One Day Be Clearly Recognized as Nations*. Calgary: University of Calgary Press.

Carey, Jane. 2020. "On Hope and Resignation: Conflicting Visions of Settler Colonial Studies and Its Future as a Field." *Postcolonial Studies* 23(1): 21–42. https://doi.org/10.1080/13688790.2020.1719578.

Catellino, Jessica. 2008. *High Stakes: Florida Seminole Gaming and Sovereignty*. Durham: Duke University Press.

Christophers, Brett. 2009. "On Voodoo Economics: Theorizing Relations of Property, Value and Contemporary Capitalism." *Transactions of the Institute of British Geographers* 35: 94–108.

Coffey, Wallace, and Rebecca Tsosie. 2001. "Rethinking the Tribal Sovereignty Doctrine: Cultural Sovereignty and the Collective Future of Indian Nations." *Stanford Law and Policy Review* 12(2): 191–221.

Coon Come, Matthew. 2015. "Cree Experience with Treaty Implementation." In *Keeping Promises: The Royal Proclamation of 1763, Aboriginal Rights, and Treaties in Canada*, ed. Terry Fenge and Jim Aldridge, 153–72. Montreal and Kingston: McGill-Queen's University Press.

Cooper, Carol Ann. 1993. "'To Be Free on Our Lands': Coast Tsimshian and Nisga'a Societies in Historical Perspective, 1830–1900." PhD diss., University of Waterloo.

Cornell, Steven, and Joseph P. Kalt. 1998. "Sovereignty and Nation-Building: The Development Challenge in Indian Country Today." *American Indian Culture and Research Journal* 22(3): 187–214. https://doi.org/10.17953/aicr.22.3.lv45536553vn7j78.

Corntassel, Jeff. 2008. "Toward Sustainable Self-Determination: Rethinking the Contemporary Indigenous-Rights Discourse." *Alternatives* 33(1): 105–32. https://doi.org/10.1177/030437540803300106.

–. 2012. "Re-Envisioning Resurgence: Indigenous Pathways to Decolonization and Sustainable Self-Determination." *Decolonization: Indigeneity, Education and Society* 1(1): 86–101.

Coulthard, Glen. 2014. *Red Skin, White Masks: Rejecting the Colonial Politics of Recognition*. Minneapolis: University of Minnesota.

Coyle, Michael. 2017. "As Long as the Sun Shines: Recognizing That Treaties Were Meant to Last." In *The Right Relationship: Reimagining the Implementation of Historical Treaties*, ed. John Borrows and Michael Coyle, 39–69. Toronto: University of Toronto Press.

Craft, Aimee. 2013. *Breathing Life into the Stone Fort Treaty: An Anishinabe Understanding of Treaty One*. Saskatoon: Purich.

Cree-Naskapi Commission. 1986. *Report of the Cree-Naskapi Commission*. Ottawa: K.G. Campbell.

Culhane, Dara. 1998. *The Pleasure of the Crown: Anthropology, Law and First Nations*. Vancouver: Talon Books.

Daugherty, Wayne, and Dennis Madill. 1984. *Indian Government under Indian Act Legislation, 1868–1951*. Ottawa: Treaties and Historical Research Centre, Research Branch, Department of Indian and Northern Affairs.

De Costa, Ravi. 2008. "History, Democracy, and Treaty Negotiations in British Columbia." In *The Power of Promises: Rethinking Indian Treaties in the Pacific Northwest*, ed. Alexandra Harmon, 297–320. Seattle: University of Washington Press.

De la Cadena, Marisol. 2010. "Indigenous Cosmopolitics in the Andes: Conceptual Reflections beyond 'Politics.'" *Cultural Anthropology* 25(2): 334–70. https://doi.org/10.1111/j.1548-1360.2010.01061.x.

De Soto, Hernando. 2000. *The Mystery of Capital: Why Capitalism Triumphs in the West and Fails Everywhere Else*. New York: Basic Books.

Deloria, Vine, Jr. 1979. "Self Determination and the Concept of Sovereignty." In *Economic Development in American Indian Reservations*, ed. Roxanne Dunbar Ortiz, 22–28. Albuquerque: University of New Mexico, Native American Studies.

Dennison, Jean. 2017. "Entangled Sovereignties: The Osage Nation's Interconnections with Governmental and Corporate Authorities." *American Ethnologist* 44(4): 684–96.

Drucker, Philip. 1965. *Cultures of the North Pacific Coast*. New York: Harper and Row.

Egan, Brian. 2012. "Sharing the Colonial Burden: Treaty Making and Reconciliation in Hul'qumi'num Territory." *Canadian Geographer* 56(4): 398–418. https://doi.org/10.1111/j.1541-0064.2012.00414.x.

Eyford, Douglas R. 2015. *A New Direction: Advancing Aboriginal and Treaty Rights*. Report submitted to the Honourable Bernard Valcourt, Minister of Aboriginal Affairs and Northern Development.

Fabris, Michael. 2016. "Beyond the New Dawes Act: A Critique of the First Nations Property Ownership Act." Master's thesis, University of British Columbia.

Feit, Harvey. 2010. "Neoliberal Governance and James Bay Cree Governance: Negotiated Agreements, Oppositional Struggles, and Co-Governance." In *Indigenous*

Peoples and Autonomy, ed. Mario Blaser, Ravi de Costa, Deborah McGregor, and William D. Coleman, 49–79. Vancouver: UBC Press.

Feltes, Emma. 2015. "Research as Guesthood: The Memorial to Sir Wilfrid Laurier and Resolving Indigneous-Settler Relations in British Columbia." *Anthropologica* 57(2): 469–80.

Fenge, Terry. 2015. "Negotiation and Implementation of Modern Treaties between Aboriginal Peoples and the Crown in Right of Canada." In *Keeping Promises: The Royal Proclamation of 1763, Aboriginal Rights, and Treaties in Canada*, ed. Terry Fenge and Jim Aldridge, 105–37. Montreal and Kingston: McGill-Queen's University Press.

Ferguson, James, and Akhil Gupta. 2002. "Spatializing States: Toward an Ethnography of Neoliberal Governmentality." *American Ethnologist* 29(4): 981–1002. https://doi.org/10.1525/ae.2002.29.4.981.

Fisher, Robin. 1977. *Contact and Conflict: Indian-European Relations in British Columbia, 1774–1890*. Vancouver: UBC Press.

Flanagan, Tom, Christopher Alcantara, and Andre Le Dressay. 2010. *Beyond the Indian Act: Restoring Aboriginal Property Rights*. Montreal and Kingston: McGill-Queen's University Press.

Ford, Lisa. 2010. *Settler Sovereignty: Jurisdiction and Indigenous People in America and Australia, 1788–1836*. Cambridge, MA: Harvard University Press.

Ford, Richard. 1999. "Law's Territory (A History of Jurisdiction)." *Michigan Law Review* 97(4): 843–930.

Foster, Hamar. 1995. "Letting Go the Bone: The Idea of Indian Title in British Columbia, 1849–1927." In *British Columbia and the Yukon*, ed. Hamar Foster and John McLaren. Essays in the History of Canadian Law, vol. 6, 28–86. Toronto: University of Toronto Press.

–. 2007. "We Are Not O'Meara's Children: Law, Lawyers, and the First Campaign for Aboriginal Title in British Columbia, 1908–28." In *Let Right Be Done: Aboriginal Title, the Calder Case, and the Future of Indigenous Rights*, ed. Hamar Foster, Heather Raven, and Jeremy Webber, 61–84. Vancouver: UBC Press.

Fraser, Nancy, and Linda Gordon. 1997. "A Genealogy of Dependency: Tracing a Keyword of the U.S. Welfare State." In *Justice Interruptus: Critical Reflections on the "Postsocialist" Condition*, ed. Nancy Fraser, 121–49. New York: Routledge.

Godlewska, Christina, and Jeremy Webber. 2007. "The Calder Decision, Aboriginal Title, Treaties, and the Nisga'a." In *Let Right Be Done: Aboriginal Title, the Calder Case, and the Future of Indigenous Rights*, ed. Hamar Foster, Heather Raven, and Jeremy Webber, 1–33. Vancouver: UBC Press.

Gover, Kirsty. 2010. *Tribal Constitutionalism: States, Tribes, and the Governance of Membership*. New York: Oxford University Press.

Graben, Sari. 2014. "Lessons for Indigenous Property Reform: From Membership to Ownership on Nisga'a Lands." *UBC Law Review* 47(2): 399–442.

Graben, Sari, and Matthew Mehaffey. 2017. "Negotiating Self Government Over and Over and Over Again: Interpreting Contemporary Treaties." In *The Right Relationship: Reimagining the Implementation of Historical Treaties*, ed. John Borrows and Michael Coyle, 164–84. Toronto: University of Toronto Press.

Gray, Kevin, and Susan Francis Gray. 2009. *Elements of Land Law*. 5th ed. Oxford: Oxford University Press.

Griffin, Mansell, and Antino Spanjer. 2008. "The Nisga'a Common Bowl in Tradition and Politics." In *Aboriginal Canada Revisited*, ed. Kerstin Knopf, 72–85. Ottawa: University of Ottawa Press.

Griffiths, John. 1986. "What Is Legal Pluralism?" *Journal of Legal Pluralism and Unofficial Law* 24: 1–56.

Gutstein, Donald. 2014. *Harperism: How Stephen Harper and His Think Tank Colleagues Have Transformed Canada*. Toronto: James Lorimer.

Haig-Brown, Mary. 2005. "Arthur Eugene O'Meara: Servant, Advocate, Seeker of Justice." In *With Good Intentions: Euro-Canadian and Aboriginal Relations in Colonial Canada*, ed. Celia Haig-Brown, 258–96. Vancouver: UBC Press.

Hale, Charles. 2020. "Using and Refusing the Law: Indigenous Struggles and Legal Strategies after Neoliberal Multiculturalism." *American Anthropologist* 122(3): 618–31.

Hall, Rebecca Jane. 2015. "Divide and Conquer: Privatizing Indigenous Land Ownership as Capital Accumulation." *Studies in Political Economy* 96(1): 23–46. https://doi.org/10.1080/19187033.2015.11674936.

Halpin, Marjorie. 1973. "The Tsimshian Crest System: A Study Based on Museum Specimens and the Marius Barbeau and William Beynon Field Notes." PhD diss., University of British Columbia.

Hamilton, A.C. 1995. *Canada and Aboriginal Peoples: A New Partnership*. Ottawa: Minister of Public Works and Government Services.

Harris, Douglas A. 2008. *Landing Native Fisheries: Indian Reserves and Fishing Rights in British Columbia, 1849–1925*. Vancouver: UBC Press.

Harvey, David. 2005. *A Brief History of Neoliberalism*. Oxford: Oxford University Press.

Hoffman, Ross, and Andrew Robinson. 2010. "Nisga'a Self Government: A New Journey Has Begun." *Canadian Journal of Native Studies* 30(2): 387–405.

Huyssen, Andreas. 2000. "Present Pasts: Media, Politics, Amnesia." *Public Culture* 12(1): 21–38. https://doi.org/10.1215/08992363-12-1-21.

Irlbacher-Fox, Stephanie. 2009. *Finding Dahshaa: Self Government, Social Suffering, and Aboriginal Policy in Canada*. Vancouver: UBC Press.

Jamieson, Kathleen. 1978. *Indian Women and the Law in Canada: Citizens Minus*. Ottawa: Minister of Supply and Services.

Johnston, Darlene. 1993. "First Nations and Canadian Citizenship." In *Belonging: The Meaning and Future of Canadian Citizenship*, ed. William Kaplan, 349–67. Montreal and Kingston: McGill-Queen's University Press.

References

Kauanui, J. Kēhaulani. 2008. *Hawaiian Blood: Colonialism and the Politics of Sovereignty and Indigeneity*. Durham: Duke University Press.

–. 2016. "'A Structure, Not an Event': Settler Colonialism and Enduring Indigeneity." *Lateral* 5(1). https://doi.org/10.25158/L5.1.7.

King, Hayden, and Shiri Pasternak. 2018. "Canada's Emerging Indigenous Rights Framework: A Critical Analysis." Yellowhead Institute. https://yellowheadinstitute.org/wp-content/uploads/2018/06/yi-rights-report-june-2018-final-5.4.pdf.

Klopotek, Brian. 2011. *Recognition Odysseys: Indigeneity, Race, and Federal Tribal Recognition Policy in Three Louisiana Indian Communities*. Durham: Duke University Press.

Kuokkanen, Rauna. 2012. "Self Determination and Indigenous Women's Rights at the Intersection of International Human Rights." *Human Rights Quarterly* 34(1): 225–50. https://doi.org/10.1353/hrq.2012.0000.

Kymlicka, Will, and Wayne Norman. 1995. "Return of the Citizen: A Survey of Recent Work on Citizenship Theory." In *Theorizing Citizenship*, ed. Ronald Beiner, 283–322. Albany: State University of New York Press.

Ladner, Kiera. 2006. "Indigenous Governance: Questioning the Status and the Possibilities for Reconciliation with Canada's Commitment to Aboriginal and Treaty Rights." Research Paper for the National Centre for First Nations Governance, Vancouver, September 15.

–. 2018. "Proceed with Caution: Reflections on Resurgence and Reconciliation." In *Resurgence and Reconciliation: Indigenous-Settler Relations and Earth Teachings*, ed. Michael Asch, John Borrows, and James Tully, 245–64. Toronto: University of Toronto Press.

Laplante, Lisa J., and Kimberly Theidon. 2007. "Truth with Consequences: Justice and Reparations in Post-Truth Commission Peru." *Human Rights Quarterly* 29(1): 228–50.

Lawrence, Bonita. 2003. "Gender, Race, and the Regulation of Native Identity in Canada and the United States: An Overview." *Hypatia* 18(2): 3–31.

Lightfoot, Sheryl R. 2013. "The International Indigenous Rights Discourse and Its Demands for Multilevel Citizenship." In *Multilevel Citizenship*, ed. Willem Maas, 127–46. Philadelphia: University of Pennsylvania Press.

Lightfoot, Sheryl R., and David MacDonald. 2017. "Treaty Relations between Indigenous Peoples: Advancing Global Understandings of Self-Determination." *New Diversities* 19(2): 25–39.

Little Bear, Leroy, Menno Boldt, and J. Anthony Long. 1984. "Introduction." In *Pathways to Self-Determination: Canadian Indians and the Canadian State*, ed. Leroy Little Bear, Menno Boldt, and J. Anthony Long, xi–xxi. Toronto: University of Toronto Press.

Loo, Tina. 1995. "Tonto's Due: Law, Culture, and Colonization in British Columbia." In *British Columbia and the Yukon*, ed. Hamar Foster and John McLaren. Essays in the History of Canadian Law, vol. 6, 128–70. Toronto: University of Toronto Press.

Lutz, John Sutton. 2008. *Makúk: An New History of Aboriginal-White Relations*. Vancouver: UBC Press.

Lyons, Scott Richard. 2010. *X-Marks: Native Signatures of Assent*. Minneapolis: University of Minnesota Press.

Macklem, Patrick. 2016. "Indigenous Peoples and the Ethos of Legal Pluralism in Canada." In *From Recognition to Reconciliation: Essays on the Constitutional Entrenchment of Aboriginal and Treaty Rights*, ed. Patrick Macklem and Douglas Sanderson, 17–34. Toronto: University of Toronto Press.

Marcus, George. 1995. "Ethnography in/of the World System: The Emergence of Multi-sited Ethnography." *Annual Review of Anthropology* 24: 95–117.

Mawani, Renisa. 2016. "Law, Settler Colonialism, and 'the Forgotten Space' of Maritime Worlds." *Annual Review of Law and Social Science* 12: 107–31.

McHugh, Paul, and Lisa Ford. 2012. "Settler Sovereignty and the Shapeshifting Crown." In *Between Indigenous and Settler Governance*, ed. Lisa Ford and Tim Rowse, 23–34. London: Routledge.

McNeary, Stephen A. 1976. "Where Fire Came Down: Social and Economic Life of the Niska." PhD diss., Bryn Mawr College.

McNeil, Kent. 2003. "Reconciliation and the Supreme Court: The Opposing Views of Chief Justices Lamer and McLachlin." *Indigenous Law Journal* 2(1): 1–25.

–. 2006. "Aboriginal Title and the Supreme Court: What's Happening?" *Saskatchewan Law Review* 29: 281–308.

–. 2018a. "Indigenous and Crown Sovereignty in Canada." In *Resurgence and Reconciliation: Indigenous-Settler Relations and Earth Teachings*, ed. Michael Asch, John Borrows, and James Tully, 293–314. Toronto: University of Toronto Press.

–. 2018b. "The Source, Nature, and Content of the Crown's Underlying Title to Aboriginal Title Lands." *Canadian Bar Review* 96(2): 273–93.

Merlan, Francesca. 2009. "Indigeneity: Global and Local." *Current Anthropology* 50(3): 303–33. https://doi.org/10.1086/597667.

Merry, Sally Engle. 1991. "Law and Colonialism." *Law and Society Review* 25(4): 890–922.

Miller, J.R. 2009. *Compact, Contract, Covenant: Aboriginal Treaty Making in Canada*. Toronto: University of Toronto Press.

Mills, Aaron/Waabishki Ma'iingan. 2017. "What Is a Treaty? On Contract and Mutual Aid." In *The Right Relationship: Reimagining the Implementation of Historical Treaties*, ed. John Borrows and Michael Coyle, 208–47. Toronto: University of Toronto Press.

Mitchell, Timothy. 2005. "The Work of Economics: How a Discipline Makes Its World." *European Journal of Sociology* 46(2): 297–320.

–. 2007. "The Properties of Markets." In *Do Economists Make Markets? On the Performativity of Economics*, ed. Donald MacKenzie, Fabian Muniesa, and Lucia Siu, 244–75. Princeton: Princeton University Press.

Morin, Jean-Pierre. 2018. *Solemn Words and Foundational Documents: An Annotated Discussion of Indigenous-Crown Treaties in Canada, 1752–1923*. Toronto: University of Toronto Press.

Nadasdy, Paul. 2012. "Boundaries among Kin: Sovereignty, the Modern Treaty Process, and the Rise of Ethno-Territorial Nationalism among Yukon First Nations."

Comparative Studies in Society and History 54(3): 499–532. https://doi.org/10.1017/S0010417512000217.

–. 2017. *Sovereignty's Entailments: First Nation State Formation in the Yukon*. Toronto: University of Toronto Press.

Napoleon, Valerie. 2009 "Ayook: Gitksan Legal Order, Law, and Legal Theory." PhD diss., University of Victoria.

Nettelbeck, Amanda, Russel Smandych, Louis A. Knafla, and Robert Foster. 2016. *Fragile Settlements: Aboriginal Peoples, Law, and Resistance in South-West Australia and Prairie Canada*. Vancouver: UBC Press.

Newman, Dwight. 2011. "Contractual and Covenantal Conceptions of Modern Treaty Interpretation." *Supreme Court Law Review* 54: 475–91.

Nisga'a Tribal Council. 1984a. *The Land and Resources: Traditional Nisga'a Systems of Land Use and Ownership*. Vol. 4 of *Ayuuḵhl Nisga'a Study*. New Aiyansh, BC: Wilp Wilxo'oskwhl Nisga'a Publications.

–. 1984b. *Nisga'a Clan Histories*. Vol. 2 of *Ayuuḵhl Nisga'a Study*. New Aiyansh, BC: Wilp Wilxo'oskwhl Nisga'a Publications.

–. 1984c. *Nisga'a Society*. Vol. 3 of *Ayuuḵhl Nisga'a Study*. New Aiyansh, BC: Wilp Wilxo'oskwhl Nisga'a Publications.

Noble, Brian. 2018. "Treaty Ecologies: With Persons, Peoples, Animals and the Land." In *Resurgence and Reconciliation: Indigenous-Settler Relations and Earth Teachings*, ed. Michael Asch, John Borrows, and James Tully, 315–42. Toronto: University of Toronto Press.

Nyce, Allison. 2010. "Wilksilaks Transfer of Knowledge: A Working Model for Maintaining Tradition." Master's thesis, University of Northern British Columbia.

Ong, Aihwa. 1996. "Cultural Citizenship as Subject-Making: Immigrants Negotiate Racial and Cultural Boundaries in the United States." *Current Anthropology* 37(5): 737–62. https://doi.org/10.1086/204560.

–. 2006. *Neoliberalism as Exception: Mutations in Citizenship and Sovereignty*. Durham: Duke University Press.

Ortner, Sherry. 2006. *Anthropology and Social Theory: Culture, Power and the Acting Subject*. Durham: Duke University Press.

Otis, Ghislain. 2014. "Constitutional Recognition of Aboriginal and Treaty Rights: A New Framework for Managing Legal Pluralism in Canada?" *Journal of Legal Pluralism and Unofficial Law* 46(3): 320–37.

Palmater, Pamela. 2010. "Opportunity or Temptation?" *Literary Review of Canada* 18(3): 6–7.

–. 2011. *Beyond Blood: Rethinking Indigenous Identity*. Saskatoon: Purich.

Papillon, Martin. 2008. "Aboriginal Quality of Life under a Modern Treaty: Lessons from the Experience of the Cree Nation of Eeyou Istchee and the Inuit of Nunavik." *IRPP Choices* 14(9): 4–23.

–. 2014. "The Rise (and Fall) of Aboriginal Self-Government." In *Canadian Politics*, 6th ed., ed. James Bickerton and Alain-G. Gagnon, 113–31. Toronto: University of Toronto Press.

Pasternak, Shiri. 2014a. "How Capitalism Will Save Colonialism: The Privatization of Reserve Lands in Canada." *Antipode* 47(1): 179–86.

–. 2014b. "Jurisdiction and Settler Colonialism: Where Do Laws Meet?" *Canadian Journal of Law and Society* 29(2): 145–61.

Patterson, E. Palmer. 1982. *Mission on the Nass: The Evangelization of the Nishga (1860–1890)*. Waterloo: Eulachon Press.

–. 1983. "A Decade of Change: Origins of the Nishga and Tsimshian Land Protests in the 1980s." *Journal of Canadian Studies* 18(3): 40–54.

–. 1989. "George Kinzadah – Simoogit in His Times." *BC Studies* 82: 16–38.

–. 1992. "Kincolith's First Decade: A Nisga'a Village (1867–1878)." *Canadian Journal of Native Studies* 12(2): 229–50.

Penikett, Tony. 2006. *Reconciliation: First Nations Treaty Making in British Columbia*. Vancouver: Douglas and McIntyre.

Perry, Richard Warren. 1995. "The Logic of the Modern Nation State and the Legal Construction of Native American Tribal Identity." *Indiana Law Review* 28(3): 547–74.

Peters, Evelyn J. 1991. "Federal and Provincial Responsibilities for the Cree, Naskapi and Inuit under the James Bay and Northern Quebec, and Northeastern Quebec Agreements." In *Aboriginal Peoples and Government Responsibility: Exploring Federal and Provincial Roles*, ed. David Hawkes, 173–242. Ottawa: Carleton University Press.

Poelzer, Greg, and Ken S. Coates. 2015. *From Treaty Peoples to Treaty Nation: A Road Map for All Canadians*. Vancouver: UBC Press.

Promislow, Janna. 2013. "'It Would Only Be Just': A Study of Territoriality and Trading Posts along the Mackenzie River, 1800–27." In *Between Indigenous and Settler Governance*, ed. Lisa Ford and Tim Rowse, 35–47. New York: Routledge.

–. 2014. "Treaties in History and Law." *UBC Law Review* 47(3): 1085–1183.

Promislow, Janna, and Alain Verrier. 2019. "Judicial Interventions in Modern Treaty Implementation: Dispute Resolution and Living Treaties." *Northern Public Affairs* 6(2): 52–56.

Quesnel, Joseph, and Conrad Winn. 2011. *The Nisga'a Treaty: Self Government and Good Governance: The Jury Is Still Out*. Policy Series No. 108. Winnipeg: Frontier Centre for Public Policy.

Rajala, Richard A. 2006. *Up-Coast: Forests and Industry on British Columbia's North Coast, 1870–2005*. Victoria: Royal BC Museum.

Ramirez, Renya K. 2004. "Community Healing and Cultural Citizenship." In *A Companion to the Anthropology of American Indians*, ed. Thomas Biolsi, 398–411. Malden, MA: Blackwell.

Raunet, Daniel. 1996. *Without Surrender, without Consent: A History of the Nisga'a Land Claims*. Vancouver: Douglas and McIntyre.

Ray, Arthur, Jim Miller, and Frank Tough. 2000. *Bounty and Benevolence: A History of Saskatchewan Treaties*. Montreal and Kingston: McGill-Queen's University Press.

Richland, Justin. 2008. *Arguing with Tradition: The Language of Law in Hopi Tribal Court*. Chicago: University of Chicago Press.

Rifkin, Mark. 2010. *When Did Indians Become Straight? Kinship, the History of Sexuality, and Native Sovereignty*. Oxford: Oxford University Press.

Robertson, Leslie A., with the Kwagu'ł Gixsam Clan. 2012. *Standing Up with Ga'axsta'las: Jane Constance Cook and the Politics of Memory, Church, and Custom*. Vancouver: UBC Press.

Robinson, Andrew. 1999. "Nihl Adagwiy T'gun Adaawaks GalksiGabin (Here Is the Story of GalksiGabin): A Modern Auto-Ethnography of a Nisga'a Man." Master's thesis, University of Northern British Columbia.

Rosaldo, Renato. 1997. "Cultural Citizenship, Inequality and Multiculturalism." In *Latino Cultural Citizenship: Claiming Identity, Space, and Rights*, ed. William Flores and Rina Benmayor, 27–38. Boston: Beacon Press.

Rose, Alex. 2000. *Spirit Dance at Meziadin: Chief Joseph Gosnell and the Nisga'a Treaty*. Madeira Park, BC: Harbour.

Roth, Christopher. 2002. "Goods, Names and Selves: Rethinking the Tsimshian Potlatch." *American Ethnologist* 29(1): 123–50. https://doi.org/10.1525/ae.2002.29.1.123.

Sanders, Doug. 1999. "'We Intend to Live Here Forever': A Primer on the Nisga'a Treaty." *UBC Law Review* 33(1): 103–28.

Sanderson, Douglas (Amos Binashii). 2018. "The Residue of *Imperium*: Property and Sovereignty on Indigenous Lands." *University of Toronto Law Journal* 68(3): 319–57.

Scott, Tracie Lea. 2012. *Postcolonial Sovereignty? The Nisga'a Final Agreement*. Saskatoon: Purich.

Simpson, Audra. 2014. *Mohawk Interruptus: Political Life across the Borders of Settler States*. Durham: Duke University Press.

Simpson, Leanne. 2008. "Looking after Gdoo-naaganinaa: Precolonial Nishnaabeg Diplomatic and Treaty Relationships." *Wicazo Sa Review* 23(2): 29–42. https://doi.org/10.1353/wic.0.0001.

Slattery, Brian. 2000. "Making Sense of Aboriginal and Treaty Rights." *The Canadian Bar Review* 79: 196–224.

–. 2006. "The Metamorphosis of Aboriginal Title." *Canadian Bar Review* 85: 255–86.

Sloan Morgan, Vanessa, Heather Castleden, and Huu-ay-aht First Nations. 2018. "'This Is Going to Affect Our Lives': Exploring Huu-ay-aht First Nations, the Government of Canada and British Columbia's New Relationship through the Implementation of the Maa-nulth Treaty." *Canadian Journal of Law and Society* 33(3): 309–34. https://doi.org/10.1017/cls.2018.23.

Soyinka, Wole. 1999. *The Burden of Memory, the Muse of Forgiveness*. Oxford: Oxford University Press.

Sterritt, Neil J., Susan Marsden, Robert Galois, Peter Grant, and Richard Overstall. 1998. *Tribal Boundaries in the Nass Watershed*. Vancouver: UBC Press.

Sturm, Circe. 2002. *Blood Politics: Race, Culture and Identity in the Cherokee Nation of Oklahoma*. Berkeley: University of California Press.

–. 2014. "Race, Sovereignty, and Civil Rights: Understanding the Cherokee Freedmen Controversy." *Cultural Anthropology* 29(3): 575–98. https://doi.org/10.14506/ca29.3.07.

–. 2017. "Reflections on the Anthropology of Sovereignty and Settler Colonialism: Lessons from Native North America." *Cultural Anthropology* 32(3): 340–48. https://doi.org/10.14506/ca32.3.03.

TallBear, Kim. 2013. *Native American DNA: Tribal Belonging and the False Promise of Genetic Science*. Minneapolis: University of Minnesota Press.

Teitel, Ruti G. 2003. "Transitional Justice Genealogy." *Harvard Human Rights Journal* 16: 69–94.

Tennant, Paul. 1990. *Aboriginal People and Politics: The Indian Land Question in British Columbia, 1849–1989*. Vancouver: UBC Press.

Thom, Brian. 2014. "Reframing Indigenous Territories: Private Property, Human Rights and Overlapping Claims." *American Indian Culture and Research Journal* 38(4): 3–28. https://doi.org/10.17953/aicr.38.4.6372163053512w6x.

Trouillot, Michel-Rolph. 2000. "Abortive Rituals: Historical Apologies in the Global Era." *Interventions* 2(2): 171–86. https://doi.org/10.1080/136980100427298.

Truth and Reconciliation Commission of Canada. 2015. *The Final Report of the Truth and Reconciliation Commission of Canada*. Vol. 6, *Canada's Residential Schools: Reconciliation*. Montreal and Kingston: McGill-Queen's University Press.

Tully, James. 1995. *Strange Multiplicity: Constitutionalism in an Age of Diversity*. Cambridge: Cambridge University Press.

Turner, Bryan. 1990. "Outline of a Theory of Citizenship." *Sociology* 24(2): 189–217. https://doi.org/10.1177/0038038590024002002.

Turner, Dale. 2006. *This Is Not a Peace Pipe: Toward a Critical Indigenous Philosophy*. Toronto: University of Toronto Press.

–. 2013. "On the Idea of Reconciliation in Contemporary Aboriginal Politics." In *Reconciling Canada: Critical Perspectives on the Culture of Redress*, ed. Jennifer Henderson and Pauline Wakeham, 100–14. Toronto: University of Toronto Press.

–. 2016. "Indigenous Knowledge and the Reconciliation of Section 35(1)." In *From Recognition to Reconciliation: Essays on the Constitutional Entrenchment of Aboriginal and Treaty Rights*, ed. Patrick Macklem and Douglas Sanderson, 164–78. Toronto: University of Toronto Press.

Veracini, Lorenzo. 2010. *Settler Colonialism: A Theoretical Overview*. London: Palgrave Macmillan.

–. 2015. "What Can Settler Colonial Studies Offer to an Interpretation of the Conflict in Israel-Palestine?" *Settler Colonial Studies* 5(3): 268–71. https://doi.org/10.1080/2201473X.2015.1036391.

Verdery, Katherine. 1994. "The Elasticity of Land: Problems of Property Restitution in Transylvania." *Slavic Review* 53(4): 1071–1109.

Verdery, Katherine, and Caroline Humphrey. 2004. "Introduction: Raising Questions about Property." In *Property in Question: Value Transformation in the Global Economy*, ed. Katherine Verdery and Caroline Humphrey, 1–25. Oxford: Berg.

Warry, Wayne. 1998. *Unfinished Dreams: Community Healing and the Reality of Aboriginal Self Government*. Toronto: University of Toronto Press.

Wickwire, Wendy. 2005. "'They Wanted ... Me to Help Them': James A. Teit and the Challenge of Ethnography in the Boasian Era." In *With Good Intentions: Euro-Canadian and Aboriginal Relations in Colonial Canada*, ed. Celia Haig-Brown, 297–320. Vancouver: UBC Press.

Wilkins, David E., and K. Tsianina Lomawaima. 2001. *Uneven Ground: American Indian Sovereignty and Federal Law*. Norman: University of Oklahoma Press.

Williams, Robert A. 1999. *Linking Arms Together: American Indian Treaty Visions of Law and Peace, 1600–1800*. New York: Routledge.

Wilson, Richard. 2001. *The Politics of Truth and Reconciliation in South Africa*. Cambridge: Cambridge University Press.

Wolfe, Patrick. 2006. "Settler Colonialism and the Elimination of the Native." *Journal of Genocide Research* 8(4): 387–409. https://doi.org/10.1080/14623520601056240.

–. 2011. "After the Frontier: Separation and Absorption in US Indian Policy." *Settler Colonial Studies* 1(1): 13–51.

Woolford, Andrew. 2005. *Between Justice and Certainty: The British Columbia Treaty Process*. Vancouver: UBC Press.

Wright, Edmond. 2003. "The Struggle to Be Recognized as Owners of Our Lands and Resources: The Nisga'a Final Agreement and the Implementation of the Nisga'a Treaty." New Aiyansh, BC: Nisga'a Lisims Government.

Young, Iris Marion. 2001. "Two Concepts of Self Determination." In *Human Rights: Concepts, Contests, Contingencies*, ed. Austin Sarat and Thomas Kearns, 25–44. Ann Arbor: University of Michigan Press.

Ziff, Bruce. 2014. *Principles of Property Law*. 6th ed. Toronto: Carswell.

Index

Note: (i) after a page number indicates an illustration.

Aboriginal (terminology), 149*n*3, 159*n*2

Aboriginal Affairs and Northern Development, 120, 128, 154*n*38

Aboriginal title: allodial title, 79; vs Crown title (colonial common law), 63–69, 76–77; definition, 69, 76; as distinct rights, 145–46; extinguishment, 9, 70–74; fee simple transformation, 55–56, 68–69; as inherent, 72–73; limitations, 68–69; modification clause (certainty), 69–76; as *prima facie* right, 67; vs private property, 84–90; rulings, 66–69, 76–77; as *sui generis* right, 55, 68; as usufructuary right, 65, 66–67. *See also* Nisga'a territory and treaty lands

Aiyansh village. *See* Gitlax̱t'aamiks village (New Aiyansh)

Alcantara, Christopher, 88–89

Aldridge, Jim, 121, 140

Alfred, Taiaiake, 7, 53

Alice Arm, 121–23

Allen, Edward, 42, 90

Allen, Frederick, 157*n*42

Alloycorp Mining, 162*n*7

AMAX Corporation, 122, 162*nn*6–7

Anderson, Benedict, 98

Assembly of First Nations, 87

Avanti Kitsault Mine, 121–23, 141, 162*nn*6–7

Ayuuk̲hl Nisga'a legal code, 42, 50–52

band council system: bylaws, 32, 44, 152*n*10; legislation and governance, 28, 29–32, 151*n*5; member status, 99; vs traditional hereditary governance, 30, 32, 151*n*5. *See also* Indian Act (1876); reserve system

Barker, Joanne, 105

Barton, Charles, 16–17, 56, 57, 58

BC Court of Appeal, 19, 41, 67

BC Liberal Party, 22, 33, 97

BC Supreme Court: environmental assessments, 121–23; self-government, 32–42; timber licences, 69; title rights, 19, 57, 150*n*16; traditional territory, 57; treaty and constitutional legitimacy, 39–42, 45
BC Treaty Commission, 20, 131
Bennett, Bill, 134
Bennett, Carolyn, 139
Berger, Thomas, 19, 150*n*16
bilateral agreements, 146–47
Binnie, Ian, 136
Blackburn, Carole, 24–26, 131
Blomley, Nicholas, 79
Borrows, John, 68, 77, 100, 132, 138, 151*n*5
British Columbia: environmental assessment requirements, 121–23, 162*n*6; formation of, 15–16; highways, 12–13; land and resource development, 73–74; legislation, 146; logging blockades, 20; mineral tax revenue, 123, 141, 147; political parties, 21–22; reconciliation agreements, 147; reserve system, 16; revenue-sharing agreements, 123, 140–42, 146–47; self-government challenge, 32–42, 153*n*22; timber licences, 12, 69; treaty approval, 21; treaty negotiation, 16–17, 19–20; treaty opposition, 21–22; treaty referendum, 39
British Columbia Forest Act, 69
British North America Act 1867 (BNA Act), 36, 38, 65, 98–99, 133
Brucejack Gold Mine, 141–42, 146–47
Bruyneel, Kevin, 46

Calder, Arthur, 16–17, 150*n*12
Calder, Frank, 18, 42, 150*n*12
Calder et al. v Attorney-General of British Columbia case: extinguishment, 9,

70; lawsuit loss, 19, 150*n*16; ruling, 9, 15, 66–67; witness, 57
Campbell, Gordon: opposition leader, 22, 32–42; premier, 153*n*22
Campbell v British Columbia (Attorney General) case, 32–42, 144
Canadian Constitution Foundation (CCF), 40, 45
Canfree (Canadians for Reconciliation, Equality and Equity), 40
Canyon City village. *See* Gitwinksihlkw village (Canyon City)
Carpay, John, 40
Carrier Lumber, 69
Castleden, Heather, 131
CBC Television, 27–28
Cherokee Nation, 105
Chrétien, Jean, 21, 96
Christianity, 11, 12, 31, 56, 112, 151*n*7
Citizenship Act, 54
Clark, Glen, 21–22
Coffey, Wallace, 53
Collison, George, 31
colonialism. *See* settler colonialism
Columbia Cellulose, 12
common bowl metaphor (*sayt-k'ilhl wo'osihl Nisga'a*), 80–84
Comprehensive Land Claims Policy, 71
Connolly v Woolrich case, 35, 43, 152*n*15
Conservative Party of Canada, 96–97
Constitution Act (1867): Indian status, 96; repatriation, 33–34, 133; self-government, 37–38; terminology, 149*n*3, 159*n*2; treaty rights, 33–34, 35, 98, 107, 118, 132–37. *See also* federal government
Coon Come, Matthew, 124
Cooper, Carol Ann, 15, 152*n*9
Cornell, Steven, 53
Corntassel, Jeff, 53
Cornwall, Clement, 30–31, 72, 80, 151*n*6, 153*n*26, 157*n*42

Cowichan First Nation, 17
Craft, Aimee, 129–30
Cree Nation. *See* James Bay and
Northern Quebec Agreement
Crosby, Thomas, 56
Crown-Indigenous Relations and
Northern Affairs Canada
(CIRNAC), 127, 138–40

Davie, A.E.B., 56
Dawes Act (United States), 86
de Jong, Michael, 33
De la Cadena, Marisol, 109
de Soto, Hernando, 88, 90
dead capital, 88–89
Delgamuukw v British Columbia case,
67–69, 74, 76–77, 136
Dene Nation, 7–8
Dennison, Jean, 47–48
Department of Indian Affairs:
assimilationist policy, 95; authority,
48; name change, 32; reserve
system, 11, 28. *See also* federal
government
Department of Indian Affairs and
Northern Development (DIAND):
band council bylaws, 32, 152*n*10;
Indian status, 96; name change, 120;
treaty implementation shortcomings,
127. *See also* federal government
Deputy Ministers Oversight
Committee, 129, 139
Diamond, Billy, 162*n*12
Dosanjh, Ujjal, 24–25
Douglas, James, 65
Duff, Wilson, 57
Duncan, William, 10, 151*nn*7–8, 155*n*7
Dunne Za Nation, 70

Elders Advisory Committee, 54, 104
England (land tenure history), 75,
156*n*35

Estey, Willard, 40
European citizenship codes, 107

federal government: assimilationist
policy, 60, 94–96, 115; auditor
general report, 125–26; "citizen"
terminology debate, 99–102;
citizenship conditions, 93; common
law vs Aboriginal title, 63–69,
76–77; Crown territorial sovereignty,
34–37, 45–46, 54, 58–60, 154*n*33;
Crown-Indigenous relationship,
3–6, 9–10, 23–24, 98–99, 138–40,
149*n*4; enfranchisement policy, 59,
94, 95; extinguishment policy, 9,
70–74; first ministers conferences,
134–35; Indigenous as member
vs citizen, 101; vs Indigenous
governance, 52–53; Order-in-
Council, 18, 59; organizational
oversight, 125–29, 163*n*22; reserve
land title policy, 84, 86–87; rights
recognition framework, 139–40;
treaty citizenship debate, 96–110,
117, 161*n*22; treaty implementation
(whole-of-government approach),
128–29, 139–40, 146, 163*n*22;
treaty implementation obligations,
shortcomings, 120–31, 162*n*12;
universal citizenship rights, 103–10.
See also Constitution Act (1867);
Indian Act (1876); reconciliation;
settler colonialism
fee simple estate: about, 75–76; allodial
title, 79; definition, 75; escheat
function, 78; legislation,
84–90; modification clause
(certainty), 69–78; private vs
communal landownership, 84–90,
158*n*52; without restrictions, 78
Feit, Harvey, 8
First Nations (terminology), 149*n*3

184   *Index*

First Nations Property Ownership Act (FNPOA), 86–87
First Nations Property Ownership conference, 88, 159*n*57
First Nations Tax Commission, 86, 88, 159*n*57
fish drying (smokehouse), 63(i)
fishing rights: management, 61–62, 128; river access, 31, 152*n*9; traditional territory (ango'oskw), 57, 61–62; as treaty right, 133–34, 135
Flanagan, Tom, 88–89
forestry industry: logging blockades ("war in the woods"), 20; logging operations, 91, 159*n*59; timber licences, 12, 65, 69
Fort Nass (Port Simpson), 15
Foster, Hamar, 155*n*7
Fraser, Scott, 141–42
Fraser Institute, 106
Frontier Centre for Public Policy, 49

Gingolx village (Kincolith): about, 10–11; band council system, 31; cemetery, 15; community court challenge (reaction), 41, 153*n*26; fishery control, 31, 152*n*9; social issues, 49
Gitanyow Nation, 150*n*10
Gitlax̱t'aamiks village (New Aiyansh): about, 11–12; band council system, 32; fish smokehouse (salmon (k̲'ayukws) drying), 63(i); government building, 51(i); social issues, 49
Gitwinksihlkw village (Canyon City), 11, 114
Gitxsan (Gitksan) Nation, 67–69, 113, 144, 150*n*10, 156*n*41
Gosnell, Eli, 62
Gosnell, James, 18, 91, 122, 134–35, 162*n*6
Gosnell, Joseph (Joe), 46–47, 62, 74, 91–92, 108, 111

Graben, Sari, 79, 125
Gradual Enfranchisement Act (1869), 94
Grant, Peter, 156*n*41
Green, Alfred, 11, 31, 151*n*7
Greenville village. *See* Laxgalts'ap village (Greenville)
Griffiths, John, 42–43
Gurney, Arthur, 56

Haida Nation v British Columbia (Minister of Forests) case, 39, 136
Hall, Emmett, 66–67
Hamilton Report (Chief Justice A.C. Hamilton), 72
Hawthorn Report (Harry Hawthorn), 160*n*4
Highway of Tears, 12
historic treaties: interpretation guidelines, 130; vs modern treaties, 3–4, 5–6, 129–30, 149*n*4; as relational vs contractual, 130; and right relationship, 130; scholarship on, 5–6, 149*n*4; surrender and release clause, 71–72; treaty making guidelines, 64–65. *See also* modern treaties
Hudson's Bay Company post, 15
hunting rights, 57–58, 61–62, 82, 113, 134, 157*n*42
Huron-British Treaty (1760), 134
Huron-Wendat Nation, 134
Huu-ay-aht First Nations, 49, 131

Indian Act (1876): amendments, 18; as "brief interruption," 27; criticisms of, 115; Indian agents, 30–31, 32, 56; jurisdiction, 44; patrilineal vs matrilineal status, 23, 94, 159*n*2; status and racial blood definition, 103–4; status Indian category, 94–95, 159*n*2; status women exclusion, 95; terminology, 149*n*3; welfare system, 115–16. *See also*

band council system; federal government; reserve system
Indian agents, 30–31, 32, 56
Indian Reserve Commission (Commission to Enquire into the Conditions of the Indians of the North-West Coast), 30–31, 151*n*6
Indigenous (terminology), 149*n*3
Indigenous and Northern Affairs Canada (INAC), 120, 125–26, 138–39
Indigenous citizenship. *See* treaty citizenship
Indigenous governance. *See* Nisga'a Lisims Government; self-government
Indigenous peoples: Crown-Indigenous relationship, 3–6, 9–10, 23–24, 98–99, 138–40, 149*n*4; enfranchisement, 59, 94, 95; fishing rights, 133–34, 135; fluid vs fixed traditional territorial boundaries, 6–7; hunting rights, 57–58, 61–62, 82, 113, 134, 157*n*42; logging blockades ("war in the woods"), 20; property pre-emption limitations, 59–60; racialization of, 102–3, 104; resistance, 7, 9, 18, 20; resource development agreements, 140–42, 146–47; rights recognition framework reaction, 139–40; socio-economic report, 49, 154*n*38; status women, 95, 104; treaty implementation litigation costs, 125. *See also* Aboriginal title; self-government; treaty citizenship; treaty making and rights; *names of individual Nations*
Indigenous Rights Recognition and Implementation Framework, 139–40
Indigenous Services Canada, 138–39
Indigenous sovereignty. *See* self-government
International Labour Organization, 93

Inuit, 71, 124, 125, 149*n*3, 159*n*2
Inuvialuit Final Agreement, 125
Irlbacher-Fox, Stephanie, 7–8
Israel, 8

Jaffe, Paul, 40
James Bay and Northern Quebec Agreement: economic development, 129, 164*n*23; non-implementation, 123–24, 162*n*12; self-government exclusion, 36; surrender and exchange clause, 71; treaty engagement, 8
Joint Fisheries Management Board, 128
Judson, Wilfred, 66–67
Jules, Manny, 86, 159*n*57

Kalt, Joseph P., 53
Kincolith village. *See* Gingolx village (Kincolith)
King, Hayden, 140
Kluane First Nation, 6, 113
KSM Seabridge Gold, 141

Ladner, Kiera, 152*n*10
Lamer, Antonio, 66–67, 76, 135–36
land claims agreements. *See* modern treaties
Land Claims Agreements Coalition (LCAC): about, 120, 161*nn*1–2; conferences, 49, 140; environmental assessments, 121; independent oversight commission, 127–29; treaty implementation lobbying, 24, 25, 120–21, 124. *See also* modern treaties
Landholding Transition Act, 55–56, 84–90
Lax Kw'alaams village, 15
Laxgalts'ap village (Greenville): about, 11; band council system, 32; community court challenge (reaction), 153*n*26; land tenure history, 60; missionaries, 31, 151*n*7

Le Dressay, Andre, 88–89
Leeson, Nelson, 25, 36, 46–47, 122, 162*n*6
liberal political theory and citizenship, 99–102, 110

Maa-nulth Final Agreement (2011): about, 20; concurrent vs exclusive jurisdiction, 43; divorce vs marriage analogy, 131; modification clause (certainty), 69; self-government, 39; treaty citizenship, 97
Mackay, David (Sim'oogit Axdii Wil Luu Gooda), 157*n*42
Maliseet Nation, 133–34
Manning, Preston, 21, 109
Marshall, Donald Jr., 133–34
Martland, Ronald, 66
Mawani, Renisa, 9
McCullagh, James B., 11–12, 112
McKay, Kevin, 25, 36, 126–27, 142
McKenna-McBride Commission, 18
McNeil, Kent, 78
Mehaffey, Matthew, 125
Mercer, Laurie, 85
Métis Nation, 133, 149*n*3, 159*n*2
Metlakatla village, 11, 30, 151*n*7
Mikisew Cree First Nation v Canada case, 136
Mi'kmaq Nation, 64, 133–34
Milewski, Terry, 27–28
Mills, Aaron, 117
Mineral Tax Act (BC), 123
mining industry: agreements, 140–42, 146–47; community benefits agreement, 141; environmental assessment certificates, 121–23, 162*n*6; tailings dumping, 122, 162*n*6
missing and murdered Indigenous women and girls, 12
missionaries, 11, 12, 31, 56, 112, 151*n*7

modern treaties: about, 3–4; vs bilateral agreements, 146–47; citizenship rights criteria, 23, 103–10; as comprehensive land claims, 19; constitutional, 33–34, 132–37; as contractual vs relational, 130; criticisms of, 52–53, 133, 142; firsts, 4, 8, 28, 33; governance powers, 43–45, 48, 154*n*28; vs historic treaties, 3–4, 5–6, 129–30, 149*n*4; implementation challenges, 119–31; implementation oversight (whole-of-government approach), 128–29, 139–40, 146, 163*n*22; internal audit report, 128; and reconciliation, 9–10; self-government exclusion, 36; self-government inclusion, 28, 33, 144–45, 147; vs side agreements, 36; survey, 49, 154*n*38; time span and written length of, 6; and treaty relationship, 142, 143–44. *See also* historic treaties; Land Claims Agreements Coalition (LCAC); treaty making and rights
Modern Treaties Implementation Review Commission, 24, 127, 147
Modern Treaty Commission, 127
Modern Treaty Implementation Office, 129, 140
Morgan, Sloan, 131
Musqueam First Nation, 135

Naas, Matthew, 56
Na-Cho Nyak Dun Nation, 124–25
Nadasdy, Paul, 6, 99, 113
Napoleon, Valerie, 113
Nass Camp, 24–25, 114
Nass River (K̲'alii-aksim Lisims), 4, 10, 31, 152*n*9
Nass River Valley: about, 4; common bowl metaphor, 81; highway, 12–13; lava beds, 13–14(i); living

conditions, 12–13, 19, 150*n*14; as traditional territory, 10; village sites, 10–11

Nass Wildlife Area: hunting and harvesting permits, 82, 113; land co-management, 79; mine tailings, 121–23, 162*n*6; resource development, 141; territory size, 4, 14

National Treaty Commissioner's Office, 140

Native Claims Policy, 71

neoliberalism, 88, 116

New Aiyansh village. *See* Gitlax̱t'aamiks village (New Aiyansh)

New Democratic Party (BC), 21–22, 96, 150*n*12

Nisg̱a'a Constitution, 51–52, 150*n*13

Nisg̱a'a Final Agreement (Nisg̱a'a treaty): about, 4–5, 15–21; approval and referendum on, 21; background, 15–21; cash settlement, 14; celebrations, 24–25; "citizen" terminology debate, 99–102, 145; citizenship debate, 23, 96–102; citizenship enrolment criteria, 102–10, 160*n*14; community court challenge, 39–42, 45, 153*n*26; as comprehensive land claim, 135; concurrent vs exclusive jurisdiction, 43–45, 48; constitutionality of, 27, 28–29, 33, 144–45, 151*n*2; core rights of, 144; core treaty lands, 13–14; court challenges, 22, 32–42, 45; criticisms of, 34–35, 45, 81–84, 144, 157*n*47, 158*n*48; elements of, 4–5; environmental assessment requirements, 121–23, 162*n*6; first modern treaty, 4, 28; fisheries and wildlife management, 128; General Provisions, 69, 73; governance powers, 15, 33, 35, 43–45, 48, 154*n*28; highway name, 13; hunting and

mineral rights, 13–14; impact of, 48–49; implementation obligations litigation, 120–31, 162*n*12; implementation oversight (whole-of-government approach), 128–29, 163*n*22; modification clause (certainty) and fee simple, 69–76; negotiations, 14–15, 19–21, 25–26, 79–84, 144, 145, 150*n*10, 156*n*41; non-Indigenous enrolment limitations, 103, 107, 108, 109, 161*n*22; opinions and experiences of, 25–26; phase-in period, 27, 151*n*2; and reconciliation, 131, 136–37, 141–42, 144; self-government provision, 5, 22–23; settlement feast, 28–29(i); socio-economic benefits, 49, 154*n*38; text of, 14–15. *See also* self-government; treaty citizenship

Nisg̱a'a Land Committee, 32, 80

Nisg̱a'a Land Title Office, 85

Nisg̱a'a Lisims Government: business forum, 114–15; chief executive officer, 25, 126–27, 142; citizenship legislation, 54; community benefits agreement, 141; concurrent vs exclusive jurisdiction, 43–44, 48; constitution, 51–52, 150*n*13; council of elders, 52; criticisms of, 45; environmental assessment lawsuit, 121–23; executive, 50; first meeting and news coverage, 27–28; governance jurisdiction, 43–44, 45, 48, 103, 154*n*28; government building, 51(i); hunting and harvesting permits, 82, 113, 158*n*48; land co-management, 79; land title (fee simple) legislation, 55–56, 84–90; lawmaking authority, 42–43, 45, 48–49, 154*n*27; legal code, 42, 50–52; legislation enactment, 27, 54, 55–56, 84–90, 151*n*1; logging operations,

188   *Index*

159*n*59; on modern treaties, 142; president, 123; quality of life survey, 49; revenue-sharing agreements (mining), 140–42, 146–47; taxation authority, 107, 161*n*22; treaty cash settlement, 14; treaty implementation obligations, 126–27; uniform rights, 113; village governments, 15, 50

Nisga'a Nation: "citizen" language, 111, 161*n*28; cultural belonging, 111–16, 145–46; economic development initiatives, 114–15; elders, 28, 52, 54, 62, 70, 104, 115; fish drying (smokehouse), 63(i); hereditary chiefs and matriarchs (*simgigat* and *sigidimhaanak̲*), 50–51, 60–62, 79–80, 157*n*42; language, 111, 161*n*28; legal code, 42, 50–52; matrilineal kinship (*huwilp*/houses), 23, 60–62, 111–12; migration, 62, 155*n*10; mineral tax revenue, 123; name inheritance, 62; non-Indigenous "taken in," 112; "not whole" origins (*w̲a'aay̲in*), 112; as one heart (*sayt-k'ilim goot*), 81; oral history (*adaawak̲*), 13, 51, 61–62, 79–80; petition, 17–18; as political community, 99–100, 106, 110, 117; president, 25; resource development agreements, 140–42, 146–47; resource-based economy, 114; scholarship on, 26; self-reliance loss (welfare system), 115–16; settlement feasts, 28–29(i), 81, 112; special assemblies, 21, 62, 81, 92, 140, 141; survey, 49; treaty meeting (BC premier), 56–60, 155*n*7; tribes (*pdeek̲*), 103, 111, 160*n*14. *See also named sim'oogit (chiefs)*

Nisga'a territory and treaty lands: boundary disputes, 79, 156*n*41; boundary marker, 83(i); collective ownership, 81–84, 158*n*50; common

bowl metaphor (*sayt-k'ilhl wo'osihl Nisga'a*), 80–84; economic development on, 84–90, 158*n*52, 159*nn*58–59; fisheries and wildlife management, 128; fishery control, 31, 152*n*9; hunting and fishing grounds (*ango'oskw*), 57, 61–62; hunting and harvesting permits, 82, 113, 157*n*47, 158*n*48; land committee, 16–17; land grant (*Hagwin-yuu-wo'oskw*), 61; land privilege (*amnigwootkw*), 61; land tenure system (matrilineal kinship (*wilp*)), 60–62; land title (fee simple) transformation, 55–56, 84–90; logging operations, 91, 159*n*59; mine tailings dumping, 122, 162*n*6; oral history about (*adaawak̲*), 61–62, 79–80, 157*n*42; private vs communal landownership, 84–90, 158*n*52; resource extraction, 91, 159*n*59; traditional land segments, 23, 55, 61–62; villages, 10–11, 15, 50, 161*n*28. *See also* Aboriginal title

Nisga'a Tribal Council: Aboriginal title and legal challenges, 9, 19, 72, 77, 134–35, 150*n*16; citizenship criteria, 53–54; common bowl metaphor, 40, 80–81; conventions, 150*n*13; at first ministers conferences, 134–35; formation, 18, 40; kinship analogy, 108; lawyers, 77, 150*n*16; mandate, 18–19, 40, 150*n*13; mine tailings media coverage, 122, 162*n*6; presidents, 18, 81, 108; side agreements, 36; special assembly, 81; treaty negotiation groups, 25

Northwest Coast Agency, 30

Nunavut Land Claims Agreement, 124

Nunavut Tunngavik Inc., 124

O'Meara, Arthur, 17, 18

Ong, Aihwa, 115–16

Order-in-Council, 18, 59
O'Reilly, Peter, 11, 30, 56, 58
Ortner, Sherry, 7
Osage Nation, 47–48

Palestine, 8
Pasternak, Shiri, 140
Penner Report (Keith Penner), 108, 153*n*19
Pigeon, Louis-Philippe, 19, 150*n*16
Plant, Geoffrey, 33
Planta, Joseph, 30–31, 72, 80, 151*n*6, 153*n*26, 157*n*42
Port Simpson (Fort Nass), 15
Powell, Israel Wood, 56
Pretium Resources, 141–42, 146–47
Promislow, Janna, 149*n*4, 154*n*27
property law. *See* fee simple estate
provincial government. *See* British Columbia; Quebec
Puck, Neis, 72

Quebec: customary law rights (Cree), 35, 152*n*15; hydroelectric dam project, 123–24; treaty rights (hunting), 134

R. v Marshall case, 133–34, 164*n*28
R. v Sioui case, 133–34, 164*n*28
R. v Sparrow case, 76, 135
R. v Van der Peet case, 135–36
reconciliation: legal meaning, 132–37; legal vs relational, 136–37; modern treaties as, 9–10; relationship, 9, 137–40, 141–42, 146–48; transitional justice, 131–32; treaty rights as, 5, 119, 131, 135–36, 144, 146–48
Reform Party of Canada, 21, 96, 161*n*22
research methodology, 24–26
reserve system: allocation grievances, 16, 30–31; band councils, 30, 32; federal vs provincial jurisdiction, 44; governance, 11, 16; land title

policy, 84, 86–87. *See also* band council system; Indian Act (1876)
Rights Recognition Framework, 24, 146
Ritchie, Roland, 66
Robinson, Andrew, 83
Robinson, James (Sim'oogit Sga'nisim (Chief Mountain)), 39–42, 45, 153*n*26
Robinson, Rod (Sim'oogit Minee'eskw): common bowl metaphor, 81; Indian Act as "brief interruption," 27–28; lava beds, 13; self-government, 27–28, 33, 54; treaty celebration, 29(i); tribal council, 18–19, 150*n*14
Romania (land ownership), 158*n*50
Royal Commission on Aboriginal Peoples (1996), 35, 131
Royal Proclamation ((1763) Indian Magna Carta), 17, 59, 63–66, 84, 142, 155*n*7
Russ, Charles, 72
Rustand, Jeffrey, 40
Ryan, John, 56

Sanders, Doug, 45
Sanderson, Douglas, 75, 156*n*35
Scott, Duncan Campbell, 95
Scott, Mike, 45
sectoral agreements, 5, 146
self-government: vs Crown sovereignty, 30, 34–35, 38–39, 43, 52–53, 54, 151*n*5; economic development, 90, 159*n*58; governance and lawmaking authority, 15, 35, 36–37, 42–45, 48–49, 154*nn*27–28; as inherent right, 27–28, 32–42, 72–73; legislative jurisdiction vs political autonomy, 38, 153*n*19; modern treaties, 28, 33, 144–45, 147; negotiations, 144; non-Indigenous rights limitations, 103, 107, 108, 109, 161*n*22; resource extraction

demands, 91, 159*n*59; side agreements, 36; vs sovereignty meaning, 46–47; as third order of government, 5, 36–37, 91, 133, 137, 144–45, 147, 153*n*19; traditional land tenure system, 60–62; tribal sovereignty, 53, 105

settler colonialism: about, 8; assimilationist policy, 8, 60, 94–96, 115; individual property ownership, 59–60; land tenure history, 75, 156*n*35; legal pluralism, 42–43; territorial jurisdiction and crown sovereignty, 43–48, 54; theoretical framework, 8–9. *See also* federal government

Sim'oogit Axdii Wil Luu Gooda (David Mackay), 157*n*42

Sim'oogit Gints'aadax̱(Kinsada/ Kinzadah), 31, 152*n*8

Sim'oogit Minee'eskw (Rod Robinson). *See* Robinson, Rod (Sim'oogit Minee'eskw)

Sim'oogit Sga'nisim (Chief Mountain (James Robinson)), 39–42, 45, 153*n*26

Sim'oogit Sgat'iin, 11

Smithe, William, 16, 47, 56–60, 63, 92, 155*n*7

South African Truth and Reconciliation Commission, 131–32

sovereignty. *See* federal government; self-government

Sparrow, Ron, 76, 135

St. Catharines Milling and Lumber Co v R. case, 65–66

Standing Committee on Aboriginal Affairs (House of Commons), 24, 33, 37, 87, 90, 162*n*12

Standing Senate Committee on Aboriginal Affairs: "citizen" terminology debate, 99–102, 111; independent oversight commission recommendations, 127; treaty citizenship debate, 40, 103–10, 117,

161*n*22; treaty implementation report, 126, 131; universal citizenship rights, 103–10

Stevens, Mitchell, 123

Sturm, Circe, 105

Supreme Court of Canada: Aboriginal title rulings, 9, 15, 39, 66–69, 76–77, 125, 133–34, 135, 164*n*28; historic treaties interpretation guidelines, 130; Indian status ruling, 159*n*2; reconciliation, 10, 135–36

Tahltan First Nation, 146–47

Taku River Tlingit case, 39

Terrace, 12–13

Thom, Brian, 6

Thomas, Mercy, 39–42

Tla'amin Final Agreement (2014): about, 20; concurrent vs exclusive jurisdiction, 43; modification clause (certainty), 69; self-government, 39; treaty citizenship, 97

Todd, Charles (Indian agent), 30–31

transitional justice, 131–32

Treaty 3, 65

Treaty 8, 65, 70

treaty citizenship: belonging, 111–16, 145–46; "citizen" terminology debate, 99–102; as "citizens plus," 160*n*4; "landed citizenship" concept, 100, 160*n*8; lawmaking limitations, 101; matrilineal ancestry vs blood quantum (race-based) criteria, 102–10; matrilineal vs patrilineal, 94; vs neoliberal good citizenship, 116; non-Indigenous enrolment limitations, 103, 107, 108, 109, 161*n*22; self-identification, 93–102; vs settler citizenship "gift," 116; status women exclusion, 95, 104; universal, 103, 106–7, 113, 145 treaty making and rights: as comprehensive land claims, 19, 135, 143; constitutionality, 33–34, 35, 98, 107, 118, 132–37; as covenant, 119; decline, 145; fluid vs fixed traditional territorial boundaries, 6–7; guidelines, 64; hunting rights, 57–58, 61–62, 82, 113, 134, 157n42; implementation challenges, 119–31; implementation litigation costs, 125; negotiation and engagement, 7–8, 19–21, 56–60, 90–91, 155n7; numbered treaties, 64–65, 70; reconciliation, 5, 119, 131, 135–36, 144, 146–48; relationship, 71, 125, 138, 143, 146–48; revenue-sharing agreements, 123, 140–42, 146–47; scholarship on, 5–6, 149n4; sectoral agreements, 5, 146; side agreements, 36; sovereignty vs autonomy, 46–47; treaty constitutionalism, 138. *See also* Aboriginal title; fishing rights; modern treaties; Nisga'a Final Agreement (Nisga'a treaty); self-government; treaty citizenship

Tr'ondëk Hwëch'in Nation, 124–25

Trudeau, Justin, 127, 129, 138–39

Trudeau, Pierre Elliott, 33–34, 96, 134

Truth and Reconciliation Commission (TRC) report: transitional justice mechanism, 132; treaties as reconciliation, 5, 9, 137–38; treaty relationship, 4, 54, 118, 143, 148

Tsawwassen Final Agreement (2009): about, 20; concurrent vs exclusive jurisdiction, 43; modification clause (certainty), 69; self-government, 39; treaty citizenship, 97

Tsilhqot'in Nation v British Columbia case, 69, 76–77

Tsimshian Nation: reserve system, 16; treaty claim delegation, 56–60; villages, 11, 15, 30, 151n7

Tsosie, Rebecca, 53

Tully, James, 138

Turner, Dale, 137

United Nations Declaration on the Rights of Indigenous Peoples, 93, 131, 134, 146, 159n1

United Nations Human Rights Council, 120

United States: assimilationist policy, 95; land privatization, 85–86; tribal sovereignty, 47–48, 105

Universal Periodic Review of Canada, 120

Valcourt, Bernard, 128–29

Vancouver, Captain George, 15

Verdery, Katherine, 158n50

Vuntut Gwitchin Nation, 124–25

Warren, Elizabeth, 105

Webster, Jack, 122, 162n6

Wesley, John, 56

Westbank First Nation (WFN), 159n58

Weston, John, 40

Wet'suwet'en Nation, 67–69

White Paper (1969), 96

Wildlife Committee, 128

William I (king of England), 75

Williamson, Paul, 38, 144

Wilp Si'ayuukhl Nisga'a ((WSN) Nisga'a House of Laws), 42, 50

Wilp Wilxo'oskwhl Nisga'a Institute (Nisga'a House of Learning), 25

Wilson, Richard, 56

Wolfe, Patrick, 8–9, 95

Wong, Randall, 40–41

Wright, Edmund, 43–44

Young, Iris Marion, 47

Yukon Peel Watershed case, 124–25

Yukon Umbrella Final Agreement, 36, 71, 124–25